Shadow Dance

Selected Books by David Richo

Being True to Life: Poetic Paths to Personal Growth

Coming Home to Who You Are: Discovering Your Natural Capacity for Love, Integrity, and Compassion

Daring to Trust: Opening Ourselves to Real Love and Intimacy

The Five Things We Cannot Change: And the Happiness We Find by Embracing Them

How to Be an Adult in Love: Letting Love in Safely and Showing It Recklessly

How to Be an Adult in Relationships: The Five Keys to Mindful Loving

The Power of Coincidence: How Life Shows Us What We Need to Know

The Power of Grace: Recognizing Unexpected Gifts on Our Path

Shadow Dance: Liberating the Power and Creativity of Your Dark Side

When the Past Is Present: Healing the Emotional Wounds That Sabotage Our Relationships

Selected Audio by David Richo

Embracing the Shadow: Discovering the Hidden Riches in Our Relationships

How to Be an Adult in Relationships: The Five Keys to Mindful Loving

Making Love Last: How to Sustain Intimacy and Nurture Genuine Connection

Shadow Dance

LIBERATING THE POWER
AND CREATIVITY OF
YOUR DARK SIDE

DAVID RICHO

SHAMBHALA
Boston & London
1999

Shambhala Publications, Inc.
Horticultural Hall
300 Massachusetts Avenue
Boston, Massachusetts 02115
www.shambhala.com

19 18 17 16 15 14 13 12 11

Printed in the United States of America
⊗ This edition is printed on acid-free paper that meets the
American National Standards Institute Z39.48 Standard.
♻ This book is printed on 30% postconsumer recycled paper.
For more information please visit www.shambhala.com.
Distributed in the United States by Penguin Random House LLC
and in Canada by Random House of Canada Ltd

Library of Congress Cataloging-in-Publication Data
Richo, David, 1940–
The shadow dance: liberating the power and creativity
of your dark side/David Richo.—1st ed.
p. cm.
ISBN 978-1-57062-444-5 (pbk.: alk. paper)
1. Good and evil—Psychological aspects. 2. Good and evil—
Psychological aspects—Case studies. 3. Shadow (Psychoanalysis)
I. Title.
BF789.E94R53 1999   98-46478
158.1—dc21   CIP

For my Fathers

Stepdad Joe Slubowski, Grandpa Philip Garibaldi,
Uncle Mike Perillo, Dad Dominic Richo,
Harry Gaunt, Roger Racette, Reverend Al Giaquinto,
Ed Murray, S.J., Rabbi Robert Goldberg, Bert Bigelow,
Don Miesen, Armando Quiros,
and Uncle Sal Garibaldi

What would life have been without your love?

Under an empty autumn sky
Stretch endless wastes
Where no one goes.
Who is that horseman riding in from the west?

WANG CHANGLING, EIGHTH-CENTURY BUDDHIST POET

Contents

Shadow Dance

Introduction

*We meet ourselves time and again in a thousand
disguises on the path of life.*

—C. G. JUNG

*D*O YOU DARE to love what you have hated all your life?
If you can entertain that paradox, this book is for you, since
it attempts to show how everything about us contains creativity and goodness no matter how bad or useless we may think
it to be. Our dark side has been called our personal shadow
by C. G. Jung. The shadow is everything about ourselves that
we do not know or refuse to know, both dark and light. It is
the sum total of the positive and negative traits, feelings, beliefs, and potentials we refuse to identify as our own.

The shadow is that part of us that is incompatible with
who we think we are or are supposed to be. It is the realm
beyond our limits, the place where we are more than we
seem. The shadow is ironically humorous because the opposite of our self-image proves to be true in spite of all our
tricky attempts not to believe or display it. Fear of that wider
self keeps it in the dungeon, but there are ways to release the
prisoner. It takes practice. This book presents it in bite-size
pieces and accompanies you through the process. It shows

you how to transform your inner demons and awaken your dormant divinities. It invites you to grant hospitality to all the pilgrim parts of yourself and make room for them one by one.

The challenge is in accepting ourselves all the way to the bottom: admitting and holding rather than denying and eschewing our arrogance, our self-centeredness, our will to coerce others, and any other dark truths we cannot face about ourselves. All these constitute our negative shadow side, which can turn out to be not so much a threat as a promise: we can find the best in us in what is bad in us. We shall see how the counterpart of every negative in the human equation is something positive. Everything is meant for good, says Saint Augustine, even what is bad.

This handbook is also about accepting ourselves all the way to the top: acknowledging and accessing the creative powers we have never believed we possessed and have never put to use. This is our darkened positive shadow side. We may admire these glowing attributes strongly in others and deny them in ourselves, just as we strongly dislike in others what may be true but ugly about ourselves. Hope grows from welcoming our positive shadow, since hope is about believing in the potential in us for a life that is greater than the one our frightened and limited ego has designed, a wisdom larger than our thinking mind can muster, and a love that is wider than that with which we embrace our immediate circle of friends.

The gnawing sense of emptiness that sometimes arises in life might be just this: our refusal to grant full suffrage to our shadow regions, our failure to see that we are more than we seem. We lose contact with our dark side when we deny our pettiness, our selfishness, our vindictiveness. We may also lose faith in our own bright merit and spiritual limitlessness:

"I am larger, better than I thought, / I did not know I held so much goodness," wrote Walt Whitman.

To think that what we are conscious of about ourselves is all there is to us puts us in danger of being run by the unconscious forces in our shadow. This is scary, since we are mostly *unable* to see or even know the full darkness of our shadow side. It is a personality with our name on it, but it was deported long ago. This part of us was banished early in life. To gain and maintain approval, we may have had to exhibit only the personality that was acceptable to our parents. Later in life we may have persisted in that self-negating routine with other adults, our partners, and our peers. By hiding the personality traits that were considered objectionable, we lost out on our chance to rework and move through them. Instead, they simply went underground. Qualities that required only some sanding and polishing were confined to the cellar, our unconscious, as useless or even dangerous. This was perhaps the fate of much potential for creative transformation. Given the chance, an ugly aggressiveness might have been trimmed to assertiveness, unwelcome controlling ways might have been spruced up into efficient leadership, fear might even have become love.

At the same time, some of the great assets or talents of our personality might also have been threatening to our parents and others in our life, and then they too had to be sequestered. These higher attributes went into the attic, our untapped unconscious potential, perhaps with the promise that they might be looked at some other day, but they were soon forgotten. Our self-doubts about our skills and potential may still be in trunks gathering dust, overlooked and seemingly above our reach.

Our dark shadow can be called a cellar of our unexamined shame. Our positive shadow is an attic of our unclaimed valuables. This is the manual that takes us down into the cellar of ourselves to retrieve and capitalize on our negative shadow and up into the attic to exult in and capitalize on our positive shadow. Unlike other books on the shadow, this one concentrates not so much on the savage darkness in us as on our practical day-to-day shortcomings and faults, not only those we fail to see but also those we clearly see in ourselves.

With great optimism we grant a hearty and fearless welcome to everything about us that might have been unwelcome before. We locate a kernel of goodness in every hard and unappealing shell. We are alchemists believing that gold can come from lead, nurturant parents trusting that little rascals will become presidents, readers suspecting that villains will become heroes, and priests believing that sinners will become saints.

How? It will not be by denying and canceling anything about ourselves but rather by acknowledging it, cradling it acceptingly, and then moving through it to its true fulfillment. In this friendly way, lead will have its full opportunity to be heavy, rascals to be mischievous, villains to be sinister, sinners to be miscreant. They will all be themselves, see themselves, accept themselves. Then they will notice how much of the energy in them is available for greater and higher purposes, how much potential they have for more joy and more giving. A shift will occur and they will become the swans that ugly ducklings become when they find out who they really are. What a wonderful prospect!

A dark side is perfectly normal for beings like us who include both sides of every set of opposites. There could be no light without the dark to contrast it with. Too much light creates a longing for night. It also follows that there is no dark without a corresponding light. This is the source of hope. It takes work to bring out the light. In these pages is a program to help us do that work and to accept both sides of everything about ourselves as fitting, understandable, and immensely useful.

Jung presents the image of the two thieves who were crucified with Jesus as symbols of the two sides of the shadow: one thief reviled Jesus while the other commiserated with him and asked for transformation. These are the opposing sides of our own souls. We fight the entry of the light into our lives and yet yearn for it. Wonderfully, both have a place in the uncovering of inner wholeness. The promise of paradise was instantaneous for the thief who welcomed the light. At the same time, it still remained available for the thief who turned away from it, if he would become willing to enter the purgatorial fires where his own interior darkness could be faced and integrated. Working on the dark shadow side of ourselves is just such a fiery enterprise. The chapters that follow are not fireproof but they are a friendly fire.

It is said that each of us has a twin. Psychically we are all Geminis. Every person to whom we react with strong fear, desire, repulsion, or admiration is a twin of our own inner unacknowledged life. We have qualities, both positive and negative, that appear visibly in others but are invisible in us and to us. Our practice is to be fascinated with those who upset or appeal to us and to find in them the hidden corners of ourselves. An archetype of twins exists in our psyche, one bad, one good. We have it in us to separate and even alienate one part of ourselves from another part. The challenge is to be on friendly terms with everything about ourselves. We can welcome what seems repulsive and recall what tries to get away. This will require a boundless curiosity about the foreign territories in our psyche that have always wanted annexation, always wanted to join the union of our self or rejoin after seceding. Such a consolidation of all our "parts" actually maintains their identity and amplifies their cohesiveness, as states maintain their rights though they join the union.

The shadow presents a challenge to us: to negotiate an alliance among all the opposing forces in ourselves. Every honest man has a dishonest side; every faithful woman has a faithless side. The courageous honesty required to look for such contradictions in ourselves creates character. Befriending both sides of ourselves allows our polarized tensions to emerge into consciousness. Then we begin to locate their creative possibilities. In this sense the shadow is a gift. Without it our ego might identify only with its light side and maintain an inflated view of itself, thus obscuring a dark glory that wants so much to peep out.

The shadow shapes our daily interactions and relationships much more forcefully than we imagine. Since it is a disowned and demonized energy, it is insidious and sly in its ways of hiding within our choices and behaviors. Nature is a metaphor for human nature. Under this visible world is another world. Digging is required to uncover it. It is full of caves and pits; the birds down there are bats. It takes special training to explore this underworld. We have to become psychological spelunkers, perhaps an unappealing and scary prospect. Our visible persona, the image we present to the world, feels threatened by exposure of its dun underpinnings. The underworld is, of course, our inner world.

In Greek mythology the Minotaur was hidden in the labyrinth, a metaphor for the shadow in the unconscious. The Minotaur killed seven Athenian boys and seven Athenian girls each year. This is an allegorical way of saying that what is hidden can destroy liveliness. The hero Theseus killed the Minotaur externally but never confronted his own inner Minotaur. In later years he drove away his son, who was then devoured by a sea monster. Thus Theseus did to his own son what the Minotaur did to the Athenian sons. We are cursed to act out the dark and desperate scenarios of the shadow as long as we keep believing it is supposed to be killed or canceled.

Like cathedrals and forests, metaphors of the psyche, we are never finished though always whole. That is wonderful news, since something complete can still be made from unfinished things. In fact, our lively energy, our life force, depends directly on our being whole but not on our becoming perfect. The only question is, How much consciousness can we stand? We can never know all of our shadow, only a piece at a time, only what we are ready for, and we will never be ready for all of it. It can never be totally tamed or befriended, but we can relate to it and horse-trade with it. When a little more each day is a good-enough bargain for us, we are liberated from both perfectionism and inadequacy, two tough features of the shadow.

The hero's journey is an apt Western metaphor for going out and working for enlightenment. The opening poem by Changling presents a powerful Eastern model of the journey of enlightenment *into* our lives. Hakuin, the Japanese Zen teacher, comments that this poem is meant to describe how enlightenment comes from emptiness. We are empty of ego fear and attachment when our mind, "sky," is clear. The void of "endless wastes" that we find in ourselves when we are free of separate ego identity—"where no one goes"—is the autumnal experience of mature spiritual life. The horseman connects humankind and nature, east and west, emptiness and fullness, light and dark. All the opposites combine. It is only this territory that enlightenment visits, swiftly, dawnward. Yet in Chinese mythology, the west is the locus of paradise and the birthplace of the gods. Thus enlightenment begins in heaven and then makes earth a heaven too, with no oppositions left standing. Changling's poem is ultimately about the human-divine journey to the east of awakening. We will refer back to it throughout these pages.

In a Bombay temple there is an image of a three-headed Shiva. The head on one side is gentle, the one on the other side terrible. The befriending head in the center looks benign and amused as it accepts both sides of itself. The challenge is to see both sides with those same eyes of welcome rather than with aggressive wishes to destroy the darker side. To acknowledge all our powers is to evoke those powers. They then tell us how we can be more than we ever thought we could be.

Shadow traits await an audience from consciousness. They are like courtiers outside a king's chamber. Each has a suit to present. Each has a wish for satisfaction or a request to adjust an imbalance. If the king of light keeps them in the dark antechamber for too long and refuses to welcome them, they mill about, grumble, and gossip. Then they may begin hatching desperate and even treasonous plots against him. The king has great power, but to keep it, he does well to hear from each of his courtiers and deal with each of them in turn and fairly. This is how they become supportive allies rather than seditious enemies. Each of us is a king and a courtier ready for alliance. As you read and work this book, you begin the dialogue and receive the royal favor.

This is not a Jungian book on the shadow, nor does it adhere to Jung's vision entirely. It is more original than derivative. In short, these pages use Jungian terms to present a new synthesis with many original applications. It will sound true if it elicits and expands the personal vision of the reader. Traditionally, the shadow has referred only to the unconscious. I am expanding it to include the known or easily known dark side of our personality, persona, feelings, and choices. "Dark" can be quite subjective. I define it most simply as that which interferes with others' rights or subverts our own deepest needs and wishes. The shadow in its widest connotation is thus about how we get in the way of others and of ourselves.

The practices that accompany the text also reflect an age-old wisdom that is interior and enduring in the human psyche. This is a workbook for individuals who are taking an inventory of themselves with regard to both limitlessness and limitation. It is not about the shadow of the world but about the shadow of our individual egos and how ready they are for light. Many books on spirituality recommend the letting go of ego. This book tells exactly how. Its purpose is not to inform us about the shadow but to help us taste it in bite-size chunks that surprise us by how nourishing they are.

The focus of these chapters is not a subject outside yourself. You personally are the subject. Read this not for information but for transformation. I have not written this book and then forgotten it. I am still thinking about it and am very much wanting the people who read it to benefit from it. This is my work in the world, and I accompany you as you find yours. The practices in the following pages serve as an examination of conscience by our adult spiritual consciousness. That happens as we befriend our negative shadow. Such befriending also serves to awaken our inner liveliness as we activate and articulate our positive shadow with all its riches, gifts, and potentials. Both dimensions of our soul thereby receive equal attention and grant equal favors. They cooperate as partners in harmony. Befriending the shadow is a dance.

We are not alone on this venture. Assisting forces are collaborating all the time. Even now, as you read these words, many saints and bodhisattvas are gathering to help you. They are attracted to the hearts of those who want to wake up and love more. They are the guardian angels who accompany us over the bridge we notice is unstable and perilous but nonetheless decide to cross.

In the darkness of anything external to me, I find . . .
an interior psychic life that is my own.

—C. G. JUNG

Our Shadow Defined

One need not be a Chamber—to be Haunted—
One need not be a House—
The brain has Corridors—surpassing
Material place—

— EMILY DICKINSON

WHO AM I IN THE DARK?

Aaron sees himself as an honest man and certainly is honest in his financial dealings. At the same time, there is a deeply dishonest vein in his personality. It appears in his relationships with women. Aaron automatically lies about who he is and presents a false front to them. He looks self-confident and trustworthy. But he has never shown or admitted his fear of intimacy and his many ways of running from closeness. Aaron does not know this about himself. Lack of authenticity, even within himself, is an automatic and long-standing habit within him. He easily sees the falseness in others and finds it despicable, but he cannot see it in himself. His honest lifestyle convinces him of his candor. When a woman points out his pretense, Aaron is indignant and feels highly insulted. He has ended several relationships in reaction to this feedback. What little chance Aaron has of finding intimacy! But that is in keeping with his agenda of avoiding the closeness that self-disclosure would introduce into his guarded life. *Is there an Aaron in me?*

Ego can refer to the strong stable center of personality. In this book we distinguish that healthy ego from the neurotic ego, which is sometimes an inflated ego with an arrogant sense of entitlement and sometimes a deflated or impoverished ego driven by low self-worth, shame, or fear. For Buddha the ego was the inner chamber of our fear and attachment. In these pages we look at this dark side of ego. The practices are meant to transform a neurotic ego into a healthy one. This happens by letting go of the former and acting in accord with the latter.

Our scared and arrogant ego has an enormous capacity not to know itself. This shadow side of our ego contains the disowned, disavowed, unlived, and excluded traits and powers of our personality. It is the dimension of our personality that is rejected by our conscious ego. It is both negative and positive. The negative shadow contains all that we despise and reject as unworthy in ourselves. It is not evil, only inferior. Only when it is denied does it gain an autonomous life of its own and become destructively evil. Our dark side is destructive when it is discredited or neglected. It is creative when it is acknowledged and attended to. The positive shadow contains all our untapped creative potential. We may have been taught to despise that side of ourselves too. In both instances, positive and negative, we usually project our shadow onto someone of our own sex since we are meeting up with the dark side of our own ego, not that of our contrasexual side.

Jung says: "The shadow is the negative side of the personality, the sum of all those unpleasant qualities we like to hide, together with the insufficiently developed functions and the contents of the personal unconscious. . . . The shadow does not only consist of morally reprehensible tendencies, but also displays a number of good qualities, such as normal instincts, appropriate reactions, realistic insights, creative impulses, etc."

Our shadow is hidden in our psyche, but we can recognize it and take responsibility for it. The dark side of ourselves can be discovered as the murderer in a whodunit. He looks like all the other characters until he is revealed as deceitfully different. This culprit looked normal as the story unfolded but was secretly up to no good. He himself knew about his malefactions. The shadow, as understood in this book, includes those aspects of the dark side that we know about too.

There is a way to recognize the shadow: what strongly attracts or repels us in others is a clue to where our own darkness lurks. As we begin accepting our shadow, we acknowledge our projections of our shadow qualities onto others as truths about ourselves. My hatred of your controlling ways may cloak controlling ways in me that I do not see. The negative shadow in us is projected onto others as strong dislike or disgust. The positive shadow is projected onto others as admiration or envy.

We may imagine that our *persona* is our true identity. This is the mask we present to the world, the image we display so that people will like us or give us what we want. We began its construction in early life and have never stopped adjusting it to what seems to be required of us. The brighter the mask of the persona looks, the more darkness it may conceal.

We imagine our persona to be our identity and reject anything else about us that might not fit its shiny, or slimy, image. In our persona is collective information that only seems personal. For instance, we know it is "in" to support the environment, so we may automatically speak up for it when we are not truly stirred by a personal concern. We choose our look and behavior in the world from a collective repertory at the expense of our own true needs, wishes, or enthusiasms.

The persona is a necessary part of our personality. It makes life and relationships run smoothly, since we are all observing similar courtesies. Following traffic signs is an example. We do not lose our freedom by obeying them; we preserve our safety and make movement more efficient. Healthy persons find ways to observe the intelligent obligations of the persona and at the same time live in accord with their own desires. We maintain our place in society and still enjoy liberty within it, integrating the civilized mainstream of life and our unique contribution to it.

Since our disowned qualities seem to be outside us but are actually projected by us, as our physical shadow is, the word *shadow* is used to describe them. The abhorred features of our own personality are projected as repulsion, rejection, or dislike of others who demonstrate the very traits we hate in ourselves. The disowned talents and creative potentials in us are projected as strong admiration of others' talents or virtues that seem unattainable by us. We may fear the negative shadow and be in awe of the positive shadow. Both of these reactions are examples of a failure to integrate our own diverse shadow components.

Jung refers to a personal shadow and to a collective shadow, an archetype of our unconscious. The unconscious for Freud is only personal, a cellar of forgotten or disavowed memories. The unconscious for Jung is both personal and cosmic, a cellar of old trunks full of family mementos and an attic of ancient volumes of cherished memories and images from the history of all humankind. It is both a family album—all of what Freud called the personal unconscious—

and a world mythology book. Both the personal and the cosmic unconscious are and contain a shadow. Our personal shadow is the rejected side of our personality and ego; our cosmic shadow is the rejected side of our higher Self. Both the personal and cosmic shadows have positive and negative dimensions.

The persona of a person may be shadow possessed. This happens when one is making no attempt to hide one's dark wishes or evil behavior. One does not put on any mask of goodness but arrogantly acts out a bullying power over others. This can happen in an ongoing way, as with Hitler or a Mafia boss or a psychopath. Some evil can only be dealt with by containment. It cannot be befriended or integrated only stopped in its tracks, as a sudden light stops Dracula. Vampires and werewolves, like Fuhrers, are examples of possession by the collective shadow.

Such possession can happen to any of us at moments in time when our defenses and pretenses are down and we let our grossest desires or actions emerge openly. The shadow is unconscious, but in these instances of possession of the persona, it enters consciousness in an out-of-control and dangerous way. The shadow is the unlived part of us that at times comes to the surface as a lived-out part. This can occur not only deliberately but also passively. What we refer to as passive-aggressive behavior is an example of the evocation of the shadow in an undercover way.

Like the coins in our pockets, the psyche contains both sides of everything. We have conscious qualities, and behind each of them is an unconscious counterpart, like tails to heads. If we are usually selfless, we have a selfish side that may never have emerged. It is an opposite if it is the selfishness of greed and self-seeking narcissism that take advantage of others. But it is a gentle counterpart if it is a healthy selfishness whereby we know how to take care of ourselves and not be consumed by our concern for others. (If we look at this in reverse, this self-nurturance is the positive shadow side of our negative shadow of narcissism.) Virtues have a negative side and vices have a positive side. This follows from the nature of the psyche.

The center of our personal life is our conscious ego; the center and circumference of our entire psyche is the Self. The ego is our psychologist, our personality with its unique attributes, powers, and limitations. It is different in everyone. The Self is our spiritual guide, our higher archetypal identity with universal powers and no limits. It is the same in everyone. *Ego, Self,* and *shadow* are all convenient terms for postulations about mysteries that defy words and cannot be contained by them. The words we use are primitive, almost autistic attempts to distinguish and describe forces in the psyche that are too intense to be grasped or defined. Perhaps every word we have ever uttered is equally provisional. The question is ultimately: What are the interior dynamics that drive us through phases of evolutionary growth to the full realization of our being? Words limp along that road. Yet we proceed with pluck anyway!

The dark side of ego is called the personal shadow. The ego cannot reconcile opposites such as light and dark or control and surrender. It separates and dichotomizes them: "I am in charge and you are at my beck and call." The ego divides reality this way because it is the guardian of our identity. We are intimidated by a split identity and inner opposition and want a simplified solution. The ego will eventually learn that opposites can be reconciled in creative and life-enhancing ways so that healthy counterparts appear. That is the task of spiritual maturity. But at least for the first half of life, the ego is at cross-purposes with the Self, which loves to combine opposites and reconcile them.

Shaping an alliance between ego and Self is called individuation, the experience of wholeness. This is the purpose of our work on ourselves, especially the work of befriending the shadow. *Metta* is a commonly used Buddhist term for this kind of friendliness: loving things as they are and ourselves as we are and others as they are. The *ego* is our unique personality. It is healthy when it is geared to fulfill our life goals of effectiveness and functionality in the world; it becomes neurotic when it is caught up in fear and desire. Our work with our shadow is meant to maximize the healthy ego and downsize our neurotic, inflated ego. For a shadow to be formed, something big has to get in the way of the light. The overinflated ego is the big, substantial giant that creates a shadow. Anything of great weight and substance will generate a shadow. Yet at the same time, only a strong, fully established ego can be individuated, that is, joined to the wholeness of the Self. The work is twofold: in the first half of our life, we build and inflate our ego, and in the second half we dismantle it and build a bridge between our healthy ego and our Self. The first half of life is about power, because that is what it takes to develop our ego. Freud helps us then. The second half of life is about meaning, because that is the focus it takes to go beyond ego. In the great synthesis, power and meaning are united in the interests of service to the world.

The *Self* is a way of referring to three graces of the human spirit: unconditional love, perennial wisdom, and the power to heal ourselves and others. It has been called the god archetype because it has and is these divine qualities. The reason we know these are the qualities of the Self is that they are the historically consistent and universally visible results of enlightened beings. Over the centuries, saints of all religious traditions have manifested love, wisdom, and healing power as a consequence of their conversion, initiation, or awakened states. These gifts of the Self come automatically to those who let go of ego and its dualisms.

In Buddhism, bodhisattvas are enlightened beings who, upon enlightenment, devote their lives to helping others toward that same destiny. There are bodhisattvas because we need assistance on our path. It takes a transcendent energy to effect awakening; it is a work of grace. Why is there a bodhisattva of compassion, Avalokiteshvara; a bodhisattva of power, Vajrapani, who brings enlightenment; Vajrakilaya, a bodhisattva who cuts through obstacles instantaneously? These forces in Buddhism are personifications of the grace required to complete our practice. They are ways of acknowledging that compassion, enlightenment, and freedom from fear and desire are ultimately gifts and cannot be conjured by effort.

A bodhisattva is not attached to personal enlightenment. Nonattachment means not identifying with, not focused on, not putting energy into. The result is that we expand our repertory of generous responses, that is, become more inventive in our ways of loving. This conversion of a personal grace into a world service is the result of the alliance of ego and Self. Formerly opposing forces now coexist fruitfully, and the other-directedness of the three qualities—the three graces—of the Self benefits all humankind.

Central authority is necessary in a society. The Self is the central authority of the psyche to which the ego is accountable. "My true Self is deeper than hell," said Meister Eckhart. The archetypal negative shadow of the collective unconscious of humankind is a principle of or inclination toward evil, not a personal attribute. It is not in us but we can be caught up in it, as individual people can buy into anti-Semitism and trust a leader with a violent plan for injustice. When the Self is in turmoil, it creates order, since it is compensatory and strives for balance. This is how the mass projection onto a savior or führer occurs. Our contemporary society lacks a unifying religious container for the resolution of its chaos, so it is easy pickings for a Hitler.

The archetypal shadow is too enormous to be integrated by any one of us. It can be faced or confronted as Jesus did Satan in the wilderness and as Buddha did the demons. The archetypal devil is a metaphor for the world shadow, which requires not integration but containment or exorcism.[1] God and Satan are metaphors for the two sides of the one valuable coin of the realm of psychic wholeness. We can sometimes project both sides onto one person, as the changing loyalties to Hitler showed. Saint Michael, an archangel, not a human, is the one who can face the collective shadow, which itself is represented by an archangel, Lucifer, since this shadow is beyond the merely human. Exactly the right personifications have been used to tell the cosmic story. (Personification and metaphor are not projections. They are recognitions of the realities of nature as psychically alive.)

The bridge that mediates between our ego and our Self is called the *soul*. This is the conjunction of conscious and unconscious. It is a treasury of images that reflect and contain the vast reaches of our psychic life. These universal archetypal images are the heritage of all humankind. They come to us in waking life in psychic realizations and via synchronicity—meaningful and fortuitous coincidences. They visit us in our unconscious life in dreams, and then we may consciously extend our dreams by active imagination, an inner dialogue with our dream figures. The soul is an ancient repository of universal images that wait to be found in each person's own

1. The psychological version of exorcism may be this: When the shadow is unassimilated, it can become autonomous and possess, gain a stranglehold over, our psyche. Then it has to be objectified and sheared away from the conscious ego. This is the equivalent of exorcism. The desert fathers were probably doing this in their "battles with demons." (Exorcism and its relation to our subject will be addressed later.)

way and time. The images are like words in the dictionary: all there in actuality, with the potential to be looked up, marveled at, and cherished one by one.

In the story of Orpheus, his wife, his soul, Eurydice, remains permanently in the underworld. This is a way of saying that our soul has to remain grounded in the unconscious and is never totally or solely conscious. The work of coming to consciousness is never completed. There is always a piece of our shadow in the underworld. Yet we can achieve and receive just the consciousness we need for a life that richly articulates our destiny. It takes work and a lifelong commitment to assemble our wholeness from the broken fragments and scattered shreds that always prove to be enough.

THE PRACTICE

The practice sections are meant to help you befriend your shadow and become a more healthy adult, both psychologically and spiritually. They combine work and playfulness, since they challenge your energy and engage your imaginative spirit. Before doing any of them, attune yourself to your inner depths and get a sense of how each one may fit for you. Pay attention to the feelings that arise as you encounter each suggestion, and notice and honor those that arise as you proceed with each practice.

Redesign any suggestion so that it coincides with your unique needs. Be sure to spend time in contemplation of the meanings you are aware of or may find. The best work flows from within you. Let the suggestions visit you within the profoundest soundings of your psyche. Then they will not lead to superficial change, because they will reflect your own interior sources and resources. Keep a journal of the work you do and of the points that strike you as significant. Write this on the first page: "Let me hear this shadow speak to me without defensiveness. I want to know what it tells me about myself. I want to hear with a childlike sense of wonder and openness as well as with the depth of my adult experience. I am ready for a shadow dance."

Be careful not to be hard on yourself. You are not meant to be perfectly successful in every part of the work. Make room for what Heinz Kohut calls tolerable failures. Having this empathy for yourself is a path to empathy for others. Do not let the work recommended in this book be another reason for guilt or self-blame. It is meant to be a joyful stretch. There is an inner timing in each individual that does not have to be aligned with the order or number of practice sections in this book. Take what you can in your own time and way. Doing one exercise and skipping two is perfectly legitimate: all you have to do is all you can do. Commitment to change and acceptance of personal timing is the combination that works best.

Walk into the work with your sleeves rolled up and your heart on your sleeve. You have nothing to lose but your limits. All that will happen is an amplification of yourself. Not even your deepest needs, values, and wishes can represent your full and final identity, since they continually change. The word *change* evokes fear. This work and play, like most work and even play, can create anxiety. This is because you are making innovations in your psyche. You are learning to tolerate competing voices: those that have told you who you are and those in this book telling you about how much more you can be. This is not cognitive work. Every practice in befriending the shadow includes feeling. Allow each feeling to arise as you proceed, trusting it to run its course in a beneficial and releasing way.

We will always have traits we are not proud of and positive potential we have not activated. As humans we cannot circumvent that inadequacy. But we can have a program in place that keeps us committed to doing the best we can. The practices in these chapters provide that program and are an antidote to regret and low self-esteem.

Befriending the shadow is incremental work that is exponentially efficacious. The practices are carefully designed technologies meant to enlist every power in your psyche in the interests of self-actualization. Whatever helps us actualize our potential brings happiness and makes us more compassionate. This is why the practices are ultimately about loving more.

• List five traits you strongly dislike about members of each of the following groups: your family, members of your profession, people of your same sex, people who have your national background, people of your religious tradition. Acknowledge each of these listings as somehow true of you. Do this by drawing a picture if that is more to your liking. If possible, share the result of this exercise with someone you trust in each of the categories.

• Notice what elicits your shadow reactions: "He's gentle as a lamb until he gets behind a wheel." "He is fine until you live with him." "Once she starts drinking, you see a whole different side of her." What are the trigger points in your life that release the negative shadow side of you? They may be money, sex, drugs, certain people, relationships, driving a car, dealing with children, religious fanaticism, ambition at work, and so on.

Triggers of the shadow might be located by attention to these questions: Are you tight with money? Do you use people or punish others with sex? Do you use alcohol or drugs for permission to go out of control? Who are the people who bring out the worst—or best—in you? Are you more aggressive behind the wheel of a car? Do your children trigger an impatience and rage that you would not dare show other adults? (Our children manifest, elicit, contain, and sometimes act out our shadow side, both positive and negative.) Ask: Do I push my religious or political beliefs on others or shame others or myself for actions that I consider not morally acceptable? Am I cutthroat at work? Do I act honestly?

If alcohol is your trigger, consider Alcoholics Anonymous, which offers a twelve-step program of recovery that directly addresses befriending the shadow. Steps one through three are *work on ourselves* to let go of ego and trust a power greater than ego. Steps four through ten are *work with others* to acknowledge accountability to them and live compassionately with them. Steps eleven and twelve are work *for the world* to share what we have learned as a gift we have received. The program thus combines effort and grace, that is, it is spiritual.

Mardi Gras and Halloween are examples of socially acceptable triggers of the shadow. They legitimize going out of character, out of persona. We have full permission then to visit the darker or less controlled corners of our imagination and act out what we keep repressed all year.

• Where do you stand today and how can you move more and more to the left side of this list?

Healthy Ego	*Neurotic Ego*
Observes	Denies or dissects
Assesses	Judges and blames
Acts in accord with assessments	Does not easily learn or put knowledge into practice
Learns from mistakes	Repeats old mistakes

Makes amends for mistakes	Denies responsibility or projects it onto others
Lives in present	Lives in past or future
Makes choices that further life goals	Makes choices that cause pain and are self-defeating
Is free from compulsions	Is compulsive and obsessive
Is not moved or stopped by fear or clinging	Is caught in fear and clinging
Lives in accord with deepest needs, values, and wishes	Accedes to the demands of others
Can relate, make and keep commitments, and show intimacy	Is unable to commit, stymied by fears of abandonment or engulfment
Will address, process, and resolve issues	Refuses to see, work through, or be accountable for problems
Has mastery in the world	Is victimized by circumstances
Is self-motivated and charged with initiative	Is driven by forces outside or impulses within
Invents creative solutions in the moment	Resorts to self-defeating or inherited habits
Has lively energy with serenity	Has nervous energy with anxiety

Technically the shadow is unconscious, but the shadow of our ego manifests consciously in the choices, behavior, and attitudes listed in the left-hand column. It is comforting to realize that the practice of letting go of the neurotic ego does double duty, installing the healthy ego at the same time.

AFRAID OF OUR OWN SHADOW

We are often afraid of our own reality. Every time we disown, discredit, and run from what we really are, our life becomes fear based. In the process, valuable powers in ourselves fail to be acknowledged. Paradoxically, these are the very powers that become resources to us when we face what scares us in ourselves. Ironically, we fear our shadow *because* we refuse to integrate it. Fear is a refusal to let in that which is threatening. When ignored, the shadow may turn on us, since it has become split off and autonomous. As in the case of disenfranchised and oppressed minorities in a society, what is kept unwelcome eventually turns on us.

When it is attended to, however, the shadow can release many wonderful powers in us. In every "negative" quality is a corresponding positive dimension. This is the power we access when we integrate our shadow. For instance, when we stop fearing our own tendency toward rage, we access our healthy and safe anger. Love integrates, lets in. Fear disintegrates, shuts out.

Anything larger than life looms over us menacingly and thus cannot be integrated. Notice how Jesus in the wilderness does not "fall down and worship" Satan as if this shadow were truly autonomous. Jesus relates to him by dialogue, that is, through active imagination. In Tibetan ritual, dancers wear masks of demon faces and then dance as if they were the demons. They believe that in this shadow dance they transform the dark forces into beneficent and cheerful spirits. This is acknowledging and trusting that everything has two sides and that direct embrace of one side will reveal and liberate its reverse.

What remains unintegrated casts a spell on us and becomes deadly and scary. Fictional personifications of this always fascinate us: Mephistopheles, Dracula, Darth Vader. The destructive, ego-driven Heathcliff is the shadow side of the desirable, uninhibited Victorian lover. Mister Hyde is the shadow side of the Victorian gentleman who, at night, when unconscious, becomes a predator. Obsession results from just such a failure to integrate both sides of oneself: Jekyll/Hyde, Othello/Iago, and Odette/Odille in *Swan Lake*. What is repressed erupts in obsessive symptoms that exhume precisely what we sought to bury.

Befriending the shadow is like the wrestling of Jacob with the angel, not like the killing of Goliath by David. What we exclude, kill off, never lets us go. What we include, work with, can have no hold on us. Integrating the shadow places us at the threshold of that life-and-death choice. We can create a barrier to our unconscious by not working with all its contents. This is a loss because it contains so many wonderful treasures, both personal and collective. It is like losing both our own jewel box and the city museum.

Fears of the shadow in us explain our penchant for prejudice, war, scapegoating, and violence. Those too scared even to know of their own absolutist inclinations might be the strongest voices against the right wing. Fears of one's own shadow find targets in the people who look the part. Our fear makes us project the archetype of evil onto others, and thus we can reject or kill them. How sadly ironic that the Ahab ego that has to win by killing what hurt him winds up lashed to the runaway whale.

We often put a face on our anxiety so it can be more easily dealt with. We can more readily fight a monster with a face and a name. Stories and films create monsters to give our anxieties a focus. We do the same thing with our prejudices: "gooks" are more easily dealt with than human beings.

Alan is upset by the devastation of the planet and the loss of so many rain forests. He goes beyond making a donation to Greenpeace. He is deeply and personally disturbed and his obsession does not go away. Alan uses expressions like "rape." His indignation has a personal flavor. How is this the emergence of a shadow issue? Nature is feminine, our mother. Alan has experienced a long-term violation of his own feminine side at the hands of dominant males. This is his personal paradigm of the pillage of nature by industrialists. No amount of sophistication can defeat the "kick in the gut" feeling that arises when the shadow appears. Alan acts from this place and it seems to be about nature, but it is really about the losses and hurts that plundered his own sensitivities long ago. He fears opening this Pandora's box in his psyche. It is easier to put all that energy into a truly legitimate and worthy cause. Alan's work is to confront this shadow side of his own past and then to approach ecology with more cool and less fever.

Shadow issues reach us at a gut level of fear, as Alan's story shows. Why are animals guides in so many myths and stories? It may be because they act fearlessly from this gut level; they act from instinct. We are mostly inept at understanding or processing from that underworld place in ourselves. This is why the work of integration will seem scary. To befriend the shadow is to face fear and work with it. The work implants the courage to reclaim what it is demoralizing to admit about ourselves. Admission that we have a dark side is the best protection from its deleterious effects and the best entry into its salubrious effects.

WHAT CHARACTERS WE ARE!

We are more than we seem. Our unconscious is not a mere absence of consciousness. It is a teeming, creative force that transcends consciousness, a cosmic or collective unconscious. Its contents are called archetypes. Archetypes are typical and recurrent themes of human experience that are articulated in images. They are innate ways we have of perceiving and ordering our experience of the world, the psychic equivalents of physical instincts. The archetypes are the meeting points of spirit and matter, the psychological and the physical, the material and the spiritual. Each archetype combines all the apparent contenders in the psychic stadium. Behind each is a psychic fact about us.

Myths embody the essential meanings of a society and of the psyche. There are familiar mythic personifications of each archetype. These are the characters of any hero story: the hero, at first a helpless or endangered child, then a fighter, and finally a victor who has won a soul mate who may first need rescuing but then becomes a profound ally. The wise old man or woman helps the hero find his or her powers or destiny. The villain (shadow) opposes the hero but ultimately helps discover and uncover the hero's potentials. The earth mother, the sky father, are the assisting forces of the hero's origins. The trickster, usually with humor, gives the hero's, or the villain's, arrogant ego its comeuppance. We are born with all these characters in our ancient cosmic memory, and at the same time, they are *character*istics of ourselves. This is why we find such immense appeal in stories that display those very themes, for example, *Star Wars* or *The Wizard of Oz*.

Our destiny, our heroic task, our psychological and spiritual work (all one and the same), is to do what the characters in the stories do: open up our personal unused potentials and then make them conscious in our lives in the service of others. Hero stories usually end with the hero bringing a boon of peace or higher consciousness to other people. The hero's destiny was not only to achieve something for himself or herself but to contribute to the welfare and happiness of all. Our destiny is the same: to find our own wholeness and then to share it everywhere. Our inner gifts and our inner work can be so deftly realized that a tranquil world is thereby evoked. For this we receive archetypal confirmation: our experience is part of a continuum of many long eras of heroic human history. Every hero of the past is a predecessor who has done the same work we do now.

Hero stories often end with marriage to a soul mate. The psychic marriage is between our own inner forces and powers. The soul mate is the anima, the feminine energy in the hero, personified by the princess. For the heroine, it is the animus, the masculine energy in herself that is personified by the dashing prince. Anima and animus are archetypes of the wholeness of men and women. We all contain our other side in gender. In this sense, male and female are not opposites but counterparts. When this side becomes the dark side, as in the macho man who refuses to show the softer dimension of his personality, the shadow appears. Saying that men are from Mars and women are from Venus divides the sexes. From the perspective of befriending the shadow, men are from Mars during a Venus eclipse and women are from Venus during a Mars eclipse.

Archetypes display themselves in personifications: mother, father, hero, wise old man, trickster, and so forth. But they can also be events of life: birth, death, marriage, child rearing. They can be things: sun, moon, serpent, and the like. (The signs of the zodiac are archetypes.) They can be motifs: task, judgment, sacrifice, journey, mission, birth-death-rebirth, feast, revolution, metamorphosis, the conjunction of opposites. All these appear in dreams, myths, imagination, and daily reality. Synchronicity—meaningful coincidence—and dreams present to consciousness an archetype ready to be befriended.[2] Life-enhancing meanings visit us and invite us to step up to our full stature. These archetypal movements beyond our control or ability to predict were once called magic, demons, witchcraft. They are actu-

2. My book *The Power of Coincidence: How Life Shows Us What We Need to Know* (Shambhala, 2007) gives information and practices on working with dreams and synchronicity.

ally the vehicles by which universal longings for and patterns of wholeness are allowed to individualize in our conscious life. Archetypes are thus psychic dispositions or instincts that enable us to activate the spiritual possibilities of the Self. Our ego may fear the emergence of this Self because it means less drama, less control, less entitlement, and fewer dramatic arguments with the conditions of human existence.

When our ego works cooperatively with an archetype, that is, lets it become conscious, we have a consoling sense of being *accompanied* on our journey. Befriending the shadow archetype, for instance, makes it a comrade, not an enemy. When the ego refuses to cooperate, complexes, diseases, or depression can result, because then an archetype has turned against us. Denial of our shadow may lead to being attacked by our shadow. The overly innocent Pollyanna may meet up with a predator and be seriously hurt. Pollyanna's shadow side is her vulnerability to victimization. An archetype often constellates to show a person's shadow and help the person's one-sidedness become more balanced. It can be a painful compensation. This is why conscious choice to look for our shadow and make friends with it is a shrewd and safe investment.

Archetypes want to be met consciously and related to rather than denied out of fear or clung to out of compulsion. Relating to our own archetypal longings for wholeness is the real meaning of working on ourselves. An archetype is prerational, so to integrate its contents we have to reconnect ourselves to our archaic inheritance. This first happens through ordinary experiences, for instance, the mother-child bond, facing an enemy, meeting up with someone we strongly admire. Unusual people exemplify the archetypes: Jesus, Buddha, the Dalai Lama, Mother Teresa . . . and Hitler too. We consciously continue the integrating work by practice. The work sections of this book present those practices.

The archetypes are numinous. Numinosity is an aura of luminosity that surrounds an archetype when it appears in powerful human experiences. It is an emotionally laden, inspiring, and energizing power. It suddenly strikes us with awe, terror, or joy, since we are encountering the divine Self, the archetype of meaning, where all the opposites coalesce. It is a spiritual incandescence and assistance that is independent of human conjuring, beyond our control, a grace. "What is above creation cannot be attained by action," say the Upanishads.

Three Greek words have a single root: grace *(charis),* joy *(chara),* gift *(charisma).* Grace fills us with the joy of a gift. Aristotle posits that something can be empirically invisible in space and time and yet be operative in them. Grace is that invisible numinous assistance that takes us a step beyond the limits of our intellect and will. It is in us but has a life of its own, ruled by forces that we cannot comprehend and that we are not in charge of. Something, we know not what, is always at work doing, we know not how, just what it takes for us to follow the trajectory of our destiny of wholeness. The emotional energy of grace downplays linear thought and frees up unlimited psychic energy. Grace cannot free us from our shadow but it can free us from possession by it.

In Buddhism our individual practice is not quite sufficient for enlightenment. In the Obaku Zen tradition and in Pure Land Buddhism, we are upheld by the supporting power of compassion from the heart of Amitabha, the Buddha of infinite light and life. This is the equivalent of the Western concept of grace: our limited intellect has to access a higher wisdom; our limited will has to be supplemented for full effectiveness.

Grace stands in opposition to fate: In *The Golden Ass* by Apuleius, Isis redeems the hero and intervenes with miraculous grace: "Ill fortune has no foothold against the lives of those whom the majesty of the goddess has saved to be her servants. Behold how Lucius, by the providence of the mighty Isis, joyfully triumphs over fate." In Isis's litany she says: "I am victorious over fate. Destiny obeys me." Grace shows the full extent of our universe. We are not alone; we are attended.

The emotional energy in an archetype feels as if it were coming from outside, hence miraculous. A miracle is a surprising transformation that connects and aligns powers from within and beyond us. We imagine special capacities only in magical or holy persons, but we have them too: "Thy faith has saved thee." The real miracle is grace, the power that assists us in reaching our destiny when all our ego powers are laid waste or laid bare, a common theme in hero stories. Miracles, grace, are our one hope of reprieve in the face of the implacable conditions of existence. "Only a miracle can save him now."

Archetypes surround the ego in pairs of opposites. Each has two balanced sides, positive and negative. There is a hero and a villain, a father and a mother, a wise kindly guide and a troublesome trickster. The positive figures meet the negative ones and the human drama is complete. This is not negative in the sense of bad but negative in the algebraic sense: a characteristic to take into account as we work toward a balance of the whole equation. An archetype is an equation of personal power. The darker side of our powers balances with the brighter side. The work is to reconcile these apparent opposites that are really complements. Every negative thing about us is balanced in our unconscious with something immensely positive. What may seem irredeemable is not only redeemable but even healing to the universe.

The true hero is the one who has found out both how inadequate his ego is and how great is the Self in which he moves. Wounded and weary, he nonetheless comes back home with gift-bestowing hands. His efforts have depleted him, but grace has made his heart replete with gifts and powers. Pinocchio saves the day but then has to lie inanimate on the shore until the fairy comes to restore him and make him real, that is, whole.

The central, most powerful, and most numinous archetype is the Self, the conjunction of opposites, the wholeness of being and becoming. The Self is the Western term for Buddha nature or Christ consciousness, personifications of the archetype of wholeness. *Whole* means containing in unity all the opposing forces in the psyche in a befriending and productive way. The image of the sacred marriage is the most common culminating theme of the hero-journey motif. In marriage, the opposites combine and love—befriend—each other. The couple also produces a human-divine (ego-Self) person. The mythic marriage of a god and a human culminates in a virgin birth: the new life is from the Source directly, a result of grace. The work of each individual is to join in that process that *wants to happen.*

Relationship itself is a concretization of the archetype of wholeness because it combines opposites. Projection is another, especially the variety that occurs in therapy, called transference. (If we look carefully, we may see that transference is about projection of the positive and negative shadow.) Likewise, our whole support system of friends and assisting forces is like satellites in harmonious orbit around our solar solitude. If these connections are kept conscious, we are befriending our shadow. If they become or remain unconscious, we are darkening our shadow.

Other concrete examples of our natural human inclination to play, and our fascination with playing with opposites, are games, arguments, competitions, debates, political parties, biases, wars. Arjuna, in the *Mahabharata*, sees the lineup of two opposing forces ready for battle. Both include his relatives, that is, parts of himself. His lifelong spiritual task is presented and encouraged by Krishna: to join in the battle and then reconcile all these opposing forces in his own soul. When there is no more strife within or without, our work has worked. Our work on ourselves is also the only chance the weighed-down world has for healing, since it can happen only one person at a time.

> *Only the living presence of the eternal images can lend the human psyche a dignity which makes it morally possible for a person to stand by his own soul, and be convinced that it is worth his while to persevere with it. Only then will he realize that the conflict is in him and that the discord and the tribulation are riches which should not be squandered by attacking others.*
>
> —C. G. JUNG

THE PRACTICE

• Who are your three favorite and long-term heroes from books or films? List the characteristics of each of them. Draw pictures of yourself with each of them. What are the qualities in your heroes that are also your own potentials? Write the words and phrases on index cards and use one of them each day as a mantra or affirmation. Simply repeat the word while imaging your hero, then switch your own face with the hero's.

• Who are your three worst villains or tyrants from books or films? List the traits of each of them. Draw pictures of yourself with each of them. What are the characteristics in these shadow figures that are also your own? Admit these to yourself and remember them for further work in future chapters. For now, acknowledgment is enough.

• Think of mother and father figures, wise guides, tricky characters, and the like, in books and films. How are any of these also like you in some way? Who are the people you have met along the way who fit into the various character/archetype roles? How have they helped or hindered you?

• The animal you love, especially if it is one most people do not like, is a clue to your positive and negative shadow. For instance, to like crows because they are naughty while most people consider them rude, impudent, and pesky may tell you something about your inner unexpressed aggression as well as your potential for assertiveness. Which is your favorite animal? Which animal scares you the most? Which animal do you find most repulsive? Which animal do you find most admirable? What are the things in nature that most appeal to you or most repel you? How do your answers to each of the above questions reveal you to yourself?

• An inner inclination in the psyche toward homeostatic balance leads us to have dreams that present images and events that compensate for our one-sidedness in conscious life. For example, if we are overly controlling we might dream of ourselves being submissive or passive. Such an unlived side of us is also our shadow. Admirable and disturbing deeds we perform and figures in dreams who seem nothing like us reveal our positive and negative shadow. Dream work is thus a crucial part of shadow work. Keep a journal of your dreams and establish a dialogue in your active imagination with the figures you meet. Notice how the practices in this book may make your dreams more vivid and how they coalesce with the themes in your dreams.

The compensatory action of the psyche happens in the day world too. We find ourselves with the very people who show us the missing side of ourselves. This coincidence is synchronicity. It is a meaningful union of apparent opposites that expands our identity to its full dimensions. Finally, it is meaningful because it cuts through the inveterate tendency of ego to divide in a binary way: male and female, black and white, soul and body, good and bad, smart and stupid, and so forth. Instead there is an acknowledgment of inner and outer coincidence, coexistence with all that is different from us, and cohesiveness with it all.

Make a two-column list, divided by decades, of the most significant events and persons in your life. In one column list the events and relationships that were based on choice and in the other those based on chance. Choice is from our own will. Chance has an origin that transcends it. Notice where the line between these polarities blurs. That is the coincidence of chance and choice: synchronicity. Is such synchronicity in our lives evidence that something, we know not what, has always been at work, we know not how, collaborating with us on destiny's path?

2

The Shadow of Ego

*Are you willing to be sponged out, erased, canceled,
made nothing? If not, you will never really change.*

—D. H. LAWRENCE

*O*UR PERSONAL SHADOW is the dark side of our healthy
ego. It is our neurotic, inflated ego, of which we are mostly
unaware. The neurotic ego is the part of us that is caught in
fear and in attachment to control and entitlement. It is the
FACE—Fear, Attachment, Control, and Entitlement—that
we show to feel safe. The ego does not know its first name,
Fear, but loves its last name, Entitlement. The ego is the face
we are trying to save in "saving face" and do not want to lose
in "losing face."

This arrogant ego can be our way of disavowing our
vulnerability to the conditions of existence: things change,
nothing lasts, things are not always fair, pain is part of life,
we are alone. Such harsh conditions are the shadow side of
our human existence but not evil in themselves. The conditions of existence can engender healthy humility. This happens best with a beginner's mind that is no longer in the grip
of a frightened or demanding ego. *Humility* comes from the
word *humus*. To be rooted in earth's conditions with an un-

conditional yes is humility. It is not to perceive ourselves as beneath all things but to be conscious of our place within all things. In that sense it is simply a devotion to the truth about us and our floating world. As the Chinese philosopher Fung Yu Lan says: "The sage *accompanies and welcomes* all that happens, both that which is arising and that which is dying. . . . This is why his joy is unconditional" (emphasis mine).

The shadow of earthly life is a source of pain, Buddha's first noble truth. To tolerate pain is the appropriate adult skill in the face of this unalterable circumstance. The alternative, refusal to accept the universality of suffering, actually makes us more susceptible to it. To accept it as a fact does not mean satisfaction with it or approval of it, only response to it. The response is mindfulness: observing with a focused and fearless awareness of the present. We then accommodate the thorns of an experience in the same way we can with a rose. The result is less impingement by the emotional charge or the ego indignation. Feelings are soothed by the gentle yes. Paradoxically, this is the best position from which to begin changing what can be changed.

Inherent in the ego is a resistance to spiritual progress because it entails the letting go of the ego's favorite props: control, retaliation, entitlement. The ramparts of our ego defend against change, against the work on ourselves that might alter our character and lead us to spiritual heights. How ironic that we are calibrated to resist what might most expand us!

The ego fears change in general because change means loss and loss leads to grief. The arrogant, neurotic ego is our scared inner opponent to the givens of existence. The ego is also the false front we present to mask our terror of this uncontrollable world. It is our long-standing pretense that we are in control and above life's threats and givens. It is the armor over our vulnerability to grief. Since vulnerability makes us lovable, this ego blockades love, which it fears and yet desperately desires. This is the ego that contravenes our best interests but is also touching and worthy of compassion. It is the frightened child within us, whistling in the cemetery, who deserves accompaniment. Making friends is the accompaniment that is most harmonious, our purpose in this book.

The work is to build a sense of our natural fit into the conditions of existence rather than to engage in an ongoing argument with them. We will lose such an argument, and depression results: a combination of grief and pessimism. Healthy people maintain an enduring sense of a healthy ego that abides throughout the painful and pleasurable vicissitudes of life. That is how nature itself is experienced, as cyclic. True optimism is not the prospect of control over pain or elimination of it but survival through it. Heinrich Zimmer says: "Everything is part of an ever-changing and ever-lasting self-revelation of the universe." There is optimism!

When we crave permanence, death is the final argument we lose. The ego also fears death and configures it as the darkest shadow. Yet death is not the shadow of life but its necessary counterpart, an ingredient, a season of the cycle by which nature thrives and renews itself. Only when it is fading does the rose produce the seeds that continue its life cycle. The scared ego runs from the pain and death programmed into healthy evolution. The fear of death is the shadow of life. To elude the facing of death, the ego uses ambition, greed, procreation, acclaim, attempts to stave off aging, and many other desperate avoidances. To face the fact of a personal ending is to stand steadfast and calm and to greet it as a return to the Source, that is, the Self. The Self is ever ancient and ever new, the ego grows old and dies at the end of a lifetime. Life and death are examples of apparent opposites that are actually in simultaneous and continual combination. Thomas Merton writes: "Life affirms itself by consenting to its end." The work is to be willing to say yes unconditionally to seasons of life and death, of beginning and ending, of arising and falling, of blooming and fading. A yes with gusto is the best sign that the work has progressed. The return to the Source is what is meant by spiritual evolution. The Source is the source of consciousness, which in all religious traditions is considered divine.

Take the thing nearest to you in nature now, for example, a tree, and picture it in each of its four seasons. Use this technique whenever you find yourself fearing death, aging, or change of any kind.

Some people were so wounded in early life that they will never see or befriend the shadow side of their ego. They are entrenched in making sure that their ego is well defended and continually advanced, which they do with verve, cunning, and creative energy. They may have something going for them that the indifferent or lackadaisical person does not have.

Bruce is a difficult man to work with or to love. He is firmly committed to his own purposes in life at the expense of those around him. He has to be first in all that he does and he does not seem to care about others' needs or concerns. Bruce's life revolves around the making of money. He already has much more than he will ever need but he feels compelled always to make more. He gives nothing to charity and is tightfisted with money among his friends. Bruce has been in a number of relationships, but none of them has worked out. He has a strong fear of self-giving, and giving in general, and this proves deadly to the fruition of intimacy. Bruce comes from a childhood background of severe emotional deprivation. He has feared ever since that he will not get what is coming to him, so he makes sure that does not happen and loses out on emotional closeness in the bargain. A man afraid to give is hard to love when healthy love means giving to one who also gives back.

Bruce *can* work through his early traumas and losses and then become less fearful about the possibility of current losses. For Bruce, anything given is lost and anything not gained is a cause of grief. The problem is that Bruce never grieves; he only looks for ways to make up for what he has lost, no matter who else may lose in the process. Ego is about fear and grasping. Bruce is inextricably embroiled in both of those. His hell is happening here on earth because of this. Bruce may not see the folly of his life's purposes and his lifestyle. He will always be able to blame others for falling behind or manipulate others into helping him climb success's ladder even higher. He would benefit from a spiritual conversion or an exposure to the work of becoming more open about his shadow. Bruce sees all that as foolishness.

But other forces, the assisting forces of the cosmic positive shadow, are looking out for Bruce and want to reinvest his wonderfully indefatigable energy into a larger purpose. Fortunately, their success does not depend entirely on Bruce. Like Dorothy in Oz, he may be tossed into the spiritual world, ready or not. Like Job, he may have everything taken from him and find something greater than anything he lost. Bruce's energy is important to the world, and that is his best chance for spiritual renewal. Built into his negative shadow is something that attracts and opens the powers of the positive shadow that can then benefit all of us.

Perhaps people who choose suicide for emotionally devastating reasons really want to commit egocide, to kill off fear-based habits, inner assailing voices, pointless quarrels with the conditions of existence, and besieging griefs. They may believe that they have no corresponding resources at their disposal to deal with these dismaying asperities. The practice of befriending the shadow provides just such a set of resources.

The ego has a personality and a nationality. There is a criminal ego, a military ego, a male ego, a female ego ("Hell hath no fury . . ."), a fundamentalist and religious ego, and an ego for every nationality, each with its own peculiar nuances. A Spanish way of referring to ego is *macho*. A baseball player socks the umpire "because he did not show respect for me as a man." That phrase might actually be "did not show respect for my ego." Sports events have become ego events in recent years. Sportsmanship means letting ego take second place to teamwork, but we do not often hear that word anymore.

Honor and *victory with honor* are terms used by the national ego to induce young men to die for an ego cause. In *Henry IV,* Falstaff speaks of honor: "Can honor set a leg? . . . What is honor? A word. What is that word honor? Air—a trim reckoning! . . . Honor is a mere scutcheon. So ends my catechism." (In Shakespearean times, a scutcheon was a coat of arms borne at a funeral, an apt reference here). How many young men have died "for honor," or was it because of a president's ego? (What hypocrisy the ego is capable of: to say it is a sacrilege for a president to have sex in the Oval Office and yet it is perfectly acceptable for president after president to plan wars there!)

As long as we are caught in the dramas of fear and desire, we are stuck in the shadow of ego and not able to access the powers of fearless love. The consoling paradox is that the more we let go of our ego, the more we *hold* our desire and fear without being overwhelmed or possessed by them. A wide compassion then emerges and we become our full selves.

Inflation is identification with archetype. Relationship to an archetype is itself conjunction, an ego-Self axis. Possession by an archetype is the disjunction of ego and Self. Being possessed by the shadow of power inflates the ego. It takes such forms as narcissism, control, and megalomania. Our work is to dematerialize this ego, to shed light on it, to transform it, to depose it, and thus to release its grip on the rest of our psyche. How is this done? The work of dismantling ego is achieved by practice *and* is received as a gift by the cosmic Self that supports our efforts with grace. (The belief that we are all there is and that only by willpower can we achieve something is ego too.)

Why do we let go of ego? We let go of ego because that is the best way to release our perhaps repressed but certainly abundant love for others. When the wall of an inflated ego falls, the long-obstructed light comes through. "Relationship to the Self is at once a relationship to our fellow man," says Jung. Crises have the same effect; they deflate our ego to release our potential for love when we collaborate with them. Achilles in his role as the inflated ego killed Hector in an act of retaliation. Later his gentled ego's compassion brought crisis and love together when the grieving Achilles said to Hector's grieving father: "Unhappy man! What mighty sorrows must thy spirit endure. . . . But come, sit beside me upon my couch."

Invested in ego, we defend against change.
Divested of ego, we work cooperatively toward change.

THE PRACTICE: Seeing What We Are up to and Changing It for the Better

Why do some things upset us so much? The neurotic, inflated ego, the shadow side of the healthy ego, is an automatic proclivity in us to control others, place ourselves first at the expense of others, or punish them for daring to cross us. This ego is what makes us believe we are entitled to an exemption from the conditions of human existence, that we are above pain and injustice. It is an arrogance that is full of the fear of grieving losses and of taking our lumps like everyone else.

Ego shows its hand when it is challenged. We sometimes notice that a reaction cannot quite be accounted for by the stimulus we have encountered. A person is curt with us on the phone and it keeps gnawing at us all day. What is making it last? Here are some possibilities:

• Am I seeing a mirror image of myself? Am *I* like that sometimes? Is it in me to treat people that way? Does it bother me that she gets away with it and I do not? Our negative shadow contains all that we strongly detest in ourselves but cannot see. We tend to see this shadow of ours in others, detesting in them exactly what is disowned in us. The work is to ask ourselves if what strikes us so deeply about others' behavior is the clue to a similar trait in us.

• Is my arrogant ego indignant? "How dare he talk to *me* that way. Doesn't he know who I am? I'll be damned if I let him get away with this. I'll get back at him somehow." These statements give us the further clue that the entitled controlling ego is enraged at not getting its way. The inflated ego has a dogged dedication to the promotion of its own self-interest, even to the detriment of others. We might say that the ego is an organ of our personality that when aroused by any slight to its grandiose sense of entitlement, becomes inflated, stands at full mast, and starts poking. Like the erect penis, the neurotic ego has no conscience or clarity.

The work is to acknowledge this and forego any punitive reaction. This requires a pause between action and reaction. Such mindfulness grants us the freedom to choose a response from a vast repertory rather than revert to the automatic settings of ego. (Ego's biggest failure is in imagination.) Saint

Thomas adds, "Beauty arrests motion." The pause also makes an aesthetic experience possible.

• "My father talked to me that way and it hurt." The curtness you met with today may trigger a reminder of a similar wound from the past. You feel hurt and powerless, a signal that your inner child has come to the forefront of your consciousness. It has come to tell you where you still feel hurt or afraid. The work is to grieve the past hurt by letting feelings about it arise. To handle the fear means admitting it, feeling it fully, cradling it as legitimate, and acting as if it cannot prevent you from getting on with your life. These are healthy ways of soothing an archaic part of yourself rather than being at the mercy of your ego/shadow.

To face and deal with our fears is a way to find our gifts. To inhale is to receive life, and to exhale is to give it back with our own unique breath. Thus, to release fear by deep breath means that *inspiration* happens when fear goes. The purpose of befriending the shadow is not to run from the dark or hide in it but to become companionable with it, to re-vision it as a necessary landscape in human becoming. Befriending the shadow is initiation: it begins in our fear of the pain in store and the unknown darkness to be entered, and it ends in rebirth.

• Which of the following sentences are characteristic of you?

What the Shadow of the Ego Sounds Like

Everyone has to acknowledge my superiority.
If I am wronged, someone will pay for it.
Rules don't apply to me.
How dare you question me?
It won't be done right unless I do it.

I deserve a special deal.

I become explosive if crossed.

I'm never wrong.

I cannot tolerate having to ask or learn from anyone.

How dare you not realize:

> I have to get my way.

> You have to do it my way.

> You cannot override my decisions, think for yourself, or act
>   on your own if you want to be close to me.

> I have to be loudly appreciated for every accomplishment.

> I can't be shown up or shown to be wrong.

> I have to be excused for every mistake.

> I may be highly insulted by the least slight.

> I have to get the last word in.

> I cannot lose face (lose ego).

> I can make demands on you but you cannot make demands
>   on me.

> I have to win, even at board games—at which I may be cut-
>   throat or cheat.

> I am fiercely territorial.

> I have to be loved, be respected, and given preference by
>   everyone, all the time, no matter what! Otherwise, I'll
>   have to get back at you.

Notice the words *have to* and how they reveal the compulsive element of ego reactions. This is the opposite of the pause that makes free choice and new alternatives possible.

The way to tell that none of the sentences listed above is operative in you is that you can take what happens simply as information. Then you speak up assertively, refuse to accept abuse, and still feel compassion for people who believe they have to be mean. Events still elicit feelings that you express, but you let go of them soon and move on. You have not been so strongly affected as to lose you own groundedness or boundaries, and you hold no grudge. Furthermore, you can receive feedback and even criticism as information rather than as a threat.

Your healthy ego may be rankled by an injustice, but it sensibly assesses its power to handle it and acts accordingly. You see a need and mindfully devise a resource to meet it. Out-of-control, or inappropriate reactions point to where your work is. They tell you what needs to be addressed, processed, and resolved in yourself. This is how overreactions to others can become valuable information about yourself. When this affirmation—which combines reasonable effort with respect for the conditions of existence—seems to fit you like a glove, you are on track: "I do my best and let the chips fall where they may."

• How can you deal with the aggressive negative shadow of others? When people come at you with ego venom, the healthy program is twofold: stand up and back away. First, stand up for yourself by refusing to accept the abuse others may inflict: "You cannot talk to me like that." "Stop, I won't be treated that way." Then move away and move on without having to get in the last word. To be compelled to win or to punish is to be caught in the same ego game your offender is playing. It takes courage to stand up and say no and it takes self-confidence to move away without a retaliatory fight. The result of these two approaches is self-respect. Try this technique the next time you are face-to-face with someone's shadow. Remember that the idea here is to act as if you were already courageous and self-confident. After repeated practice, you will do it naturally. Authentic virtue is the result of work.

You may notice that someone in your life is utterly incapable of receiving feedback or constructive criticism of any kind. She acts defensively, seeking to justify herself or to show that you are wrong. Remember that the ego is tone-deaf to voice inflection. The slightest criticisms are heard by the *en garde* ego as if they were sharped. A person's ego actually hears even gentle feedback at a higher pitch than you are using. This activates the predictable reaction of self-protection and makes hearing you impossible. Perhaps our frustration at and boredom with this may give way to compassion someday, the same compassion we feel for someone with a physical hearing problem.

• Some people after being hurt feel no hatred toward their persecutors. It seems that they have no need to retaliate to recover from a blow to the ego. Instead, anger, grief, and forgiveness serve that purpose. When a vulnerable self has fragmented by reason of disappointment or betrayal, rage may arise. This is a result of uncontained—and unexperienced— anger. An intact person uses healthy anger to register an "Ouch!" *How do I keep myself afloat? What does it take for me to recover?*

• Find one example of a strong reaction that occurred this week and look for your shadow in it. Acknowledge this shadow possibility from now on, whenever you are strongly upset by something. Write about it in your journal but also share it in the moment, with the person who incited it, and then later with a friend.

• Find an example in your own life of holding a grudge or of attempting to get back at someone for what he has done to you. Instead of the silent treatment or any other form of punishment, approach the other with love and ask for amends without blaming him. This is acting in accord with a standard of friendliness no matter what someone has done to you. If the other person does not respond in kind, notice how good you feel nonetheless, since you, at least, have done the loving thing. After practicing this for a while, it will matter less and less whether others respond as you wish. Your compassion for them will grow and that self-expanding feeling in yourself will be sufficient reward. You will notice that it feels better to do good than to get even. Then you understand why love is the essence of spirituality. This results in freedom from fear: "Perfect love casts out fear because fear brings punishment." (I John 4:18)

• Ego is not a personal fault. It is a conditioned response to the collective setting in which we have always lived. It is a bequest from the unawakened world. But the awakened world bequeaths us something too: this work and our spiritual practices. We are indebted to the past archetypally and at the mercy of it ego-collectively. In the same way, the work is not for personal enlightenment but for the benefit of all. We do not reject the world, nor do we become enmeshed in it. We are witnesses in it and of it. How can this become true in your life?

• The neurotic ego has another side: the sense of unworthiness that is self-abasing and pusillanimous and harbors low self-esteem. The *FA* of FACE, the fear and attachment, are the central traits of this depleted ego. Control and entitlement refer more strongly to the inflated ego. The impoverished ego is the opposite of the inflated ego. It is the shadow of the shadow.

CREATIVE OPTIONS EGO OFFERS

The hero whose attachment to ego is already annihilated passes back and forth across the horizons of the world, in and out of the dragon, as readily as a king through all the rooms of his house. And therein lies his power

*to save; for his passing and returning demonstrate that
through all the contraries of phenomenality the Uncreated Imperishable remains, and there is nothing to fear.*

—JOSEPH CAMPBELL
The Hero with a Thousand Faces

The FACE of the neurotic ego, like everything human,
has a positive, creative side. We find this positive shadow side
of ourselves not by defacing or effacing ourselves but simply
by *losing* face. Here is how: The *F* for fear becomes an acknowledgment of our vulnerability while contacting the excitement on the other side of fear. Then we find ourselves
acting bravely with fear but not because of it. The *A* of attachment becomes bonding in a committed but nonpossessive
way. The *C* for control becomes power *for* not *over* others.
The *E* for entitlement becomes speaking up and standing up
for our rights self-nurturantly but then letting the chips fall
where they may. Each feature of the FACE of ego causes pain.
Fear is first because it is the origin of the other three and
because it may have happened first in our lives. We attach
because we fear loss. We control because we fear grief. We
demand entitlement because we fear the condition of existence that warns us things are not always fair. There is a
higher power than the scared-child ego. It is the adult power
of ourselves that can work a program of change, such as this
book presents. The higher power spiritually is the grace that
shifts us into transformation. Work on letting go of ego is
ultimately a spiritual practice.

Yet many changes are accessed automatically when we
begin to notice and break our negative ego habits. (They are
negative not because we are bad but because they do not
work, they prevent us from giving or receiving love.) "Accessed automatically" is the clue to grace at work cooperatively with our efforts to dismantle our ego holdouts. We lose

nothing; we gain wonderfully empowering and valuable gifts. We lose face and find heart.

Here are the gentle and healthy changes that occur in each of the negative features of the ego when we let go of having to act out its agenda in arrogant and neurotic ways:

As I let go of having to	*I become more able to*
Get my way	Cooperate with others
Be noticed and appreciated by everyone	Ask for, give, and receive appreciation
Insist my misdeeds be overlooked	Apologize and make amends
Insist I not be shown up or shown to be wrong	Do my best and still be open to feedback
Be utterly devastated if I lose face	Admit an error and protect myself from being shamed
Make demands on others	Ask for what I want and be able to accept no for an answer
Win, be loved, be respected, and be given preference	Do my best, ask for rightful credit and let go
Have to get back at others	Have a sense of justice that asks for redress or amends without the need to punish
Assert the implacability of ego	Discover the indestructibility of soul

Everything in us and in the universe is driven by an urgent yearning for wholeness. Any one-sidedness in conscious life is compensated by the Self, the ever vigilant shepherd of the straying ego. An archetypal energy is at work to open our healthy ego potential (and our spiritual potential). Our part of the work is to undo automatic shadow ego reactions, for instance, punishing, self-justifying, and the like. A God who has to reward and punish is made in the image of the shadow of the human ego. (A necessary reward contradicts the freedom of grace. A necessary punishment contradicts divine mercy and human transformation.) Such a God rejects the Sermon on the Mount and is the higher power of the ego, not of the soul and the universe. The signature of ego and the ego god is retaliation: saith *that* Lord. Deeply rooted in the Christian psyche may be a sense of being deputized to get back at the Jews for the killing of Christ. The work of letting go of ego is foregoing "the law of talion" that is so deeply rooted in us. This "eye for an eye" law has long-standing historical roots in superstition. For instance, in ancient times it was believed that steam from the blood of a murdered man followed the murderer as a phantom all the rest of his life and then passed on to his descendants. The ego wants to believe it will ultimately get its revenge. Unconscious of the real plan in the universe, we project a plan. Justice or karma then becomes the guarantor of the law of talion.

Injustice leads to rightful indignation, attempts to repair the abuse, and grief about the loss. Grief is scary mainly because it seems to equal powerlessness. Its alternative, revenge, is resistance to grief, since it substitutes retribution for sadness. It grants a false sense of power because it is power over others, not power for resolving unfairness or transforming human beings. Capital punishment is an example of a historically legitimized form of revenge. It is rationalized as deterrence. Our wounded ego engages the state to assure we can get even and not have to grieve so ardently or be so much at the mercy of life's conditions. Once we let go of ego, love gains precedence in our hearts and we cannot be satisfied with punishment. We want the transformation of the offender, restitution to us or the community, or the offender's heartfelt restoration to humanity. There is an admirable organization dedicated to this idea called "Families for Reconciliation." It is made up of people who oppose capital punishment even though their loved ones have been criminally hurt or killed.

The Christian recipe for divesting ourselves of ego violence and retaliation is in the Sermon on the Mount. There we find the unpalatable recommendation that we turn the other cheek, bless those who hurt us, love those who hate us. In short, reverse every automatic reaction of ego. The left column of the list above is about those aggressive reactions. The right column is a recipe for nonviolence and freedom from fear. The requirements of nonviolence seem extreme to the rational mind. They are not taken literally because to do so would mean losing face, that is, letting go of ego. Nonviolence is a shortcut path to letting ego go and letting love in. If, then, in protesting an injustice, we are not doing it out of love for those we disagree with, it is not authentic.

There has always been a tradition of nonviolence, even in pagan times. The ancient Greek playwright Aristophanes says in *The Frogs:* "From ancient times the great poet Orpheus gave us the Mysteries of Eleusis and taught us it was wrong to kill." The ego flame of retaliation is deep-rooted in us humans, but so is the spark of nonviolence.

The Dalai Lama says that the only way to peace is peace, not war or violence. In nonviolence the objective is to resolve and reconcile, not gain an advantage. Pope Benedict XV wrote to the Allied powers at the end of World War I, pleading, unsuccessfully, that they not humiliate the German people: "Remember that nations do not die. They chafe under the yoke imposed upon them, preparing a renewal of the combat, and passing down from generation to generation a mournful heritage of revenge." The challenge of shadow work is to define sanity not simply as rationality but as a sense of justice and a permanent eschewing of violence. That is the essential challenge in letting go of ego. Vietnam veteran

James Brown must have been referring to the insanity of war when he said, "We the unwilling were led by the unqualified to do the unnecessary for the ungrateful." Would we refuse to vote for a candidate who did not believe in war? Are we antiwar in principle but definitely want a standing army to defend us in a time of crisis? Are we involved in ongoing peace work? These questions make us look more deeply at our commitment to nonviolence.

Einstein said: "Look deeply into nature and you will understand everything human." Since nature is the best place to look for the meaning of our personal story, here is an example from nature that is quite telling. Remember the cowardly lion in the *Wizard of Oz?* A study by Dr. Craig Packer at the University of Minnesota suggests that there are two types of lions in a pride: one type goes forth to challenge and fight intruders and another type shirks such duties and yet shares in the bounty created by the courage of the others. The fearless hunting lions accept freeloaders without punishing or excluding them. Lions have no apparent hierarchy, so leaders do not lord it over laggards. It is just matter-of-fact that some do the work and some do not. This is the forsaking of ego in favor of cooperative dominance. The lions do by instinct what it takes work for us to actualize.

BEYOND PUNISHING AND PLACATING

Our ego often reacts to painful interactions with others in hackneyed and automatic ways. For instance, when someone snubs us or disappoints us, our arrogant ego may react with a plan to punish him with "eye for an eye" vengeance, distancing, sarcasm, or some other retaliation. Our ego in its victim mode, on the other hand, may feel intimidated and react to such rejection with conciliatory or fawning gestures such as giving in to someone or overcompromising. Both sides of the ego are in all of us. We may punish when we are outraged or placate when we are intimidated. Punishing masks our grief and rage; placating masks our fear. Wanting him "to get his" also arises from fear: we avoid our own grief by the satisfaction of making the other pay for his trespass against us.

I may punish you for not placating me.

You may placate me so that I do not punish you.

Everyone is occasionally rejected or intimidated. The ego takes poor treatment by others as a personal affront and injury. Punishing and placating are neurotic attempts at controlling and avoiding the painful feelings that arise when we have to confront these normal predicaments of human existence. The alternative program consists of fully admitting and feeling our grief and fear, maintaining self-protective boundaries in relationships, acting assertively, consistently overriding the impulse to punish or placate, feeling compassion and forgiveness, letting go and going on. We move on gently. It does not mean rejecting our ego but simply finding a new focus in life, as teenagers move from focus on toys to focus on cars. They do not have to break their toys, only drive on without them.

Have I found that it is utterly intolerable that I be rejected in any way by anyone? Do I complain about the way it happens so coldly or irresponsibly as a ploy to blame the other rather than grieve my own loss?

What are we avoiding in the space between our fear and rage? Just vulnerability, the essential ingredient in loving. We imagine it to be the unsafe, scary vulnerability of the victim. Instead, it can be the open, empowering vulnerability of the hero. The space is then *utter reconcilability,* the essence of humanness, the essence of divinity.[3]

---

3. These words *utter reconcilability* came to me in a dream. I went to sleep musing on this section of the chapter, and I dreamed of myself pondering

THE PRACTICE

• In the face of rejection, we let ourselves be vulnerable both
to it and to our own grief about it and strong enough to take
what has happened as information. We do this by allowing
ourselves to feel our sadness, anger, and fear (the components
of grief) and by assenting to this rejection as a given of human
existence with no wish for an exemption: "I am human.
Things like this happen to humans. This can happen to me
and has. I also have it in me to live through it and get over
it." Grief and acceptance are precisely how.

• Our self-centered ego shows us the shadow side of our motivations. It is normal that some self-interest may characterize
our motives. Rather than attempting to eliminate this element, it helps to acknowledge it openly. "I did this for you
but I can see that I did it also to make you like me more."
This is embarrassing to say, but losing face is what letting go
of ego is about.

Embarrassment can be a practice that deflates the pride
of (and fear in) ego. Paradoxically, as our ego becomes matter-of-fact and catches itself red-handed in its defensive game,
it no longer fears losing face. This is the homeopathic remedy
of shadow work: we use the problem as part of the cure.

I am embarrassed as someone walks out on my lecture.
My ego is scared and bruised, so I make a crack that is meant
to embarrass the person who is daring to leave. I catch myself
and then admit to the audience that my remark is retaliatory
and I take it back. This embarrasses me even more. I have
now found egoless humility by using the same device on myself that I was inflicting on someone else. The difference is

---

the avoided space between my own fear and rage, when I heard a voice
say: "In that space is utter reconcilability."

that I am not being retaliatory but repentant. I am calling myself on something publicly. The public witness reinforces the seriousness of my commitment to turn the hose on the shadow of my ever flaming ego. (Souls in the *Inferno* of Dante are not there because they are sinners but only because they have refused to *repent*.)

• Intimidation does not make us cower once we are both brave enough to admit feeling afraid and strong enough to stand up to others and to refuse to let them come at us that way.

In all the above encounters, we are becoming conscious of our responses and combining defenselessness with resourcefulness.

A healthy person can tolerate intimidation without having to appease the intimidator. He or she can tolerate rejection without having to get back at someone for a personal affront. Fearlessness is simply "no contest" in the face of these conditions of existence and relating; it is defenselessness. Fearfulness is an inability to be that vulnerable; it is defendedness. This is why fear is the opposite of love. Fear is a renouncing of vulnerability to hurt or grief. Love says yes to vulnerability. In the powerful vulnerability of love, we act lovingly and look lovable. We have personal standards that do not falter in the face of, nor at the mercy of, others' behavior. People may hurt or scare us, but that no longer compels us to punish or placate them. Our ruffled ego no longer suborns us with fear of losing face or the desire to win. Love impels us instead to the warmhearted alternative it always finds.

Explore your automatic reactions to rejection and intimidation. How can you redesign them, if necessary, to fit this model of vulnerability with power?

• There is a shadow character in the crime world who preys specifically and successfully on the shadow of ego. It is the confidence person who knows just how to capitalize on the predictability of the greedy and vengeful ego. A confidence ring could never exist if it were not for the easy pickings of the shadow side of the ego. "Here is a deal in which you can make a killing, and I am in it too." The seduction is twofold: you can get away with making a quick fortune doing something slightly illegal, and someone else is in on it who already has experience. After you are fleeced, the confidence person knows your injured ego is ready to be fleeced again, this time by the chance for retaliation. He sets up another scam and you lose one more time. Could there be a more instructive trickster for the ego? (The trickster is the archetypal mischievous power that deflates the arrogant entitlements of the inflated ego.) Have you encountered this trickster? How can you forgive and let go while protecting yourself for the future? How have you conned others? How can you make amends?

• Someone offends or hurts you. There are two options: to follow the blueprint of the neurotic, inflated ego or to follow that of the healthy ego:

Neurotic Ego Reactions	*Healthy Ego Responses*
I *act* with animosity and retaliation	I *ask* for amends or an apology
I seek to continue it by ongoing resentment	I seek to finish it by compensation or restitution
This equals threat	This equals dialogue
This leads to alienation	This leads to reconciliation
The person who does this is feared and hated	*The person who does this is trusted and respected*

The reactions listed on the left are automatic, ingrained with many years of fear and inhibited rage. The responses on the right do not come easily; it takes practice. Our ego will fight the work tooth and nail. Only a spiritual program will help us reach this level of sane and humble love. We can begin by *acting as if* we were moving to the right side. On which side do I mostly find myself? How can I act from the right side at least once today?

• What to do with hurt feelings:

We humans have a long history of being mean to one another. In the face of this unfortunate fact, the ego has a repertory ready to be employed: attack in a vengeful way or withdraw in an alienating way. What is the alternative adult spiritual response when someone hurts your feelings, acts inconsiderately toward you, or is downright mean to you? The spiritual practice is to forego the options of the vindictive ego and to choose the path of loving-kindness. As you live in accord with standards that transcend your ego's habitual strategies of fight and flight, you evolve as a more human being. You find new ways of turning the other cheek.

Here is what the commitments of a defenseless and resourceful program might look like:

• I let myself feel this hurt fully without any defense against it.
• I vow not to retaliate.
• I declare directly to the person the impact of his or her behavior on me without blaming or shaming. I ask for amends if appropriate.
• I accept the fact of occasional inconsiderateness or meanness as a given of human life.
• I am determined not to be mean myself.

I dedicate these five commitments to the welfare of others, both those who are hurt and those who do the hurting:

May compassion increase in me and flow from me as a result of what I suffer.

May love grow in others as the result of my commitment not to inflict suffering.

Following are examples of what to say when circumstances of hurt arise (notice how the emphasis is on the behavior and my reaction to it, not on the person or his or her character):

"We had an agreement to meet. I felt hurt and confused when you did not show up and did not call to cancel."

"What seems like sarcasm in your statement to me really stings and leaves me feeling hurt."

"Your involvement with my partner has devastated me and my relationship. I have been crying, not eating or sleeping, and feeling completely bereft since I found out about your affair. This is what can happen to partners who are betrayed and I want you to know that it is happening to me."

When I commit myself to nonviolent ways of responding to hurt, my self-respect grows accordingly. I let go of the vulnerability of a victim. I find the vulnerability that has and leads to power. I like myself more as I access such courageous gentleness no matter what the cost or provocation. Anyone may hurt me and I will not only survive but become more spiritually conscious in the process. No one can make me swerve off my course toward or give up my standards of loving-kindness. This is the basic meaning of groundedness: to no longer be moved off center by what others may do. "When love is my only defense, I am invincible," says the Tao.

Being rejected by others brings up hurt feelings most keenly. Yet every one of us is rejected every day: the mail carrier did not bring the letter we hoped for; the neighbor drove by without waving; the salesclerk did not notice us.

The healthy response to rejection is grief, and the ego fears grief. To defend against that feeling the ego resorts to its familiar repertory of vengeful or escapist protocols. What if we were to accept rejection as a condition of relating and use our same defenseless and resourceful program as a response?

• To let go of ego is to admit our fear and then to act against it by saying yes to the conditions the ego was set up to protect itself against. It might even be as simple as using affirmations such as these:

> • I embrace my aloneness and open myself to support.
> • I accept the changes that keep happening around and in me.
> • I grieve and let go of what is passing away.
> • I embrace what is coming to pass and feel excited by it.
> • I live through pain and am transformed by it.
> • I keep finding creative responses to the unpredictable surprises of life.
> • I grieve about unfairness and act fairly in all my dealings.
> • I acknowledge that some burdens are too hard for me and ask for support from beyond myself.
> • I open myself to the graces that keep inviting me to let go of ego.

To return again to where I am, I make this journey.

—DANTE, *Purgatorio*

• Is the motivating force of my life the assertion of my ego over others or the practice of love? If it is ego, I am compelled to defeat, compete with, punish, and fear others. If it is love, I am impelled to open my heart, seek and make peace, forgive, reconcile, and show compassion. The capacity to forgive is the capacity to let go of ego.

We have a reflex to grab and hold our hand when it is suddenly hurt. That reflex is in us psychologically too. Would it not follow that the same reflex is in us to reach out and hold others in their hurt? Pain makes no distinctions. It takes a choice on our part to override the inborn spiritual instinct to be compassionate.

Compare these statements:

★ Everything we do, every little ruse, charm, and smile, every plan and relationship, has as its purpose to shore up, inflate, and maintain our ego.

★ "The whole purpose of our lives is to put everything we do into the channel of universal love." (From the diary of Quaker John Woolman)

Which one is more like me? What can I do today to move more of my life into the channel of universal love? It happens just like that, in daily, even momentary, ways.

WHY IS IT SO HARD TO LET GO?

Petals of poppies,
How willingly
They drop.

—ETSUJIN

The theme of letting go keeps appearing in our work of deflating our egos. Why do we not let go as easily as the poppy petals do when their season ends? Why is it not automatic in us, as this phrase of Rilke's suggests it can be: "Make it as easy as the earth makes itself ready for spring"? To ask why surrender does not happen without pain is like asking why we do not have strong muscles without working out.

It takes practice—both psychological practice and spiritual practice that have as their purpose to grant an unreserved assent to every human predicament we find ourselves in. The ego cannot do this; it has too many vested interests in survival based on its props of control and entitlement. Only the grace of the Self can teach us to pronounce the unconditional yes. Psychologically we have no motivation for letting go. It is a spiritual and risky venture that happens in its own time. This is probably why humility and patience are associated with saints. Rumi is an Islamic saint who prayed: "May the dissolver of sugar dissolve me just in time." Only that which arises in our dissolved state can be touched by grace and become compassion.

Another reason it is difficult to let go may be that it involves change. Steel needs to be tempered in fire. Pruning is necessary to bring out the full potential of a tree. Since we are part of nature, these same hard rules apply to us. The difference is that nature is one immense and ever resounding yes to the facts of life, and we are often plaintive plaintiffs. It takes an arduous, ego-effacing journey to arrive at the shrine of Yes. Our frightened, restive ego keeps qualifying and opposing the yes of unqualified consent that all of nature pronounces so faithfully. Nothing less is required than a demolition of the ego's edifice of control and entitlement and a rebuilding from its ruins. The ordeal of death and rebirth is meant to abolish worldly time and recover primordial time, time that does not corrupt. This is how the spiritual Self is born in the lowly stable of our surrendered ego. Surrender of ego means letting go of the multiplicity of our fears and desires to return to the source of serene love. This is how the surrendered ego is the passport to paradise. It is also true devotion. Rebirth is another way of saying that energy cannot be destroyed, only recycled. It refers to "something in the soul that is uncreated and uncreatable," as Meister Eckhart writes.

In the past it was thought that fasting, self-flagellation, asceticism, made a contribution to one's own holiness/wholeness or to that of others. These practices were reproved by the Buddha, who saw them as life negating. Our best offering to the world is in capitalizing on our own vast body-soul potential. What helps us toward wholeness and what helps others is the release, not the inhibiting, of our hidden reserves. This release is found especially in meditation, yoga, body-oriented therapies, dream work, and active imagination. The central purpose of these practices is the letting go of ego, not the splitting of mind and body. The mind's subjugation of the body can be another ploy of the ego to keep us divided against the Self. Ego thrives on oppositions, so defeat of oppositions is the true letting go of ego.

A body image is the ego's version of our body. We confuse these two and think they are the same. Actually, our body is a marvelous tool and full of wonders unguessed by the mind. The ego version of the psyche does not give the complete picture of who we are either. Dreams, poetry, imagination, and projection give clues that there is more to us than ego. In body and mind we are more than we seem.

An encounter with the agenda of the Self is frightening to the ego. Losing face can feel like a deathly defeat. Our ego transformation carries an image of bodily death. Yet this is not about an annihilation of our existence. It is a liquidation of our past, our limits, our fear of spiritual heights, as grapes are liquidated to become wine. The grapes are not thereby destroyed but fulfilled. Ego disintegration is not final in any myth but is always the bridge and means to rebirth.

Why does initiation involve learning the hard way? It is precisely the pain and shock of the initiation ceremony that initiates. The sacrifice of ego means releasing illusory control over our lives in order to release our authentic power. Death, for primitive peoples, was not a cessation but a rite of passage. This is a metaphor for how we are always dying to what is not essential. Every event in life forms part of one birth-death-rebirth experience. Every event has that multilevel meaning. To find meaning is to see and welcome a similarity between our own and nature's cycles.

Nature beats on a cyclic rhythm: high tide and low; full moon and new, waxing and waning; light and dark; sound and silence; spring and winter; summer and fall. All cycles contain and honor antinomies. In us and in nature there is no warring of opposites, only combinations of them. Every cell of our bodies survives by cycles of oppositions: breathing in and breathing out, the pumping of blood through our heart with dilation and contraction, the rising and falling of pulse rate and respiration (peaking during the day, descending to a low point in sleep). Holding opposites rather than lingering in one of them *is* physical health. Psychological health is in the same alternating rhythm. This is why befriending the shadow is a form of psychological and spiritual health.

An intriguing metaphor for the dissolution of ego is the metamorphosis of the caterpillar. When it becomes a cocoon, it goes into dissolution, becoming an undifferentiated mass. This is a necessary stage before it can be adorned in its splendid butterfly raiment. We will feel like an identityless mass when we let go of ego. Our first reaction may then be fear, and that makes us hold on more tightly to the FACE we do not want to lose. We fall back into the old patterns of control and combativeness. In reality, the time has come to let go of those ingrained habits and to allow dissolution. It is time to lie still, as mummies do. In fact, a mummy is a cocoon, lying quietly for as long as it may take for its new life to open. Sometimes the work is to dissolve rather than solve. Letting go of ego proves to be what wants to happen in us. It is not a goal but a program already and always in place for beings like us, so infused with urgent yearnings for wholeness.

We know we *can* let go willingly, because we do not scream and cry when the poppy petals fall. Pain does not happen because something passes away but because we think it should not do so. The "we" here is the entitled and untrusting ego. A poppy buds, blooms, and fades. It seems that the dying flower is less valuable, and yet *only in it* is the seed of new life. The beauty of one poppy is promised in the bud. The assurance of an ongoing cycle of poppies is guaranteed in the falling petals. Every beautiful thing in nature is in the service of a wider life than its own. The transience of life is precisely what makes life endure. This combination of opposites is the true law and gift of survival. The enduring and equally paradoxical Self might say with Thich Nhat Hanh:

> *No coming. No going.*
> *Everything is pretending*
> *To be born and to die.*

BEYOND CHANGE

Change is the result of psychological work on our ego; transformation is the release of love, perennial wisdom, and healing power from our inner Self. Change is the automatic result of effort; transformation is the possible result of grace, though it is often responsive to our spiritual practices. Psychological work is meant to lead to a healthier ego, that is, sanity. Spiritual practice is meant to release the inestimable riches of the Self. This is sanctity.

An analogy of the combination of effort and grace can be made with playing cards; we win by a blending of skill and luck or chance. Skill in this analogy is the work we do psychologically on ourselves. Luck/chance is the metaphor for grace, a gift that comes to us beyond our control and irrespective of our skills. Recognition of a power greater than ego is built into human nature. When we first sucked our mother's breast, we were demonstrating both that we did not come into the world equipped with all we needed and that we did have a way to access it. In other words, we were both defenseless and resourceful. We require a power greater than our skill, but skill is nonetheless required. In the spiritual world, this power is called grace, and it complements our efforts.

In a card game, the skill element is perhaps 40 percent and the luck element 60 percent. Perhaps it follows that in life the choice element is 40 percent and the grace element is 60 percent. Synchronicities and strange turns of events account for so much of the shape our lives have taken. There are assisting graces and afflicting forces: relationships that work or hurt, sudden opportunities or crises, encouraging or impeding people, inborn talents or disabilities, being at the right or wrong place at the wrong or right time. It is all in the combination and the continually shuffling ratios.

St. Paul says: "The *Spirit* brings love, joy, peace, patience, kindness, goodness, gentleness" (emphasis mine). As we saw above, the ego has no motivation for nor interest in these virtues. They might deflate its grandiosity. The Self alone will want to generate these qualities. Yet it is also true that the Self cannot work without the engagement of ego. The gifts of the Self are only potentials until the ego becomes their agent in the world. A budding actor can be of Academy Award caliber, but without an agent to land her some good parts, she is only a wanna-be.

Our work is to make friends, to establish an axis of ego and Self so that they can dance together and benefit from one another. Only the Self, grace, can make us authentically loving. Only the ego can make love concrete in the here and now. Our healthy work on our ego is required to make love work. Virtue is a habit of acting that the healthy ego forms through practice; virtuousness is a state of being that comes as a free gift of the Self. Virtue is change; virtuousness is transformation. Why is it difficult for us to be virtuous? Because it is not a matter simply of doing good but also of overcoming an inveterate ingrained proclivity toward vice. Vice is an energy that aims at eradicating virtue. It is a feisty habit struggling in us not only for ongoing survival but also for sovereignty. Yet virtue can do the same. The choice is ours. We make the choice when we do the practice work that gradually replaces a bad habit with a good one.

Change is a transition from dysfunctional behavior to functional behavior. Functionality means skill in achieving healthy goals, for example, becoming more assertive instead of remaining passive in our dealings with others. We might then be able to address rather than deny, process rather than run, resolve rather than leave things unfinished. To cope is to put up with a painful situation and live in hope of change. To change psychologically is to become skillful at handling things better now than we did before. To *handle* is to work out and follow a plan for change:

1. I become so upset and frustrated with my kids that I hit them.
2. I work on this by participating in a support group with other parents who have similar issues.
3. Thereby I learn that I am doing to my children what was done to me.
4. I then grieve my own abusive past and thus deal with a personal unfinished issue in myself that was not resolved.
5. I learn stress management techniques.
6. I participate in couple and family therapy.

The results: personal change, I can deal with my children without hitting them, and transpersonal change, I make a contribution or volunteer time to a charity for abused children. Change is a psychological event; transformation is a spiritual gift.

Transformation, unlike change, cannot be achieved; it happens. Transformation means love, wisdom, and healing in thought, word, and deed so that an equation results between the inner Self and our healthy ego choices. We begin to display in our daily routine the timeless powers of our psyche. In this sense, transformation is a holy communion of our psychology and our spirituality. It always goes beyond the narrow limits of psychological change; for example, I *change* when I drop my need for revenge against this person here now. I am *transformed* when I reach out and create reconciliation here and everywhere. Transformation is not limited to this instance here and now but widens to include all behavior:

Change: I'm fair in my relationships.
Transformation: I'm generous.
Change: I took this and give this back.
Transformation: I give away what I am attached to.

What I give is love, the letting go of my soap opera ego for you. When I really love you, I drop my ego defenses. When I love myself, I have the resources to match. This is because letting go of ego fear and ego attachment empowers me to realize my capacity to love you and everyone.

At the same time, even dropping the need for revenge against one person flows from a grace of transformation. The scared, arrogant ego has no motivation for such a move. An assisting force of the Self is at work and the ego assents. Its greatest asset is this ability to say yes. Perhaps every change that makes for more love is, after all, transformation and the gift of grace, a power beyond what ego can conjure on its own. Any time I transcend my present limits and fears and move in the direction of loving more, I am doing more than changing. I am undergoing a transformation. Even becoming more healthily ego assertive may be geared this way. Less and less of the work then seems merely psychological; more and more is spiritual too. Perhaps the attitude of thanks makes the most supreme sense as we contemplate this fact.

I am still what I always was so I must also already be what I will become. In this sense, life is not about how I change but about how I finally happen.

TRANSFORMING OUR EGO: THE SPIRITUAL WORK

• Wholeness implies that we have all the virtues as potential within us, that is, in our positive shadow. For instance, courage is always resident in our psyche. Like all virtues, it can be activated in any of four ways: It can happen by effort: keep acting as if you were courageous and eventually you will build the habit of courage. (A virtue is a habit.) It can also happen interactively as the natural result of experiences that provide encouragement. For instance, if a person is appreciated by others, she may notice herself becoming more generous. Likewise, our sense of self-worth and power in the world may be built up by people who support us and by events that we handle well. As a result we notice that we automatically have more courage. This is the interactive dimension of virtue.

Virtue can also happen by grace, which takes two forms. It is sometimes available in an *essential* ongoing way so that it seems to be part of our personality. Sometimes grace is existentially available, suddenly granted in the here-and-now moment of need. When the grace is essential, courage is an innate gift that we have always been able to access. The daredevil you remember in grammar school may be an example of someone with that gift. When the grace is *existential,* courage comes to us suddenly: we see someone in need or are confronted with a challenge and we respond courageously without thinking. It seems to come from nowhere, not from familiar ego resources but from a power beyond our limitations; hence it is called grace.

So, virtues manifest in four ways: by effort, interaction, essential grace, and existential grace. Look within yourself and ask how courage lives in you. Has it come naturally (essential gift) or occasionally (existential grace)? Is it happening through experience and support? Is it taking effort: you feel afraid but are overriding the fear and acting as if you had all the courage you need? Who is there to thank?

• Here are some virtues: love, trustworthiness, courage, honesty, humility, gratitude, openness, conviction, compassion, cheerfulness, simplicity, hopefulness, generosity, courtesy, candidness, flexibility, appreciativeness, confidence, loyalty, justice, serenity, respect, humor, forgiveness, truthfulness, cooperativeness, and the ability to temper desire.

Write each one on a separate index card. Working with one card each day, keep the word in mind throughout the entire day. Write it out and hang it in a prominent place or carry it in your pocket to help you remember to do this. As you begin in the morning, ask for cooperation from your assisting forces in the practice of the virtue. Say the word in your head or aloud throughout the day. As often as you can, form an image of yourself practicing that virtue in some specific way. Look for ways to practice it with the people and events of the day. At the end of the day, draw a picture of yourself practicing the virtue of the day. Give thanks for all those who helped you in this work.

• Here are specific examples of the building of a virtue by devising a plan and following a practice: The virtue of justice means respect for the rights of others. This includes honesty in our dealings and accountability for our actions through responsible behavior. If when you drink you act violently or engage in behaviors that are risky to yourself and others, the plan has to be to stop drinking. Alcoholics Anonymous is the program already in place for this. Given your circumstances, joining it and staying with it is building the habit/virtue of justice. If you speed on long trips, the plan is to form a conscious intention of slowing down. If that does not work, you might take a plane or hire a chauffeur or install a governor on the accelerator. The point is to notice when you stray into dangerous territory in your behavior and not simply to regret it or think of yourself as stupid for doing it. Holderlin says: "Danger itself invites the rescuing power." There is always a program to put into place that intelligently and effectively changes things. It is a virtue even to be the kind of person who uses this approach whenever you notice yourself in the wrong. It is a way of taking preventive measures to become more responsible rather than promising yourself you will do better and leaving it at that.

> *To be human is to be born into the world with some-*
> *thing to achieve, namely, the fullness of one's human*
> *nature, and it is through the virtues that one does so . . .*
> *The virtues are the only guarantee against a wasted life.*
>
> —PAUL WADDELL, C.P.

• The heart continually generates electromagnetic energy. Egoless love makes the heart's waves harmonic and serene, and the rest of the body follows suit. Our autonomic nervous system comes into balance and we are then less vulnerable to disease. Stress is considerably diminished and our lively energy is released. The neurocortex of our brain, responsible for higher-level reasoning, works more efficiently and our decisions have a sounder base. All this happens in a matter of seconds. David McClelland, a Harvard psychologist, has generated research that suggests that heartfelt, that is, egoless, love actually leads to a greater production of antibodies (salivary immunoglobulin A: IgA) that help in fighting flu viruses. Letting go of ego and feeling loving builds the immune system.

All her adult life the great Spanish mystic Saint Teresa used a practice of devotion as she drifted off to sleep at night: she formed an image in her heart of her favorite scene from the life of Jesus, his prayer in the garden of Gethsemane. What if each night we were to picture in our heart the spiritual scene, person, situation, or place that has been most moving to us in life. This might even be a recollection of being loved by someone. It is important to do this in the context of falling asleep so that it can be the heart's bridge between the conscious and the unconscious. The heart can combine these opposites; the mind only divides them further. To try to fall asleep while thinking does not work, but images do, as those who visualize sheep jumping a fence have noticed.

- Use these affirmations:

  - As I let go of being subject to desire, real joy enters my life.
  - I am brave when I return good for evil.
  - I am heroic when I forgive.
  - I let go of the option of retaliation even in my mind.
  - I bypass and override my ego's appeals and seductions.

- What I criticize in others may be true of me.
- I look into my motivations and actions and endow them with gentle love.
- I create my path by walking.

• Every religious tradition recommends the letting go of ego by humble compassionate service and nonviolence. Nonviolence is not submission to injustice but an alternative way of resisting it. It is the healthy ego's creative response to injustice rather than the inflated ego's automatic reaction to it. Basically, this means letting go of the will to retaliate in favor of self-transformation and the desire to transform others. It is found in Christianity, Hasidism, Sufism, Buddhism, Hinduism, and elsewhere.

Those who have chosen the path of nonviolent love have often suffered or died for it. The crucified Christ and the assassinated Gandhi bear witness to this. In some medieval pictures Christ is actually depicted nailed to the cross by his own *virtues*. The path of egoless love is not about safety. It is about love at any cost. This is why it may not be for everyone and is often thought of as requiring a special call and a special grace. To participate in the initiation rites of Isis in ancient times, one had to be personally called by her in a dream. A force beyond ego has to grant to ego the strength to let itself go. This is the paradox of egolessness.

What follows are several passages from five religious traditions that describe this path. Read them in your own voice onto a tape and listen to them repeatedly. Let the words and concepts penetrate slowly. Write one page of each of the passages out, longhand, each morning. At the beginning and end of each writing or listening, say: "This is what it will take for me to befriend my ego and I commit to it."

The Sermon on the Mount is the Christian model for the dismantling of ego:

Blessed are you when people abuse you and persecute you and speak all kinds of calumny against you on my account, rejoice and be glad, for your reward will be great in heaven. This is how they persecuted the prophets before you.

Do not resist an evil person. If someone strikes you on one cheek, turn the other to him also. If anyone wants to sue you and take away your tunic, let him have your cloak also. If someone compels you to go one mile with him, go with him two.

Love your enemies, bless those who curse you, do good to those who hate you, and pray for those who abuse and persecute you, that you may be sons of a heavenly Father who makes the sun rise on the evil and the good and the rain fall on the just and the unjust.

Here is a saying of Muhammad in the Islamic tradition:

No one of you is a believer until he desires for his brother what he desires for himself.

This is from the Talmud:

What is hateful to you, do not do to others. This is the entire Law; all the rest is commentary.

A Hindu statement from Shantideva's treatise *Entering the Bodhisattva Practice*:

My body, its pleasures,
And any merit I have gained
I will give without a second thought
To help other beings. . . .
Let them despise, strike,
Even murder me at will.

Let them play with my body.
Let me be the object of laughter and scorn! . . .
But let no harm come to them
For anything they do.
May anything they do to me
Result in benefit to them. . . .
May whoever accuses me, curses me, or insults me,
Have the fortune of enlightenment. . . .
Today in the presence of the Buddhas,
I invite all beings to this joyful feast
Till they attain enlightenment.

These words are from *Stanzas for Training the Mind* by the eleventh-century Tibetan Buddhist monk Geshe Langri Thangpa:

With a determination to accomplish
The highest welfare of all sentient beings
Who surpass even a wish-granting jewel,
I will learn to hold them supremely dear. . . .
In all actions I will learn to search into my mind
And as soon as an afflicting emotion arises,
Endangering myself and others,
I will firmly face and avert it. . . .
When others, out of jealousy, treat me badly
With abuse or slander,
I will learn to take all loss
And offer the victory to them. . . .
When one whom I have benefited with great hope
Unreasonably hurts me very badly,
I will learn to view that person
As an excellent spiritual guide. . . .
I will learn to offer everyone without exception
All health and happiness directly and indirectly

And respectfully take upon myself
All harm and suffering of others.

The *Dhammapada,* a compilation of sayings of Buddha, adds:

Hatred does not come to an end by hating but by not
  hating. . . .
I will be assailed by abusive words the way an elephant
  receives an arrow in battle.

The four qualities of the sangha, the Buddhist community, are:

If someone harms us, we do not harm him.
If someone is violent toward us, we are not violent toward
  him.
If someone insults us, we do not insult him.
If someone accuses us, we do not retaliate.

*As long as space abides, and as long as sentient beings
remain, may I too abide to dispel their suffering.*

—THE DALAI LAMA'S PRAYER

3

The Mystery of the Self and Its Shadow

*The silent mystery that tastes like nothingness
because it is infinity.*

—KARL RAHNER

*T*HE SELF IS not like a thing; it is like a field, electromagnetic, gravitational. A field is an area that makes it possible for certain powerful phenomena to occur. For the Self, these phenomena are unconditional/universal love, perennial wisdom, and healing power. We do not contain these powers; we are epiphanies of them, and so is all of nature. The Upanishads speak often of the inner Self of all beings, not only of humankind. When Heidegger said, "Persons are not things or processes but openings through which the infinite manifests," he was forgetting to look beyond persons to include the reindeer and the rose.

The Self is the psychic totality, which both contains ego consciousness and transcends it. This is the window to the infinite to which Heidegger referred. The Self is the conjunction of opposites that underlies the process of human individuation. Individuation is the Jungian term for spiritual and psychological wholeness. By it, our lives become a unique display of the Self's eternal design; the transpersonal psyche makes a personal appearance in our individual ego, the "opening to the infinite." How fascinating that the Greek word for psyche means butterfly. Something with wings emerges from the chrysalis of ego. Something earthbound has the whole sky as its home.

Individuation happens when there is an axis of ego and Self. This axis occurs when we let the light of consciousness enter our daily-life choices and behavior. We do this by making explicit, that is, conscious, the implicit attributes of the Self. In fact, the Self summons our ego to mount an exhibition of its wares. Every time I act with love instead of self-interest, every time I listen to wise counsel instead of to my own scanty knowledge, every time I choose reconciliation over revenge, I create an axis of power between my limited ego and the infinite Self. Wholeness happens as external choices match interior qualities. It is activation of potential. This is why the work is ultimately so simple; it is already done. It is only a matter of realizing it, of practicing it.

The Self is pure unbounded potentiality. It is space not mass, like all reality. It is described in Eastern philosophy as the diamond essence because it is clear and yet hard and indestructible, another paradoxical conjunction of opposites. The reason we are indestructible is that we are pure space. Our existence is in the Self, a space unconditioned by the conditions of human existence. This may be why Saint Clement could say: "When you know yourself, you know God." Only the ego is vulnerable to the givens of life as only wood is vulnerable to fire. The diamond in the wooden house remains imperishable. The Self is thus not determined or influenced by human predicaments. It uses external reality to accomplish its sacred task of manifesting in time the timeless love it has to show and wants so urgently to give.

How do we find out about all this? The whole teaching is contained within the wisdom dimension of the Self. It is an archetypal heritage that is geared to funnel through our unique personality. Our insights are actually rediscoveries of the insights of philosophers and enlightened people of all the ages. This universal consensus about the nature of life and its truth was termed by Aldous Huxley "the perennial philosophy." It is an ageless treasury of wisdom in our souls that is revealed and then rerevealed in new words and paradigms by a succession of teachers and students throughout history. Perennial wisdom is not something old that now is to be rediscovered. It is continuous with the past, ever renewing and evolving. Something in us is greater than we. We know this wisdom more profoundly than our ancestors did and yet it is the same, as we know the moon better than they did and yet it is the same.

The contents of this perennial philosophy are not produced by individual intellect or experience but by the collective community of humanity. Each new generation recognizes and reaffirms its truthfulness. This is why they are ever assented to, preserved, and cherished. We have the wisdom in us and yet receive it too. "Wisdom is that power of revelation which is time's last gift to the mature and powerful mind," says May Colum.

The ur-message is in our humanity so ineradicably and irrepressibly that if all teachers were to die and all books were to be burned, we would reconstruct the entire body of enlightened truth in no time. Wisdom is so big that no one person has it all. We need one another to piece its fragments together in successive moments in time. This is how the timeless makes its entrance into our puzzled and puzzle-solving world. "I have seen the ancient way, the old road that was taken by the all-awakened and that is my path too," said Buddha. The treasury of images in the soul of each of us is also the archetypal treasury of the wisdom of all of us.

An owl is the symbol of wisdom because it flies in utter

silence and with lightning speed, combining the opposites of dark night and clear vision. Wisdom cuts across the sky of mind in one instant swoop of wholeness just like that. The "horseman" of enlightenment in our epigraph poem by Changling does the same.

The Giza sphinx is another ancient symbol of perennial wisdom. The sphinx is the metaphorical guardian of the sustaining meanings of life that evade the human ego. He faces the rising sun of clarity with his human face, and buried deep beneath and between his lion's paws is a chamber-library of wisdom texts that wait to be discovered. An imaginary triangular line from this chamber extends directly to his heart. Thus the human heart, *my heart*, is likewise the custodian of eternal wisdom that waits to be discovered and yet is already known in the perennial philosophy. I am my age in body but ever ancient, ever new by reason of this wisdom.

Here are some elements of the perennial philosophy:

• All reality is one and this oneness can be contacted as a spaciousness behind all the appearances we see. That spaciousness on the human level is what we call soul. Its dark side is called the void.

• Nothing is to be taken literally in the spiritual world. All is a metaphor for the transition from ego to Self, the personal journey to the transpersonal Source.

• Nature is alive and is the divine mirror by which we see ourselves and the transcendent power "whose center is everywhere and whose circumference is nowhere."

• Human fulfillment happens in the alchemical transmutation of our dark ego into the gold of our spiritual Self. This dark gold Self is no different from the reality of nature and the divine. The three levels of being—human, natural, and divine—are all composed of opposites that unite.

These perspectives are founded on the correspondence between microcosm and macrocosm; every person and thing is simultaneously everything and all. The Self has an existence in the universe at large, and out of it the ego has evolved. Ego and Self refer to different experiential levels of one archetypal process: "This perishable nature is meant for imperishability; this mortal frame is meant for immortality," wrote Saint Paul. The Self is the vehicle of an unconditional yes to the conditions of human existence with all its dust, and a yes to the condition of human sanctity with all its grandeur. The Self brings us to an awareness of an archetypal meaning that has become personal. This has been called conversing with angels, the "light" referred to in religious experiences. It is our name as it is written in heaven, love as it is now and here, already and always embracing us.

The healthy ego is the hero that struggles successfully to be free from fears and attachments so that he or she can join the forces of the light. Our interior journey throws that light of consciousness on every holdout of the ego. Spirituality then comes to mean that love has released us from the ego-bound world. We treat others with respect and drop our ego defenses as we let go of the need to be right, to be in control, to use or abuse others, and so on. Love between people who have let go of ego is reciprocal individuation.

In the *Mahabharata*, the lawful sovereigns, the Pandavas, have been driven out by a blind king, Dhritarashtra, who usurps the throne. He represents the ego, blinded by fear and grasping, supplanting the Self. Arjuna, the hero, as we saw above, does not want to join the ensuing fight. As an integrated ego-Self, he does not want to enter a battleground of his own inner forces opposing one another. His reluctance about fighting is: "How can I kill part of myself?" Our work toward individuation will often feel like just such an inner division. But the Self will find an axis of power with the ego if we enter the fray, as Arjuna finally did: deflating the neurotic arrogant ego, raising the banner of the Self, and making the peace that passes the ego's understanding.

The Self is the Buddha nature, our essential wholeness that waits for full awakening. Our work is to take steps in that direction. Then the shifts occur in our consciousness that engender compassion because they actualize that potential of the Buddha nature. This is why when we are awakened from the slumber of ego, the first thing we say is: "May all beings benefit from my work and from my gifts." The compassion happens when and because we realize we all have this same enlightened nature, but some of us are so caught up in ego fear and desire that we miss our access to it.

The Self, Buddha nature, Christ consciousness, is our essence, always and already whole. It is existential as well, cultivated by our daily practice. The purpose of spiritual practice is to display in our lifetime the timeless life of the Self, our Buddha consciousness. Existential work unveils the essential reality. This essential reality is described as a void or emptiness because it is empty of separate, self-standing existence. This is the central wisdom of the Self about the nature of reality. Things and people are like Ping-Pong balls, mostly inner space. Emptiness means the absence of a stable identity but not the absence of existence. The void affirms the existence but denies the solid enduring identity of things and us. We and things exist only in this present moment. True emptiness is unconditional reality, beyond concept, time, and division. In this freedom from division is the access to awakening and to compassion.

The coconut is another apt symbol of the psyche, the hard shell of ego outside and the milk of the real Self inside, the fruit of opposites. The work is to crack it open without

losing the valuable inner core and still find a use for the remaining shell. Even in pieces it has value, since the way things
appear is only part of how they exist. Behind the appearance
of opposition is unity; behind brokenness is a readiness for
healing wholeness. This, paradoxically, is the emptiness that
is also an openness, a boundless potential, not defined or limited by separate identity. The conventional, subjectively filled-
in reality and the nondefined, nonreified reality are actually
one and the same: form is emptiness; emptiness is form.

The ego/Self axis as well as the shadow/persona axis sig-
nifies freedom from dualism and the bridge connecting us to
the highest reaches of ourselves. In Eastern religions, all the
gods have both a wrathful and a benign side. They thus combine and are composed of opposites. When we combine opposites in ourselves, persona and shadow, for example, we
become epiphanies of that divine unity.

The Self cannot be defined. It is an *unlimited within,*
what Campbell called the Uncreated Imperishable, as in "this
perishable nature is meant for imperishability" referred to by
Saint Paul. It is a mystery, known only by being initiated into
it. The word *mystery* in Greek also connotes initiation. The
work exercises in this book are initiation rites through the
labyrinthine ways of the shadow of ego and Self. A mystery
is not something hard to understand because it is so complex.
It is rather that it is not graspable by the analytically, linearly
limited ego that has the wherewithal only to solve problems.
A problem is something to be solved; a mystery is something
to become involved in. The deeper we reach into a mystery,
the deeper it becomes, that is, the *more* mysterious. The reach
takes letting go of ego, which is the point and aim of spiritual
initiation. Meditation and active imagination (dialoguing
with images that appeal to us or engage us or with figures we
meet in dreams) are two of the many paths into mystery. Its

door cannot be broken down by effort but may open easily to spiritual practice and grace.

The healthy ego is built by psychological work. The Self requires no work at all, being already perfect and impervious to events and time. It is meant to be visited and discovered over the years and in the midst of life events. The ego is in us; we are in the Self. We work on our ego; we let the Self work in and through us. Together these form the ego/Self axis that is the fulfillment of our human destiny.

> *I shall savor, with heightened consciousness, the intense yet tranquil rapture of a vision whose coherence and harmonies I can never exhaust.*
>
> —TEILHARD DE CHARDIN

THE PRACTICE

How do we access the powers latent within the Self? We gain access only by acknowledging them as a birthright we received and now are choosing to manifest and maintain. When we let go of ego, we open ourselves so that this can happen. Our unconscious requires the sacrifice of ego as the Minotaur required the annual sacrifice of the seven Athenian boys and girls. His labyrinth is our own unconscious, where we often lose our way. To find the path to liberation, the ego is useless on its own; it needs the anima, the soul, as Theseus, the personification of ego/spirit, needed Ariadne, the personification of the Self/soul, to find his way through the labyrinth. Hero stories provide a blueprint of the initiation process. This is another way of seeing how the archetypal themes of humankind are our personal themes and that the collective Self is the ego's soulful friend.

How do we allow our soulful powers to assist us? It happens every time we let go of the inflated-ego shadow traits that represent and reinforce our fear, acquisitiveness, control, and entitlement. It happens whenever we grapple with life experiences in nonviolent ways. Actually, the purpose of human experience is to give us opportunities to let this happen. We have a story *so that* we can fill in the journey from neurotic ego to healthy ego to spiritual Self. Our destiny is to make our unconscious Self-powers conscious, palpable, and visible in the world.

Psychologically we address, process, and resolve issues that arise within and among us. The reason we humans use these powers so poorly is that we have gained them so recently in the course of evolution. We are still amateurs in the use of sane logic, integration of will and knowledge, processing, resolving amicably, trusting loving solutions, and making peace. Only yesterday we were using clubs and now bombs to solve problems among us.

Spiritually we let go of ego, increase our compassion, and simply stay, as silent witnesses who do not judge or convict in the court of any of our life experiences. Notice the paradox: we deal with things actively *and* we sit and observe. When we see no contradiction in these, we are in the Promised Land, the unlimited within that is the Self. The Promised Land is an archetype of ourselves when we complete our journey, that is, befriend our shadow, do our work.

Ego	*Self*
Symbols: yang, sun, human, male	Symbols: yin, moon, divine, female
Operationally: acts as a functional adult moving toward goals, or as neurotic, caught in fear and attachment so that drama and pain result	Ontologically: is spiritually awake; already has love, wisdom, and healing within; and uses spiritual practices to manifest them

Uses knowledge, intellect	Accesses wisdom through meditation and imagination
Has personality	Has presence
Has personal history	Has mythic roots
Seeks perfection	Enjoys completeness
Thrives on dualisms	Creates balances
Is limited by self-doubt, etc.	Is unlimited
Is fear-compelled	Is love-impelled
Holds on	Lets go
Places accent on willpower or willfulness	Places accent on willingness
Leads to inner war and division	Leads to the Promised Land within
Can be changed and improved by effort	Is revealed and opened by grace

AN EASTERLY DIRECTION

The Self spoken of by Jung is the Buddha mind, the Original Mind. Buddha is the historical person of the sixth century BCE. But as with all gods and sages, literalism misses the point and can make us idolaters. It is not the Buddha of history that is significant but the archetype of wholeness he personifies. The historical Buddha embodied wholeness, and now the venerated Buddha represents it in order to evoke it in us. The history of Buddha (he) is not as important as the nature of Buddha (we). In fact, in the Buddhist perspective, Gautama Buddha is only the fourth of one thousand buddhas who will appear in this golden age. Every being, without exception, has the potential of becoming one of the nine hundred and ninety-six to come.

The Buddha nature/Original Mind/Self is actually in all of us as an ever present potential for full awakening. As long as we fill ourselves in with identifying ego marks, desires, and fears, we do not notice our Self as Buddha did. Gautama sat under the Bodhi tree, a fig tree, in silent meditation, paying attention to his breath and to the elusive spaces between the story lines in his head. In other words, he sat mindfully, letting go of every ego attachment, seeing through every ego trick. Then one day he serenely and mirthfully awoke to what had been in him all along, the pure love, wisdom, and healing in his/the world soul Self. The attachments, fears, and tricks of ego were all that had been in the way. This is enlightenment, this is Buddha nature.

Buddha is not out there or back then but a here-and-now consciousness in us. Buddha, enlightenment, is a consciousness that Gautama articulated in person in history. Now it is transhistorical in anyone who embraces it. A poem by the Zen sage Hakuin says it all. This poem is referred to as the lion's roar because it wakes up the sleeping (unconscious) jungle: "All things are from the very beginning Buddha: this very body: the Buddha, this very moment: eternity, this very place: the lotus paradise." (Buddhism: what a prodigious contribution to humanity's experience of itself!)

In the Taoist tradition, the lion's roar is equated with the voice of the fearless man. It is only in freedom from bondage to the fear and desire in the ego that the indissoluble oneness of the Buddha and ourselves comes through. In Buddhism the true Self includes the world we live in, as the present includes past and future. This is why the Self is a world soul.

How are we one with the buddhas? Their enlightened practice is continually carried on throughout the world, for and with all sentient beings. We are all participants by the power of their devotion and by our own baby steps. From the time we first aspire to the Way until we attain enlightenment, both practice and attainment are carried out with all enlightened beings and ourselves. The work outlined in this book is meant to join us to Buddha's practice of enlightenment and to join Buddha to ours so that it becomes clear that there is only one of us. Sincere readers and workers of this book may now have noticed that they are not alone in their practice. Many saints and bodhisattvas are gathered around the tree under which we sit.

Both Buddhism and Western psychology have the same view of the functional ego. Both see the sense of a separate self (ego) not as innate and self-standing but as evolving out of our relations with others. What we call our self (ego) is an ever reassembling, temporary, and often fictional selection of internalized images from our encounters with the world. Like matter, it is mostly space that looks solid. Our linear mind fools us into seeing it as stable, unchanging, and continuous. This illusory sense of self is the subject of both Buddhist and Western psychologies. The Freudian concern was the danger of a lack of a stable sense of self. The Buddhist concern is the perpetuation of a sense of a separate self as the deepest source of suffering, ultimately futile and self-defeating. Yet just to doubt separateness for a moment is liberation. We are so close.

There seem to be three equally legitimate stages in life. In the first we make things happen. In the second we let things happen. In the Zen-like third phase, we let things happen *or not*. We usually go kicking and screaming from one phase to the next, since we are so reluctant to let go. We desperately attempt to stay in control of our children once they are grown up, for instance. We will not grant ourselves (or them) the gift of letting them do it their way. Our body and psyche says: "Let it happen!" Our invested ego/shadow says: "I'll be damned if I let them make this mistake!" They refuse to listen and then they do it their way, for better or for worse. There is a merry symmetry in this: we start letting go when we have less skill in getting our way.

One benefit of a strong ego is getting what we want. We can let go only when that no longer matters. Otherwise we are like the osprey that tenaciously holds a fish in its talons though it is being pulled farther and farther under water until it finally drowns. What an image of the self-defeat awaiting the ego in its compulsion to win at any cost! "How can you fight the dragon once he has eaten you?" Jung asks.

The issue is not self or no-self but both self and no-self in phase-appropriate order. We need ego formation and healthy "self" esteem. (What we call self-esteem is ego esteem, since the archetypal Self needs no esteem, being always and already infinite and perfect.) The healthy ego is not the one we let go of in our spiritual practice. The target is the neurotic ego with its attachment to fearful and grasping habits and illusions. The goal is not the dissolution of something valuable and real but the recognition of the essential unreality that we have called our identity. The work is to dismantle a Potemkin village. Once the cardboard structures are removed, the spacious reality of the healthy ego-Self axis can appear.

The Dalai Lama says: "This seemingly solid, concrete, independent, self-instituting I that appears under its own power, actually does not exist at all." I as ego is simply the act of pointing and projecting. It has no reality to back it up. Actually, not even external objects have a reality corresponding to their name. A house is a product of pointing mind too, since it is only a collection of assembled parts. The house facing me is really *in* me. It depends on a particular shape for its unifying reality, ultimately only a name, as we give ourselves names. Independent existence is only an imputation we make. If our ego were self-instituting, if it had within itself the power to exist on its own, it would be real. Changling's poem suggests that enlightenment happens only where *no one* goes.

At the same time, identity *is* real in a conventional, provisional, and convenient sense. We do exist, but only as dependent arising and disappearing. If there were an independent, inherently existing ego/self, there would be something permanent and unchanging onto which we could affix our attachments. There would then be no chance for liberation from our painful attachment to fear and grasping. It is thus in the best interests of our liberation that there be no such self. Yet each of us does exist as a relative, ever shifting personal entity through which the life force flows and has continuity. It is not that the world is an illusion but that we treat it like one, that is, as if it had permanent self-standing reality. There really is nothing fixed. This is why the proper etiquette around things is letting go. It is also why heaven is *here:* "This very place: the lotus paradise." (The lotus is considered the birthplace of the gods.)

The metaphor for this realization is arrival at the Promised Land, the inner realm of security and peace that now appears *anywhere I am.* It is a map without sharp demarcations between psyche and universe or even between self-preservation and service of others. After Black Elk returned from his vision on Harney Peak in the Black Hills—the Sioux center of the world—he said that now he knew that everywhere was the center of the world. (The center of the world is any place in which we realize that.)

This anecdote comforts us because it shows how nature is in on our story. Everything in nature, persons, and life events joins in for our wholeness. The urge for wholeness is not only within but everywhere around us. Our identity is more than our deepest needs, values, and wishes. It has a wider scope and purpose: unconditional love, perennial wisdom, and healing power.

Some day an accident will unexpectedly cause in you a sort of mental revolution, and thereby you will realize that the Pure Land of Serene Light is no less than the earth itself, and that Buddha is your own mind.

—D. T. SUZUKI

INNER WHOLENESS: ALREADY AND NOT YET

You already own the costly elixir that will heal.
You have only to use it. . . .

—RUMI

Individuation is the natural process of maturation for which the psyche instinctively yearns and which it is geared to complete. It is inhibited by choices that perpetuate ego and nurtured by choices that transform or transcend it. Our work is to redeem the Self hidden by the neurotic, inflated ego and make it ready for an epiphany in the healthy ego. The incarnation of a god is an apt metaphor for human individuation. Incarnation is to a god what individuation is to humans. This incarnation/individuation happens when the ego gives up hegemony over our psychic processes and lets go of its need to control human circumstances. Only then can there be a revelation of the Self as the true center of the human psyche, its divine nucleus. Individuation is the greater unity attempting to emerge in everything we experience. Nathan Schwarz-Salant calls it "the process by which the ego is challenged to develop toward wholeness as imaged by the Self."

The Source, the divine nucleus of psyche, has a yearning for incarnation and wants to find human form, give oracular knowledge, and benefit the world in our lifetime. Its path moves this way: from the Source (Self) through our unique personality to higher consciousness. Psychic energy is dammed up by ego habits, self-limiting beliefs, and fear of what is greater than ego. To let it come up and through is what the practice of befriending the shadow is about. It is a collaboration of conscious and unconscious resulting in superconsciousness.

Mark Antony, at Caesar's death, says: "Now let bloody treason flourish over us!" This is a metaphor for what may happen when the world is ruled by the neurotic ego instead of its true governing principle, the Self.

World of Ego	*World of Self*
Punishment	Rehabilitation
War	Negotiated settlements
Competition	Cooperation
Win-lose	Win-win
Feud	Reconciliation
Retaliation	Asking for amends
Grudge	Forgiveness
Sarcasm, ridicule	Harmless humor
Control	Freedom
Fear-based decisions	Courageous risk
Worst will happen	Best can happen
Greed	Generosity
Me-first	We-always
Use others	Respect others
Take advantage of weakness	Treat weakness with kindness

All the archetypes are recruited for the epic task of individuation. We integrate, in our own unique way, our hero energy, our shadow energy, our male and female energies, our wisdom energy, and so on. The striking paradox is that through cosmic consciousness we experience our own individual uniqueness. In this awareness of our world-Self, primacy is no longer given to the accidental circumstances of our story. From our center of pure awareness we observe our ego and its predicaments but are no longer seduced by them. Instead the Self rides the ego to beatific vision. Individuation is thus an integration of our psychological and spiritual work. How?

By Psychological Work	*By Spiritual Practice*
Become more functional: what I do leads to my goal, and less dysfunctional, less distracted by fear and desire	Access and release the Self: love, wisdom, and healing, by openness to assisting forces: grace
THIS I ACHIEVE	THIS I RECEIVE

Integration means being involved in both of these at the same time. This is combining effort and grace. Grace is that which takes me beyond the limits of my effort, willpower, and intellect. It is the advocate archetype, an assisting force on the path to individuation. We cannot be whole by willpower alone or by spiritual practice alone. It will always take more, an intervention by something greater than our ego, that is, the Self. Kneading dough takes effort by us. But the rising of the dough takes something we cannot provide. Writing a poem takes concentration, but writers know that a muse has to endorse the inspiration for something wonderful to result. If so much is double-edged like that, our arrival at wholeness must be shaped that way too.

THE PRACTICE

Here is a list of the building blocks of healthy self-respect. Ask yourself how closely you approximate each of them on a scale of one to ten. Make an enlarged copy of this list and hang it where you will see it often. Show it to your partner, your best friend, and one family member and tell them you welcome their feedback about your progress. This list integrates your psychological and spiritual qualities so that wholeness becomes visible in your daily life.

I am sincerely looking for my own truth and design my life accordingly.

I am happy when I appear as I am without pretense, no matter how unflattering.

I notice times when I am not in touch with my adult powers. I do not feel ashamed of myself nor do I blame others. I simply acknowledge my inadequacy, ask for help, or try something new.

I am not perfect but I am committed to working on myself. I welcome feedback that shows me where I am less loving than I can be, where I am less tolerant, where less open. I make a plan to change for the better in accord with what I learn.

I have passed through painful experiences and have endured them by addressing, processing, and resolving them whenever possible. In this sense, my life is an heroic journey.

I keep my commitments and finish the tasks I agree to do.

I have reason to be proud of some accomplishments. Thoreau wrote in his journal: "A man looks with pride at his woodpile."[4]

I occasionally resist the challenges on my path. I accept this as part of the journey. I make room for occasional mistakes and procrastination.

I ask for what I want without demand or expectation, take

4. Reader: Your serious commitment to the practices in this book can be your "woodpile."

responsibility for my feelings and behavior, have personal boundaries, and at the same time I act gently toward others.

I have standards of rigorous honesty in all my dealings and I live in accord with them. If I fall down in this, I admit it and make amends. I easily and willingly apologize when necessary.

I act towards others not as they act toward me but in accord with personal standards of fairness. I am committed to resisting evil and fighting injustice in nonviolent ways.

I do not knowingly hurt others. If they hurt me, I do not retaliate only open a dialogue and ask for amends.

I look at other people and their choices without censure.

I am always aware of the pain and poverty of those less fortunate than myself. I find ways to respond that combine generosity and personal contact.

I can see goodness and something touching in any person. I look for an opportunity for growth in any predicament. I have lived through pain and been transformed by it by holding such opposites.

I am able to say "Ouch!" to inappropriate pain in jobs, relationships, and interactions with others. I take action to change what can be changed and to move on when things remain abusive. I do this without self-pity or the need to make others wrong.

I confront the inherited or deep-rooted governing principles of my psyche rather than placate them. For instance, if I operate on a scarcity model—being ungenerous because I fear there will not be enough for me—I admit it and act as if I believed in abundance.

I am responding to an inner call to me to find and live out my vocation and my personal potential. I make the choices in life that make room for new possibilities.

I have goals and I am doing what it takes to reach them. I am engaged enthusiastically in something meaningful and this is the source of my bliss.

Confronted with the suffering in the world, I do not blame God or man but simply ask: "What then shall *I* do?" I respond to pain in others with a plan to help, even if it has to be minimal. Meeting needs with resources is lighting one candle rather than cursing the darkness. T. S. Eliot says: "I sat upon the shore with the arid waste behind me. Shall I at least set *my* lands in order?"

I have an unwavering sense of myself as a person of conviction while still being flexible. I am able to change, to drop outmoded beliefs, and to make alterations in my lifestyle that fit the ever-evolving demands of my world. I see an identity crisis as an opportunity for enlightenment!

I have it in me to put off immediate or self-serving gratification in favor of long-term goals and with awareness of the needs of others.

I tread gently and appreciatively on the earth with what Saint Bonaventure called "a courtesy toward natural things."

I learn from my own reactions: Tears at a movie invite me to look at my personal griefs. Attraction and repulsion invite me to look at my shadow. Memories and images that tug at me invite me to stay with them and to follow their lead into my own unopened spaces.

I live in accord with my deepest needs, values, and wishes while loving others more and more.

I have spiritual self-respect by honoring the divine life within me by acting with love, wisdom, and healing power.

An inner wholeness in the psyche presses its still unfulfilled claims upon us.

—EMMA JUNG

4

The Rest of Me You Do Not See

*The boundless resolve, no longer limitable in any direction,
to achieve one's purest inner possibility.*

—RAINER MARIA RILKE

THE LIGHT THAT WAITS TO SHINE:
OUR POSITIVE SHADOW

Our *personal positive shadow* is the life potential we have
not yet activated. It is our truth-in-waiting. Full potential is
like the seed of a rose that contains the whole rose if the
appropriate conditions are in place. Like our psyche, our positive shadow is twofold, personal and collective. Personally,
it is our ego ideal not yet realized. It is the light we may have
hidden under a bushel. It comprises all our unopened reserves
of talents and gifts. Archetypally, it is unconditional love, perennial wisdom, and the power to heal ourselves and others,
the attributes of the higher Self, our Buddha nature. To be
true to this most godlike part of ourselves is a form of faith.
The positive shadow calls for faith in our own capacity. The
legacy we leave the world does not have to take the form of
a book, a painting, or a place in history. It can be a virtue, a
love that makes a difference, a life honestly lived. We are as

successful as Jonas Salk or Abe Lincoln when we give the gifts we were gifted with, be they ever so humble.

The positive shadow, psychologically, is our healthy ego; the positive shadow, spiritually, is our Self. Both the positive personal talents and virtues of our healthy ego and the marvelous cosmic powers of the Self may be denied or ignored. We may believe that everything about us is inadequate and wrong. This happens because the part of us that might imagine otherwise has been lulled to sleep by that habitual self-defeating belief. We may be passive and fearful in our behavior. If so, we can be sure that we have active courage waiting to be accessed. What we act out existentially is actually backed by an unlived essential capacity for its opposite. We also contain the counterparts of every negative attribute in positive potentials. Within fear is the useful counterpart of caution *and* healthy vulnerability.

Saint Irenaeus said: "The glory of God is the human person who is fully alive." The positive personal shadow contains a higher quality of life than we ever imagined. This potential wants to reveal itself. The main way it does so is by projection of itself onto others in the form of admiration or envy. We imagine certain traits or qualities to be in others only when they are also a mirror reflection of what is in us. Our strong reactions of awe or envy give us the clue that we are in the picture we are looking at. The strong reaction is the result of an excitement in our psyche about seeing its long-hidden twin. Everything about us joins in the urgent enthusiasm of our psyche to become the midwife of wholeness.

The positive shadow refers to attributes and traits, not specific skills. For instance, we may admire or envy someone's prowess in sports or proficiency in music. Shadow projections are not about others' inborn or practiced talents but may be about the confident or admirable *manner* in which they show their talents. Our positive shadow may be constellated when we esteem the extraordinary result of someone's practice. We then may have it in us to put energy into our own unique talents and develop them with equal success. But the specific talent that someone else was born with is not necessarily the one in us.

Each of us was born with just those talents that fit perfectly with our purposes on this planet. Our physical makeup is appropriate to our talents. My scholar body is not your wrestler's body. Our brand of intelligence is suitable to our natural inclinations. Our bliss appears and our destiny is reached when all this comes together as we locate and live up to our gifts. It takes humility to accept the limited number of our gifts in comparison with the apparently more numerous gifts of those we strongly admire. *Can we live beyond compare?*

At the same time, we can be proud of our own unique gifts and appreciate them as that which makes us who we are. We are thankful for our gifts but also clear about our efforts in putting them to use. "How can God make Stradivarius violins without Antonio?" asked Antonio Stradivari in a poem by Robert Browning. Our potential is activated in two ways: by the unfolding of what is in us by grace, and by work and practice to enliven and animate it. Inherent in that which is potential is a will to open, as the chick in the egg surely knows. It takes effort to peck at the shell and open it. It takes nature's grace to make the bill strong enough to pierce the shell. Both are necessary and it all happens synchronously.

Our gifts, like our virtues, are meant to become embodied in our life's work. The trainer of Rin Tin Tin was asked what made the famous movie hero-dog so special. After trying to explain and not succeeding, the trainer said simply: "Rin Tin Tin is dignity in the form of a dog." *Can I be love in the form of myself? Can I use my every gift for that?*

Some of us have spent years on the wrong path, perhaps

trying to make it in business when our gift was in art. We made money a goal in life when artistic creativity was our real talent. We grieve the money we lost when actually we might more appropriately grieve how we lost our way and looked for something that was never meant to be ours. (Our real gift will never be only a talent but will also be a virtue.)

Here is an example of projection of the positive shadow in the context of envy in relationship: James resents his wife, Loretta, for her gutsy strength. This envy tells him about his own unacknowledged strength. He resents in her what he has not uncovered or manifested in himself. To envy is, ultimately, to hate one's own potential. It will be disastrous to their relationship if James attempts to subvert Loretta for her power rather than work on releasing his own. If only he would take her example as an assisting force in his own life. Loretta is mirroring his own unexplored riches. James can discover himself by identifying with the part of Loretta that carries and shows him his own potential. Can James let go of his ego competitiveness long enough to do such a good thing for himself? If he can, the relationship will be successful. It will lead to mutual happiness and respect that will free up James's positive shadow. James will find his own untapped potential for strength in facing things and he will even have the guts to get things done. Loretta will find her strength mirrored and appreciated and this will lead to her increasing it. She will share it with James once she sees he is no longer threatened by it.

Our positive personal shadow is our deep unexplored identity. It is a center of song in us where, like the nightingale of Keats, we sing "of summer in full-throated ease." We *are* more than we seem. There is so much more to us than anyone has noticed, least of all ourselves. Could there be a tragedy more heartrending than a heart that has never had its chance to open as much as it could? We have so much love, wisdom, power, joy, talent, feeling, and rapture inside that wants to emerge. There are moments when we allow it to happen, when we dance it out into the delirious air. Befriending the shadow means expanding and multiplying those moments more than ever before. *Can I stand that much blooming?*

Yet that center of melodic power in us can be projected, for example, by following a guru or fundamentalist religious or political perspective in a life-absorbing and self-effacing way. We may see a teacher or leader or dogma as infallible or even as omnipotent. We are half right, since the Self has these qualities, but we have limited the possibilities for our own growth by projecting the Self onto one person or ideal. As long as someone or something is above and beyond our reach, we miss "the many-splendored thing," our "purest inner possibility." Once we assume our full stature, we no longer need to people our world with either giants or pygmies. We will all be companions.

> *It is very much lamented, Brutus,*
> *That you have no such mirrors as will turn*
> *Your hidden worthiness into your eye,*
> *That you might see your shadow.*
>
> —CASSIUS TO BRUTUS IN *Julius Caesar*

Our *positive collective shadow* (the shadow of the Self) is projected onto gods and heroes. Emerson said: "History is an impertinence and an injury if it be anything more than a cheerful parable of *my* being and becoming. . . . All that Adam had, all that Caesar could, I have and can do. . . . Suppose they were virtuous? Did they wear out virtue?" Religious figures, heroes, sages, and champions of all kinds reveal the qualities in us that wait for integration. Every icon can become a mirror, as every photo in our family album becomes more and more a mirror of us throughout our life span.

With every passing year, I see myself looking more and more like Grandpa. What keeps me from seeing the pictures of Buddha or of the heart of Jesus as more and more like myself too?

It takes work to match the capacity we have always had: "All beings are from the very beginning Buddha." "Learn of me for I am gentle and humble of heart." Where have statements like that landed in us? Did we ever allow ourselves to know that they were descriptions of an inner Self that is waiting to make a personal appearance in our lives?

In Egypt the pharaoh is sometimes pictured venerating his own image. He is the perfected human, one who has returned to the Source and come back with gifts for all. He venerates himself because that Source is within him, and this is also why he was adored as a god. This is what is meant by returning to the Source: to come back to the riches that reflect the divine Self, to find one's divine identity, to end the dichotomy between ego and Self. It is precisely the axis-forming practice of befriending the shadow.

The ancients were not foolish enough to take things literally; they found their most compelling truth in metaphor. There were always wise people who knew that "the pharaoh" was an *inner* reality. By the end of the Old Kingdom, everyone could be initiated and thereby return to the Source. What perfected the pharaoh was his expanse into the fullest stature of his being, into divinity. The god Amon, not ego, was considered the source of the pharaoh's power. Anyone can do the work and receive the graces to achieve and receive that too. To adore is to self-diminish unless it is a mirroring of the one Self, always and already in us, in others, and in nature.

We see now that our ego cannot portray us fully, since we have another dimension to us, the vast potential of the Self. The shadow is the vessel of that potential, and this is why there is such joy in befriending it/ourselves. In the Christian view, Jesus returns to the Source by his ascension into heaven. He returned his material body back to its spiritual source. This is a metaphor for our work: to take everything material and gritty in our lives and relocate it all in our spirituality. Then our life on earth is "as it is in heaven." The *Egyptian Book of the Dead* summarizes it: "Your essence is in heaven; your body is on earth." Such a transfiguration is what is really afoot in befriending our shadow.

The positive collective shadow of the Self/God is love, wisdom, and healing. This is what we see in the provident Father, the redeeming Jesus, the compassionate Buddha, the wise Krishna. Sanctity is the human articulation of this archetypal shadow. Our positive shadow side is thus personified by gods and saints. Individuals who act from pure motives are the saints who devote their lives to acts of goodness and thereby cooperate in the collective positive shadow activity of the Self. The Dalai Lama and Mother Teresa seem to have lived humbly in accord with a cosmic will toward love, with no motivation of self-aggrandizement or profit. They make eminent contributions to the treasury of graces that we can all access as an assisting adjunct to our efforts. Not only their example but their co-presence on our planet in our day is an assisting force, a blessing to us. Saints are the proof that the work works and that personal work is collectively beneficial. Every saint embodies and exemplifies one unique piece of our inherent potential. The positive shadow of heroic people reaches us in healing ways. Unconditional love and the healing powers of the psyche are truly one and the same. For instance, Mother Teresa reached us as lonely when she reached out to the lonely. She reached us as needy when she fed the hungry. She touched us in our isolation and lostness when she found a place for the homeless. As long as our human identity happens in relation to others, our personal growth is a direct path to intimacy and compassion.

A human person can achieve a clear, accurate, and all-embracing grasp of the nature of his or her own and the world's reality. This is the experience of utter openness that comes with freedom from any fixed or limited identity. It happens by befriending the positive shadow. Buddha's teaching included a call to just this befriending. He was showing people their potential for light and offering them a technology to let it through. The spiritual potential of the human psyche is its ability to experience itself not as separate and ego driven but as a loving and generous member of the mystical body of humanity. In this body one is contained securely while at the same time embracing it all: enfolded and enfolding. This can happen only when the ego relaxes its grasp and the only option is the close embrace of love.

You are the light of the world.

—JESUS TO THE PEOPLE, MATTHEW 5:14

THE PRACTICE

• Read the following poem by Emily Dickinson slowly, first silently, then aloud. Copy out the last line in longhand. Ask yourself honestly how it is true for you. Which phrase of the poem strikes you the most? How does this book ask you "to rise"? What steps are you taking in the practices in this book that help you release your "royal" energy?

We never know how high we are
Till we are asked to rise
And then if we are true to plan
Our statures touch the skies—

The Heroism we recite
Would be the normal thing
Did not ourselves the Cubits warp
For fear to be a king—[5]

• The unconscious contains our life purpose not in the fact
that it conceals the past but in how it unfolds the future. Our
inner life has a story that parallels the external one. As we do
the work, we gradually notice what psyche is up to, how it is
always coordinating our destiny and urging us on to it. Our
inner life keeps giving hints of the wholeness at our core. This
wholeness is the meaning of our life. Events and crises are the
vehicles by which the inner meaning is revealed and unfolded.
The goal of our psychic life is to activate the potentials that
appear in those challenging moments and to release them
generously in our lifetime. As each potential opens, we are
aware of even more possibilities. These are intimations of
prodigious powers that transcend ego limits. Our experience
of meaning is thus the same as contact with the transcendent.
The infinite is taking shape in the finite events and persons of
our life. The recognition of this personal incarnation is what
makes us speak of "God within." The highest and the deepest
are one and the same: spiritual Everest is the deepest reach of
our psyche.

A sense of emptiness may not represent loneliness but a
lack of trustworthy roots or a stable footing in my own inner
world. How much contact do I have with my own depths?
What is the story of my inner life? I look over the chapters of
my life and ask where my focus was in each phase, for example, in the sexual or creative aspect. I ask which fears pre-
sided. How much energy went into repressing my creativity
and how much into releasing it? What was the core of per-

5. p. 523 in *Complete Poems*.

sonal meaning from which I operated? How much of my activity was running in place, how much was tied to habits and repetitions, how much was about the forward processes of evolution? Was I at my most creative when I was repressing myself or when I was expressing myself? Do I mostly make choices that increase my freedom or restrict it? The fact that I have abused my freedom at times does not mean that I cannot use it productively now. Do I see that an abuse does not take away a use? Or do I fear freedom in myself and/or in those around me?

• We activate our potential when we break out of our sheltering routines and when we let go of our rigid unexamined beliefs. What are these for you?

• A single person is not comparable to a single planet but to the entire solar system. We integrate diverse and complementary energies and that is what allows the system, ourselves, to flourish. Astrology can help in re-visioning ourselves in this more expanded way. The purpose of astrology in the archetypal perspective is not to predict the future; it is a symbolic description of human completeness. It challenges each of us to live through the entire cycle of human experience. Our birth sign is only a single snapshot of a moment in our lifetime. The full opening of our personal potential is in the full experience of the zodiac. Our destiny is to receive and live out what each sign offers. (In medieval times a jury was formed of twelve men who each had a different astrological sign so that the full amplitude of human judgment could be represented.) The signs take us through the seasons of the year, and these seasons reflect our own human unfolding and the successive phases of our individuation: we begin with Aries, the birth of consciousness, and end as Pisces, the transcendence of ego in favor of cosmic attunement.

Look into this further if it appeals to you. Find the meaning of each of the signs and present it to yourself as a challenge. Notice that each sign has a positive and a negative shadow side. Take each one as true of you in some way using the befriending techniques you are learning in this book. You might even work on the qualities of each sign during its own time of the year.

Look at the moon tonight. Picture it in all its phases. A smile is visible in the full moon, though it soon wanes and even disappears. This is nature telling us how life goes and how it can simultaneously have a lighter side. Am I stuck in the FACE of ego: fear, attachment, control, entitlement, or gazing at the mirthful face in the moon?

WHEN LIGHT MEETS LIMIT

There came a time when staying tight within the bud became more painful than the strain it took to bloom.

—ANAÏS NIN

Potential is related to actualization as a seed is to a flower. We have a storehouse positive shadow that awaits a greenhouse attentiveness. It is hard to be effective gardeners if we doubt ourselves. Inner critical voices may be rebuking us for our limitations. They usually hearken from the reproachful messages of parents, teachers, authority figures. They are internalized by us early on and maintained over the years. The work is not to banish the inner critic but to hear in its voice some clues to our own shadow traits. Since inner critical words are introjected from others, they are actually alien. The early messages contradict our present sane beliefs about who we really are. We can easily see the falseness of them at the intellectual level, but our belief system keeps us stuck in them. The part of us that knows better, our adult logical self, joined in the developmental process rather late. The more primitive inner-child part of us already believes firmly in the messages that came from our parental shadow, no matter how offensive or life-effacing they are: Don't want anything. Don't go. Don't give yourself, show yourself, to anyone. Don't think a man or woman will want you. Don't let anyone know what you are thinking. Don't let anyone get too close or go too far away. Don't be enthusiastic about anything. Don't be exuberant. Nothing you do matters or will come to anything. You are inadequate, ineffective, weak, failing, failed, doomed. Don't be. When these don'ts are internalized they can become rigid, self-defeating mind-sets.

Self-negating messages characterize the neurotically deflated ego. They whisper to us in our own voice: I don't deserve happiness; I may as well put up with abuse; I am a victim; I can't change anything; I am in despair; there is something faulty in my character if I am weak or inadequate to a task. These verdicts conflict with the inner voice that says, "I am acceptable as I am and I can smooth out my rough edges. I am both all right and in need of some change." This combination of apparent contradictions is the great advantage of the practices of befriending the shadow.

The core of the shadow is the archetype of the enemy or stranger. We are required to be careful about strangers if we are to survive safely in early life. This is why family violations are so insidious; they do not fit the stranger-danger archetype and so they confuse us. We do not have a program within us to watch out for danger from that quarter. Our instinct is to trust family members and not to eschew or even confront them. It is frightening to contradict the early injunctive voices of authority. Challenging the voices at the emotional level brings up deep anxiety because it seems to be contrary to survival. We are not instinctively calibrated to defend ourselves against our own mothers. We are preprogrammed to trust and love those who care for us. This is why we originally let in self-defeating shadow messages without question. Our discriminating ego was not yet formed, so the messages proceeded directly into the unconscious with no questions asked. When we can adopt an attitude of comfortableness with our split-up state, then we are no longer under its power, no longer manipulated by it. As we befriend our own shadow, we discover our inherited shadow and befriend it too.

We may also be holding on to values and wishes that we inherited from our parents or from society. We may have tried to match our gifts to their plans for us. Maybe we were trying to play basketball with a football player's body. Success is congruence between our own gifts and our own choices, between our feelings and our expression of them, between our conscientious standards and our daily dealings. The positive shadow, our untapped potential, is the same as our deepest needs, values, passions, and wishes, our gifts and our identity. We are successful when we do all we possibly can with our gifts, thus activating our potential. We lose our chance to do this to the extent that we maintain limiting beliefs and thoughts: "I cannot do that," "I will never get to that point," "I am too old, too young, too late, too soon, too weak." Such verdicts against ourselves prevent access to our authentic needs and wishes. It is also true that these inherited beliefs were not proven facts about us but what others imagined were our limitations. Our own imagination can likewise revive us: by affirming and picturing ourselves with the powers that we now repudiate in ourselves, we access them abundantly.

We can even declare that we are what Byron saw: "a rose with all its sweetest leaves yet folded." Eventually we realize that whatever in us has remained folded up is really that about us that was never loved. This is the sadness in the folded rose of ourselves. What was not confirmed and loved by others, especially our parents, did not have full permission to emerge. It is up to us to find this confirmation now from within ourselves, our relationships, and our spirituality. Joy results from permission to unfold. The alternative is melancholy or depression.

When we realize, to our dismay, that we are not even close to capacity in our activation of our talents or in our own ability to give or receive love, we may feel a discouraging melancholy. If our range of physical motion is inhibited, we may feel an ache in that area. That ache psychologically is melancholy. After a while it becomes a feature of our undeveloped inner landscape and we take our stunted life for granted.

The ugly duckling lamented because he had no proper duck feathers. He considered his voice ugly because he could not quack and his body uncoordinated because he could not waddle. Little did he know what gifts he was born with! One day a swan made him realize what his real gifts were. Then his whole life made sense and all his inadequacies were reassessed as assets. He found his unique place in the universe, and it was a much prouder and more splendidly beautiful place than any duck could occupy. We have all perceived ourselves as ugly ducklings in some way. To find the same happy ending is our task. Befriending our positive shadow is a path to it.

"You've had the power all along," Dorothy heard from her assisting force, the good witch Glinda, who was pointing to the final unconscious capacity in Dorothy. This was true of Dorothy *essentially:* she had the quality she admired in the wizard. Glinda then says, "All you have to do is click your heels together." This is the work she had to do, the *existential* action that activates the unrealized potential. The successful combination of essential capacity and existential action leads us to manifest what we had always thought we could only receive from others. Now we know the way home without asking. This is finding what was "too bright for our infirm delight, the truth's superb surprise," as Emily Dickinson said.

Plotinus, a Neoplatonist of the third century, was said to be the discoverer of the unconscious. He believed that potentials are unconscious in us because they are at a higher level of development than we are. It is thus not a matter of none but of not quite yet. An acorn is not a defect, only a not-yet. It has the capacity for oak tree-ness, but that will take the work of planting and watering, joined to the collaborative grace of friendly environmental conditions. The essential capacity is meant to be complemented by the existential work. Our task is to match our effort to our capacity. We put ourselves down often and we deny our potential. Yet there lives an urge in us toward higher consciousness that is latent even in the deepest self-denial. If this were not true, enlightenment and evolution would be impossible. We are each as ideal as our untapped potential and as real as the energy with which we strive to activate it. *Unconscious* means, in effect, unconditional potential. I am unbounded potential that can neither be created nor destroyed, like imagination that can receive or create any image, or like an empty room awaiting either tawdry or elegant furnishings.

Ultimately, life is a battle not so much with our inadequacy as with our belief that we are inadequate. What I hide from in myself is a crucial ingredient of myself. It is my own liveliness that has become scary and unacceptable. When I disown it, I disown my full identity. I live from my neurotic ego and persona only, with no acknowledgment of my healthy ego and my spiritual Self. For example, I notice a desire to hurt someone in retaliation for what he has done to me. Now I know there is a spiteful vengefulness in me. Yet there must also be its counterpart in me, the nonviolent loving response that looks for redress of injustice but also for mutual transformation and reconciliation. (I trust this because I have grasped that my psyche and all things are opposites complementing one another in a vast array of wholeness.) To choose the nonviolent response will take effort, turning the desire for vengeance inside out, looking for creative ways to confront the person who hurt me. I can tell him how I feel hurt. I can ask for amends. I am now doing something that takes me beyond ego, unconditionally loving while sanely protecting myself. If my choice is vengeance, I am living out my neurotic shadow ego with all its slash-and-cut limitations. I am doing to someone else what he did to me. Nothing moves and changes. No transformation happens. As an alternative, I may take notice of my shadow and look for ways to tame and befriend it. This is how shadow work leads to spiritual growth.

Just as the work leads us beyond our limits, it is also not limited in its effects. In the world of the higher Self, there is a treasury of images and of wisdom gathered throughout all the history of humankind, universally and continually available. Every person who achieves any amount of consciousness contributes to it. Every ray of light that enters us shines through us into the common treasury, as light enters and illuminates a cathedral. Anyone can draw upon the treasury of light. It is an assisting force along the human journey to wholeness. When our ego engages in the practice of befriending its shadow, it is transformed, and that is a deposit into the treasury of graces for all humankind. Deposits are made one person at a time, the same way peace happens. Our personal work has a transpersonal impact; one small step by a person is one giant leap for humankind. Jung says: "If the individual is not truly regenerated in spirit, society cannot be either, for society is the sum total of individuals in need of redemption. . . . Anyone who has found access to his unconscious automatically exercises an influence on his environment."

Thus, to do personal work is also to do collective work. Christ's descent into hell after his crucifixion is a metaphor for how the work of shadow befriending and individuation embraces the unconscious and lost pieces of ourselves and others. Christ's harrowing experience of hell is the metaphor for the ego's choice to go down into the unconscious to recover the worthy powers buried there, not for oneself but for all. Thereby we defy the lord of death: "The dead are, for me, the voices of the unanswered, unresolved, and unredeemed. . . . I cease to belong to myself alone, . . . but to all," wrote Jung.

Admiration for creativity is universal, so creativity must be part of the hidden reserves of all of us. What has been disregarded, suppressed, forgotten, or hidden holds and holds down our most creative powers. That power has a force that upsets and cuts through our tragic flaw of limiting ourselves. The energy invested in hiding or repudiating our bright potential may be misdirected but it has not diminished. With creativity we can release and redirect the derailed energy. This involves a renunciation of conditioned responses, of hand-me-down, obsolete, self-defeating beliefs, and of the inveterate habits of ego.

An immense lively energy lies in the dark spaces, the gaps, the uncertainties, the imponderables, the enigmas that open between beliefs and habits. To be creative requires that we be able and willing to visit all the dark regions of our psyche, no matter how primitive or disturbing. To lose touch with our shadow is to be despoiled of our lively energy. The creative impulse is a path by which we can acknowledge our truth and not be overwhelmed by it. Creative people even know how to protect and soothe themselves by means of creative activity.

THE PRACTICE

· Make the inner negative voices explicit by speaking their words aloud and you will be less likely to act on them. Speak in the second person (as you first heard them) and then reverse them and resolve to act as if that opposite were true of you for the future.

· When you hear the inner critic admonishing, reproaching, shaming, or inhibiting you, do not try to silence it. Instead, use active imagination to open a dialogue between the critic and another voice that also exists inside you: the kindly uncle or aunt or the nurturant parent or the best friend. Let this supportive voice that you recall from your past or that you are aware of from life experience respond to the critic within. Let this voice defend you, stand up for you, be your advocate. This is your inner assisting force that gives a self-empowering answer to your inner afflicting voice. Since we contain all the opposites, we have both voices within ourselves equally. It is only a matter of letting the kindly voice be heard and letting it gain ascendancy. Shamans in trance became possessed by spirits of dead ancestors who spoke words of comfort and advice to the tribe through them. There is thus a long human history of access to the healing voices within. Notice how one line of *The Rime of the Ancient Mariner* changes to another: "A thousand slimy things lived on and so did I" becomes "Sure my kind saint took pity on me and I blessed them."

Persevere in confronting and questioning ingrained beliefs every time they arise. Access an alternative voice of power. This is how their stranglehold finally weakens. What are the images and beliefs responsible for my present self-limitation? What are the thoughts on which I have become fixated? They are not accurate assessments but outdated flotsam holding down the ship. Fixation is staying too long; regression is going back too far. Where do I stand?

• Identify your central, most familiar negating belief about yourself. It may be the governing principle behind all your decisions. It may be sabotaging your chances at healthy intimacy. It may be a source of despair, a reason to keep giving up on yourself. Usually, this self-defeating belief originated in early life and is cellularly imprinted in you. In other words, it is not responsive to mental injunctions but is in the very cells of your body. It even directs gestures and behaviors in unconscious ways. The experience of shame or inner emptiness may be a tuning in on this belief. It may be the discordant channel on which you relate to others and judge yourself. Unless you take action to unseat this belief, it continues to gain ascendancy in your life choices. It dictates to you and lies to you. It makes you believe it is all that is true of you and all that is authentic in you. Such a core self-negation can be the result of abuse and even a way of blaming yourself for it.

Complete these sentence stems with a variety of endings: "My most familiar negative belief about myself is . . ." "My truth is . . ." Breath and relaxation exercises are necessary here, as is mindfulness meditation, since core beliefs are deeper than the intellect and require a redirection of physical consciousness. Incorporate yoga and other disciplines that help balance your mind and body. Look for your familiar gestures and bodily responses that seem automatic and see how they can change when this more holistic attention is brought to them.

• In moments of despair, you may be a person who occasionally says to yourself: "Well, I can always kill myself!" Make a commitment right now that that is no longer an option for you. You are committed to lifelong looking for a solution to whatever distresses you. You will not choose self-destruction as your way out. Remind yourself of this commitment if the suicide solution comes into your mind again. "No, that is not something I will ever do. I will honor my predicament by working things out. I have it in me to handle whatever comes my way." Now you are an assisting force to yourself. *That* is what empowers you to handle whatever voices say or life brings. The predicament itself is an assisting force we can lean on rather than be crushed under. "Life is or has meaning and meaninglessness. I cherish the anxious hope that meaning will preponderate and win the battle," says Jung.

• At times of dark despair or depression, sit with the disturbing feelings with no attempt to dismiss them. Pay attention in a cradling way to the dismal spaces in yourself. Visit these dim and uninviting deserts with curiosity and compassion. Let yourself feel as bad as you feel and stay with yourself in a nonabandoning way. You will notice that something shifts, after a while, all by itself. Your lively creative energy will appear in an effortless way. When you simply remain faithful to your own reality, you evoke the creative forces in yourself that lie just below the lunar surfaces of your psyche.

• Use whichever of these affirmations help you stretch:

  • I dissolve the boundaries I have set on my potential, specifically . . .
  • I allow myself to see the expanse of my untapped potential, especially . . .
  • Where I was contracting, I expand. For example, I am limiting myself at work by not asking for a promotion. I will ask.

- Where I was isolating, I connect. For example, I will break the silence between me and my friend by calling her and initiating a reconciliation, a great challenge to my capacity for love and creativity.
- I acknowledge and act on my gifts, specifically . . .
- I feel joy about all the gifts I have and how they fit me so perfectly.
- I consecrate my gifts to the benefit of all humankind.

- Our choice of friends gives us a portrait of our positive shadow. We enjoy being with our friends not only because of who they are but also because of who we are when we are with them. They bring out the best in us, that is, our positive shadow. They also have attributes that we admire, and in this way too they reflect our untapped potential. List three admirable qualities of each of your three closest friends, attributes you do not believe you also have. Write affirmations that make them your own. Tell your friends about this exercise and express appreciation for their presence in your life.

- What about gender potential? As long as a man's self-image relies on the presence of a woman in his life, and vice-versa for a woman, the full potential of the man or woman is truncated. Examine your feelings and needs regarding the opposite sex: What am I really up to, what do I really want, how is this man (woman) a crutch? How does this man (woman) or all the men (women) in my life contribute to or diminish my sense of myself as a man (woman)? How can I integrate independence and interdependence?

THE DARK THAT OPENS TO THE LIGHT: OUR NEGATIVE SHADOW

> *While looking for the light, you may suddenly be devoured by the darkness and find the true light.*
> —JACK KEROUAC

The negative shadow is all that we find unacceptable, unlovable, and ugly in ourselves. It is not a missing piece of ourselves but an undeveloped piece. We fear and hide from our own dark side. We may strongly despise in others what we unconsciously deny in ourselves. This is the negative shadow side of us, our own inner darkness, an offensive thing we may be doing and not noticing. We also suffer from blurred vision in looking at ourselves, but we see sharply into others. We thus see negativities through a glass darkly in ourselves but with face-to-face clarity in others who have traits that reflect our own.

The negative shadow seems below and beneath us, as the positive shadow seems above and beyond us. It is the unconscious side of our false persona and our neurotic, inflated ego. It comes up especially in times of stress or frustration, and this may account for our being kind to people generally but then, at times, unwittingly, quite mean. (Jane Austen's novel *Emma* is about just such a person.) The negative shadow is that which exposes and embarrasses us. We are ashamed of whatever in our ego does not fit into our ego ideal. Our ego feels defeated in knowing we are not as kind as we can imagine ourselves to be.

The unacceptable negative shadow refers not only to unwholesome traits but to any denied feature of our character or mood, for example, the depression or bitterness that may lurk behind a cheerful exterior. The darker, unknown face of Maurice, the fey young lothario, comes out when he plays a mean or humiliating practical joke on one of his friends. He is ordinarily the life of the party, a morale builder. His persona is supportive of everyone; his shadow is out to get anyone. Occasionally Maurice is caught in the act of his aggression. He makes light of it and goes underground for a while, acting nicer than ever. Maurice is very concerned about not letting his nice-guy image be sullied. He wants his good looks to represent him, not his bad manners. He is afraid of being found out because his life revolves around people's admiration and appreciation of him. Maurice will never find his shadow as long he sees his aggression as "all in good fun." He will not see the cruel barb in his behavior until he is caught red-handed and admits his darker purposes. (Insight can also happen through therapy or in a spiritual awakening.) Maurice is acting out the retaliatory compulsion of ego. Perhaps he was treated cruelly in childhood. Perhaps little Maurice was humiliated, shamed, made fun of. That was a blow from which he never quite recovered. The shadow of Maurice was in the works before he had the chance to defend himself from it. Now he offends to get back at the world that has hurt him. He can work things through by addressing, processing, and resolving his inner-child issues. Perhaps, also, someone will come along and care about Maurice, someone who will understand his plight and, instead of judging him for it, will love him as he works through it. This is an assisting force that makes befriending the shadow easier.

The *negative personal shadow* is the dark side of ego with all its defects. These defects can easily become conscious and can turn into creative impulses if we search for them, make an inventory of them, and commit ourselves to the practices of befriending them, our extensive focus later in this book. Jung said: "The repressed personal shadow is not evil. . . . It is merely somewhat inferior, primitive, maladapted and awkward, not wholly bad. It even contains childish qualities which would vitalize and embellish human existence—but convention forbids." The personal shadow is not *intrinsically* evil (since it is a lawful part of our variegated nature), but it can become evil *operationally* when we repress it and then act it out. Some parts of our shadow appear clearly to us only because we act them out, for instance, through meanness to those we know we love or with tyranny and control when we are in a position of authority. This may take subtle forms such as taking initiative in a group with such force and alacrity that we do not give others the time to process the issue at hand. This is how ranking can take precedence over linking.

The shadow shows us up, something the inflated ego refuses to tolerate. In this way, the shadow is the truest mirror of ourselves, the one that reveals to us that we are not Snow White. The work is to act like the prince, not the wicked stepmother, while admitting we have both energies within us. *Let dark reach into me but not reach out of me.*

The *negative collective shadow* is the dark side of the Self. It is the God archetype in its destructive form. Dissolution in nature is part of evolution. Shiva in the Hindu pantheon represents destruction but only as a form of release. Since destruction is part of the cycle of creation, the dark aim can be to show us where to let go, not to annihilate us. The devil is a metaphor for the pernicious, annihilating dimension of the Self that usurps its legitimate powers and instigates havoc in the world. The universal archetype of and negative energies. The "wrath of God" is the Judeo-Christian shadow of God. In Hinduism, Shiva the destroyer (of ego) balances Brahma the creator. The trinity is rounded out by Vishnu, the preserver, the reconciling third between the opposites. In the mythic Persian trinity, Ahura Mazda is the light aspect of the deity Ahriman, the dark aspect, and Mithra is the mediator between them.

It comes as no surprise that such an eminently spiritual place as India tests a bomb more deadly than that used on Hiroshima. Opposites are the flora and fauna of the psyche. As long as God is the all-perfect goodness—the summum bonum—there has to be an Evil One. This is the split god of the ego that dichotomizes opposites. Only the whole psychic life of individuated humans can see the inadequacy of that model. Its alternative joins both light and dark, the reconciliation of oppositions in one divinity. Dark, in this context, does not mean evil. Evil is the *destruction* of wholeness.[6] *God* and *the Self* are ways of referring to wholeness, and thus they do not contain evil. Good and evil are the one set of opposites that cannot be reconciled. To say that God and the Self have a dark side is to acknowledge their capacity for evolutionary destruction. This darkness is the destructive force as we see it in nature. It is part of a built-in and necessary cycle by which evolution proceeds. (What we call evil is the afflicting force that seeks to upset the cycle by controlling or halting it.)

Most ancient religions have a female divinity. In Christianity the Virgin Mary comes nearest to holding the female aspects of God. Yet her image is limited to the nurturant mother and lacks the dissolving quality of the dark side. The psyche abhors one-sidedness, so at least two results of Mary's one-dimensionality have been visible in history. First, the dark side has been projected onto women as a destructive and dangerous force to be controlled or crushed. "Witches" were generally women close to nature who were persecuted by the male establishment. Not at all curiously, precisely at the times when the devotion to Mary was on the rise or exaggerated, the persecutions of witches increased.

Second is the phenomenon of the black Madonnas. From pagan times, the Great Mother goddess was worshiped in the form of a black meteorite stone. From the beginning of the Catholic era, in every country there have been statues and pictures of Mary in which her face has turned black and remained so. In Switzerland, for instance, there is a black Madonna at Einsiedeln, which means "hermitage," an appropriate metaphor for the psyche, nature, and God all coalescing in the enclosure of a feminine divinity.

---

6. The circle of flames around Shiva, god of destruction, is the fire of cremation that burns away mortality and preserves immortality. At the same time, it is energy in its purest form and om, the basic sound of creation. Teilhard de Chardin says: "Little by little we shall see the universal horror unbend, then smile upon us, and take us into its more than human arms."

The androgyny of God is a universal intuition for mystics. The wholesome vision is not of antagonizing personifications but of connected resources, as the roots of a tree in the darkest depths of earth are the same tree as the topmost leaves in the brightest heaven. *Can I make that connection?* Opposites that are left unreconciled amass great and terrifying power. Gods and demons are larger than life. This is a way of saying they represent the positive and negative aspects of the world, rather than the individual shadow. The dark side of the collective Self/God is larger than any single human life and cannot be integrated by any individual. Individuals collude with it in history by joining its juggernaut of aggression actively or by standing by silently in the face of its advance. Nuclear war, genocide, the holocaust, and such things articulate the collective negative shadow and show us what is in it. When our personal shadow enters the service of the collective shadow, holocausts happen. We deny this potential for savagery in ourselves. We imagine that only monsters could be responsible for genocide. This is because there is something terrifying hiding in us that we choose to externalize. Gandhi said: "The only devils are the ones in our own hearts. That is where the battle should be fought."

In Book Six of the *Odyssey* "Athena instills courage in the soul of Nausicaa." In the New Testament "Satan put it in the heart of Judas to betray. . . ." In former times virtues and vices were thought to be the direct result of supernatural forces. Now we understand that the personal shadow in all its dimensions is part of the original equipment of every human psyche.

We may actually be like cats whose true nature appears only after dark. Neruda calls them "the secret police of the tenement." The wolf man and Dracula are personifications of this predatory quality in us. Actually, genocide and evil are calibrated into the collective negative shadow of human nature. They lie impotent there until they are activated by the personal shadow of individuals who choose to act out their dread demands. The work begins with acknowledging that we are capable of everything that humans do, be they like the deeds of Hitler or those of Saint Francis.

Scapegoating is imposing the collective shadow on individuals. It is done by a group or by a leader who then commandeers others to join in. Lynching of blacks, bashing of gays, drafting of youth, are all examples. William Tecumseh Sherman said it quite clearly: "We must act with vindictive earnestness against the Sioux, even to their extinction: men, women, and children."

In biblical times, lepers were shadow figures and were scapegoated for the sins of the community. The Self contains healing power, so it makes sense that Jesus, as an archetype of the Self, cured lepers. This form of healing is a metaphor for the fact that the collective shadow can be befriended and integrated only by the grace of the Self, not by human, that is, ego, effort. When lepers were cleansed, they gave thanks in the temple, a metaphor for sacred space, that which is "greater than" ego limits. This is another way of acknowledging the necessity of the Self dimension in the integration of the world's shadow. To "carry the weight of the world on our shoulders" is to scapegoat, victimize, ourselves. It is also to equate the power of our ego with that of the Self. Our sense of guilt for not doing enough to solve the world's needs may arise from that same misunderstanding.

In 1996 I visited the Wailing Wall in Jerusalem. Along with many other mourners, I leaned against it and silently confided the griefs of my life and those of all my family and friends. I did not feel any strong reaction. As I was about to leave, I noticed a curious doorway to my left. I gingerly entered a strange, large, cavernous chamber. It was narrow but quite long. There were many men there dressed in black coats and hats, some holding books. There were books along the walls too. I remember a glass plate in the floor and something that was perhaps meant to be venerated beneath. The whole atmosphere was dreamlike in the sense that I could not name the place (synagogue? library?) or understand what it was really about or what the people there were doing. I did realize very clearly, however, that the men with the bobbing heads and the gutturally repeated prayers were acting out some kind of religious ritual.

Suddenly, out of nowhere, a thought rode into my mind: "This is how harmless Judaism is and yet Hitler wanted to destroy it." What happened next I will never fully comprehend. I broke into a paroxysm of grief such as I had never felt in all my life. I sat in the nearest chair and cried, sobbed, and even convulsed with total and relentless abandon. I knew I was powerless to stop this and that I had to let it happen. The strange thing was that I did not feel painfully sad, only *full*, and I was somehow fully liberating grief. In this sacred space, I seemed to be releasing a shadow greater than my own, but perhaps one I had tried too long to carry.

I wept so many tears that I could see them falling to the ground below me. Men walked by me and looked at me but no one disturbed me or tried to restrain me. They took my reaction in stride as if they had seen this many times before. Beside me was sitting an old man who was offering—or selling?—a green herb, perhaps basil, to those walking by. He felt like a protective presence for me somehow. After a long time, I rose and left, reverently, slowly, and very humbly. I felt washed or renewed in some way. I have never tried to understand this experience lest I sully the purity of it. I want it to remain a mystery until and unless it reveals itself to me spontaneously in its own time.

I am not a Jew, though my grandfather was an orphan

and family lore has sometimes mildly conjectured that he may have been part Jewish. This never made a deep impression on me. I have, nonetheless, always been uncommonly and mysteriously sensitive to the Holocaust issue and have reacted strongly to the details of it, which I seek out and yet recoil from. One night, for instance, I was watching *Judgment at Nuremburg* on TV. In one sequence, Jewish children are lined up in a concentration camp, showing the serial numbers on their arms, apparently following the orders of a commandant we do not see. The coat of one girl was the same as that of Kathy, a best girl friend from my childhood in the forties. I suddenly flew into a frenzy of weeping. The sadness ran with such force through my body that I fell off the sofa onto the floor. It was painful that time.

My shadow has spoken in these and many other ways in my life not only about the Holocaust but also about Vietnam, a source of pain and protest in my youth. (Such personal "sources" are probably strongly implicated in how we work out our destiny to return to the Source.) At the Vietnam Veterans Memorial in Washington, the long wall of names, I felt the same mournful stirrings. It does not stop; it happens over and over with respect to both those cataclysms of the collective shadow. I am actually glad to have heard so touchingly from the world's uneasy and unfinished gloom in my own life, and I hope this book makes a contribution to its peace.

(A week after writing the above account, I woke up one morning thinking of the phrase "out of nowhere," and I remembered the poem of Changling: "The horseman of enlightenment comes out of nowhere into the nowhere of emptiness but moving in the direction of the dawn.")

How Karma Works

With us, violence is an ancient evil that seals many destinies. This land, famed for its history, its beauty, its

art, suffers from an invincible cruelty that hides behind
the oleanders, the sycamores, and within the ancient
ruins. It vibrates in the air scented with lemon blossom,
and, in the night, strikes the sleeping Nicholas.

—ENZO BIAGI

The lines above were written by a Sicilian author and
journalist to a father whose little son, while asleep in the
backseat of his car, was shot by bandits. People in the news,
or beside us, show us the karma of humankind and our part
in it. Karma refers to the fact that our actions, both positive
and negative, have consequences in our lives and in the lives
of others. Like the meanest person we know, we too can be
cruel. Everyone has that deadly capacity. It is the shadow side
of our immense kindness. We are sometimes malicious in our
behavior toward others, often because of envy, vindictiveness, or ambition. We are sometimes so self-centered as to
demand or connive for what we want at others' expense. The
choice to satisfy our own greed or narcissism *at others' ex-*
pense is the essence of immorality. But karma is not simply
what we did wrong and now have to pay for. Any punishment for evil is inherent in the evil itself.[7] This is because evil
splits us off from others. Since we humans want contact more
than anything else, even more than happiness, alienation is
the fiercest penalty for our misdeeds. This may explain why a
person would risk his or her own life for another. Something
ancient, an immemorial kinship with other humans, has sur-
vived even the densest narcissism. That is the courage and
healing that is always and already alive in us. This is what

7. The Dalai Lama adds: "The actual protector and destroyer is not Buddha but your own karma. What really helps you is your own virtuous
action. What really harms you is your own non-virtuous action" (*The*
Good Heart: A Buddhist Perspective on the Teachings of Jesus. Boston:
Wisdom Publications, 1996).

makes us jump in to save someone when our own life is thereby endangered. "Our true reality is in our identity and unity with all life," wrote Joseph Campbell.

In the spiritual way of configuring life, painful events that try us are forms of initiation. We thereby become people of character and strength who can also have compassion on those who suffer as we do or have. Suffering is thus a program for spiritual maturation. In this sense, the real sin is to flee the condition of existence that includes pain as part of growth. An inner archetypal truth about the necessary affliction of the hero tells us this. Such initiatory anguish is not punishment but the pulley to destiny. (This may be why initiatory rites are for the young. It is then clear that the pain has nothing to do with penalty, as they are still so clearly innocent.)

Karma is not only about reaping what we sow; it is also about reaping what we did not sow. We sometimes have to pay for what we did not do. That is the archetype of an original sin: we seem to owe far more than we ever borrowed in the course of life. At the same time, we often draw on the treasury of graces from others' work that expands our own effort. We are illumined, without meriting it, by the work of those who bring more light into the world.

Karma also promises synchronicity: we will meet up with exactly the people and situations that show us how to open to our full potential both for light and for dark. Karma helps us see how we share in the malefactions of all our human brothers and sisters. This knowledge alone reduces our ego pretense about being "above all that." Our best friend is the one who impolitely looks in our cupboards and drawers, under and behind our private things, and places them before us saying: "What's this?" We may be hiding the fact that we are no different in our secrets than others are in their disclosures.

Karma in Sanskrit simply means deed or action. It has been expanded over the years to signify a spiritual law of cause and effect by which good and evil deeds ricochet back on us in this life or in a later life. It is then a psychic inheritance of good and bad accruing from previous deeds, our own or others'. Actually, karma was never meant to confirm the retaliatory ego's system of reward and punishment. The conditions of existence forbid such a reliable level of predictability. Guaranteed reward and punishment is an extension of our vengeful ego's wishful thinking. Karma is simply a way of referring to the *fact* of cause and effect. Karma is not judgmental, only observational.

In the Hindu tradition, karma is related to the belief in rebirth. Karma and rebirth are two sides of one coin in that every action has a moral dimension and a result. The action takes any of three forms: that which is being done, that which is the fruit of what was done, that which is being stored up. Karma is the universal law over gods and people. People can make up for negative karma by making a pilgrimage to and purifying themselves in sacred waters (for instance, the Ganges), by making a pilgrimage to a holy city and dying there, and by acts of charity and gifts to the gods.

Popular Buddhism in the Mahayana school accommodated karma and rebirth. Buddhism emphasizes the present only. Buddha said karma was a way of referring to the condition of being unliberated, still caught in the chain of birth and death because still caught up in fear and attachment. Buddha proposed psychological rebirth. Here is a metaphorical example of this concept: When I am gluttonous, I am in that instant (since only the present is real) being reborn as a pig. Since all life forces are in us, any psychological metamorphosis is possible. The spiritual metamorphosis happens when I let go of ego.

Karma can be a poignant way of looking at our assisting

forces in life. The goodness of all human beings in all times and places helps each of us. Their kindnesses fill the repository of graces that make scarcity unthinkable. My progress does not entirely depend on my works. I am supported by many sources, known and unknown. They are drawn to me by my visible enthusiasm and resolve to become more loving and more wise.

Like assisting forces, afflicting forces are also forms of karma that figure in our human story. There are always powers at work that want to interrupt our journey or win us away from our path, like Lampwick or Honest John in Pinocchio's story. Such tempters or injurers can ultimately become shadow graces, dark afflicting forces that can turn out later to be brightly assisting ones: I am fired from my job and thereupon go into business for myself, finding happiness in my work and a wonderful new lease on life. An unhappy relationship that afflicted me for so long now remains in my memory accompanied by gratitude for all the lessons I learned. But we cannot rely on such happy reversals. Our commitment to turning a sow's ear into a silk purse or crystallizing carbon into a diamond may fall flat. We can still wind up with a thin soup or a lump of coal. Karma is a guarantee that there are no guarantees.

Pope Leo XIII declared Saint Thérèse the patroness of missionaries even though she never traveled anywhere out of Europe. She had promised: "I will spend my heaven doing good on earth." His choice of her was based on the belief that love, no matter how hidden or seemingly insignificant, reaches everyone, everywhere, in life-changing ways. No one knows the extent to which the silent act of love and caring of others is helping him or her right now. Is this the real mystery of the human heart, humanity's heart?

The mutuality in our evolution is an archetypal perspective and an ancient one. The death ritual of the Mayans was believed to provide a pathway for the souls of the dead to move on to rebirth. In exchange, the souls were expected to guarantee fertility, by being buried. The goal after death was not to float up and away selfishly but to stay and help the community. The Christian belief in the efficacy of the prayers of saints in heaven for those on earth includes the same consoling and isolation-defying promise.

THE PRACTICE

How do we detect the presence of our shadow? It may appear in

- Crisis and transition
- Dreams
- Surprising or sudden impulsive behavior
- Quantum leaps in intuition, virtue, or talent
- Envy of someone who has a quality we lack
- Our reaction to people who bring out our worst or best
- Synchronicity
- Paranoia and bigotry
- Miraculous and healing powers
- Seeing or hearing of evil deeds
- Friends' ways of acting or of reacting to us
- Doing to others what we hate their doing to us (the Golden Rule is a shadow practice)
- Inner parallel voices that tempt us to act meanly
- What slips out in humor

Which of the above are familiar to you? Presuming that all of them are at work in your life, which ones seem most in need of attention?

Regarding humor: the shadow is the feared side of us and humor releases the fear. What strikes us as funny is often a clue to our shadow side. For example, American Indians were unusually chaste, inhibited, and strict about sex, but they loved ribald stories about the coyote, their image of the archetypal trickster, with an oversize penis and freedom from moral restraint. Humor compensates for the hidden shadow.

Kindly, healthy humor pokes fun at oneself or the foibles of others in good fun, with no intent to put down or hurt anyone. The shadow side of humor, however, is sarcasm, ridicule, pranks, practical jokes, and bias. What do you find funny? Consider the jokes you tell and the ones you laugh the most at. Do they scapegoat a group? What biases do you have? How do you show them? Can you make an agreement with yourself never to tell another racist or minority-debasing joke? Can you refuse to listen to any? These are simple but challenging ways to grapple with the personal shadow as it connects to the collective shadow.

• Consider this quotation from Saint John of the Cross and how it fits with your own religious views. "The nearer the soul comes to God, the darker and deeper the obscurity. . . . So immense is the spiritual light of God and so greatly does it transcend our understanding, that the more we approach it, the more it blinds and darkens us."

• Perform a ritual in your own religious or spiritual tradition to honor those who died in the holocaust of the Native Americans by the settlers, of the Jews and others in the Second World War, of the Tibetans by the Chinese,[8] and of any

8. A positive consequence of the Chinese invasion of Tibet is the dissemination of the Tibetans' gentle Buddhism to the rest of the world. Tibetan monks were living in isolation at a time when humankind was desperately in need of their message. The attack and genocide were unjust and savage,

other genocides or violations of humanity that you are aware of. Confront yourself about avoiding news of present-day genocides. Reverse that by exploring what is happening and responding to it in a public-spirited way, for instance, by writing to a congressman. This is a practical example of how individuation becomes engagement, how the psychological work becomes a spiritual gift to the world. Hence, Jung says: "Individuation does not shut out the world but gathers it to oneself. . . . You cannot individuate on Everest."

NEWS AND ENTERTAINMENT

The shadow is our unlived life. We keep some of our human possibilities concealed from ourselves. This is a good thing with respect to a criminal negative shadow. It is a bad thing when we do not live up to our full potential for goodness. Both film and news media serve a compensatory function for the shadow sides of us. We see characters acting out potentials for good or evil that we would never act out. We are negatively possessed when we are glued to our TV sets watching the O. J. Simpson trial. We positively identify with it when we are among the sixty-five thousand people who went to Iowa to see the "field of dreams" within a year after the movie of that name was released.

We were fascinated while the hero, O. J. Simpson, was fleeing the police or while Andrew Cunanan was on the loose or during the trial of Timothy McVeigh. Each of them was

---

but the best has come from the worst. This is an example of an entire nation befriending the shadow of the world. It is not that pain *had* to abound that way but that grace did the more abound. Padmasambhava prophesied in the eighth century: "When the iron bird flies and horses run on wheels, the Tibetan people will be scattered like ants across the world, and the Dharma will come to the land of the red-faced people."

accused of a sordid and ghastly crime. O. J. went free. Cunanan killed himself. McVeigh was condemned to be executed. Their respective fates were also fascinating, because they are precisely the three most frequent consequences of evil in the ego's world. The news presents shadow figures and shadow reactions that compensate for and resolve the personal shadow fears and desires of all of us.

The news also portrays the collective shadow: the Swiss collaboration with the Nazis and their robbery of Jewish gold, the germ warfare of the Iraqis, the sinister plans and deals of the tobacco companies with Congress, the FBI and Waco, the genocide in Rwanda, China's arrogant cruelty and unchecked disregard for human rights. Is the list endless because it takes that much to feed our need for a compensatory experience of the shadow we keep denying in ourselves?

Strange animal sacrifices and grave robberies have recently been committed in the Bible Belt South by children who style themselves devil worshipers. Nowadays there are alarming numbers of murders of young people by young people that are often linked to satanic cults. Cults may appeal most to woebegone or highly intelligent outcasts who want to follow a leader. The added element of the "satanic" in a population that is steeped in Christian fundamentalism is evidence of the shadow, which constellates the extreme opposite of that which has become dualistic, severe, or obsessive. When there is an adherence to inflexible rules and an insistence on only *one* way, there is more likelihood of an embrace of evil as if it were the *right* way. Animals and children are the victims because they are representatives of the positive shadow in this attack by the dark side. Such possession by the negative shadow gives people a false sense of mission. They believe they are obliged to carry out its retaliatory and ritualistic demand against those whom they consider ignorant or uninitiated. They are acting out the model of punishment they learned in Christian fundamentalism. Both sides represent the shadow side of ego under the guise of righteousness. The grotesque crimes of satan worshipers are the visible manifestation of the biased belief system they were molded by. The shadow denied makes the shadow inflated.

From time immemorial the story of our shadow has been told in imaginary ways too. The faces aglow around ancient campfires are the same faces around the TV or in dark theaters today. We want to hear and have our own stories told in safe ways. Since *Ben Hur* we have looked with horror or rapt attention at parts of ourselves projected on the screen. We come to see ourselves reflected by heroes and villains on film in order to live vicariously the possibilities in us that will never come to light consciously or actively.

Joseph Campbell says: "Myths touch and exhilarate centers of life beyond the reach of reason." The most widely loved films integrate our deepest needs, values, and wishes with the ego-transcending mythic themes of human destiny. From *The Wizard of Oz* to *Star Wars*, great films develop the motifs of the hero's journey: an ordinary person risks leaving his or her home; confronts, and survives confrontations with, the dark side; and receives a gift of power by befriending or conquering the shadow. It is always a hazardous venture.

Most of us never commit murder or serious crimes, yet almost every dramatic film includes them as the central focus of the story. The *Godfather* series was an example. Half of the novels by Jane Austen have been made into films. They seem, at first glance, to be about the jejune concerns of genteel and inhibited young ladies of the eighteenth century. Yet each of them is about the deeper shadow side of those characters and their society. This combination/composition of opposites appeals to our psyche in compelling ways and may account for their success. It happens when a film articulates the meanings in our interior world.

Films like *Forrest Gump* and *Field of Dreams* captured the imagination of movie audiences because they showed the positive untapped shadow potential of ordinary human beings like ourselves. Some films combine positive and negative shadow experiences, for example, *Witness, First Night, Lone Star, The Crying Game,* and *Edward Scissorhands.* Some combine the personal and the collective shadow: *Gone with the Wind, Ryan's Daughter, Sophie's Choice, The Last Emperor, The Mission, Contact.* It seems that the most memorable films are about the shadow and how to handle it. Films like *Ordinary People* and *Ice Storm* show the danger in the repressed shadow side of the clean-looking middle-class family. They, like the Greek plays of the past, serve a crucial function for us: to act out and show how. They are the fascinating moments in time that so authentically and uncannily flash the timeless themes of our lives before our wondering eyes. We cannot look away from something so near.

I bring forth the universe from my essence and I abide in the cycle of time that dissolves it.

—MYTH OF MARKANDEYA

5

Our Shadow Denied

Consider them both, the sea and the land; and do you not find a strange analogy to something in yourself? For as this appalling ocean surrounds the verdant land, so in the soul of man there lies one insular Tahiti, full of peace and joy, but encompassed by all the horrors of the half known life.

—HERMAN MELVILLE, *Moby Dick*

WHEN WE DENY our shadow, we are like a father sleeping downstairs in a house while his son is having a seizure upstairs. Father and son in this analogy are two parts of one person. Denial is symbolized by the fact that the father is in the dark, at a lower level of the psyche, that is, the unconscious, sleeping through a crisis happening to another part of himself. He is thereby unable to hear the cries of his son and does not rescue him. His destiny as a father is thus unfulfilled. Denial of our shadow happens at just such great peril to our unfolding. It is a life-and-death issue when life means nurturing all the parts of ourselves and living out our full potential. We lose sight of the needy side of ourselves *and* of our resourceful side too. Denial of the shadow is thus a denial of our destiny of completeness. Are we *fearing* our own full fruition and full fruitfulness?

The child having the seizure will be angry at his father for not hearing him. It is the denied shadow that becomes unruly and aggressive. The shadow that is attended to and befriended does not react that way. Another metaphor might be of the wild child or the child kept prisoner, who will be fierce and intimidating when she emerges from her constricting cell. When a child is found in the closet where her parents kept her prisoner, those who free her feel compassion and wish to hold her and help her grow. This applies to the closeted, repressed parts of ourselves; shadow befriending is loving and holding the lost that has been found. It is thus a compassionate and spiritually evolved work.

Our unconscious is always at work in our decisions, and we deny that it is a residence of personal choice. Trying to muffle the voice inside that wants a hearing is a form of fear of the truth about our full selves. Only *with* this truth can we turn our shadow into an ally. This is why the unconscious dimension of the shadow is the first to be addressed as we move toward befriending it. We begin by admitting we have a dark side. Even in Alcoholics Anonymous, that is the "first step" toward recovery.

Alexis is considered a "nice" person. She is always doing something for someone else, always putting herself second. She sees herself and everyone in her world sees her as an ideal friend. But Alexis cannot stand women who are assertive or strong-willed. There is no in-between for Alexis; she finds them all repulsively controlling and manipulative, though she does not admit this to herself or to others. As a supervisor, she will pass over such women for advancement, preferring the more mild-mannered workers on her team who remind her of herself. Alexis is thus unfair and allows her judgment to be influenced by her undercover anger at strong women. She does not see this vindictiveness in herself nor would she believe it if it were pointed out to her. Alexis rationalizes that courtesy and femininity are lost values in today's world and that she is trying to change that. She has no room in her vocabulary for healthy female self-declaration. Alexis calls that aggressiveness, and yet she herself acts aggressively toward the strong women around her.

The "nice person" of Alexis's persona seems to be all of her. Yet she has another side: she is also an angry and spiteful woman who is afraid of female power when it is expressed directly through a healthy ego. Alexis has inner strength, but she has not yet accessed it. That is her positive shadow lying fallow in the negative ground she does not know is hers. It can only be released when she stops denying her anger and indignation. Alexis will have to call her sense of justice by its rightful name, retaliation. As she breaks through her own lies and admits her own unsavory truth, she will automatically access her healthy anger with a sense of fairness. Then her unilateral decisions can yield to a dialogue between her and other women, and something valuable to all will result. It is gratifying to see how individual work on the shadow benefits others.

In *Jane Eyre*, Charlotte Brontë portrays the shadow of the Victorian women of her time. Hidden away in the attic is the wild, uncontrollable, impulsive first wife of Mr. Rochester. She screams her presence in the night, and the gentle, rational, conscientious Jane can hear. She inquires about this presence in the house, that is, in the psyche, but the shadow woman's reality is denied to her until she attempts marriage to Mr. Rochester. Then she meets her counterpart in his life, the shadow of herself.

What we cut off saps our energy. As we have seen, the shadow becomes a problem only when we deny it. Then it leads to projection or possession, two versions of the same phenomenon of self-disavowal. If the shadow possesses us, we are overwhelmed by its malice and we act out the worst traits of our ego. A vampire is a metaphor for this draining descent into the darkness.

In projection we see our own traits in others but not in ourselves. The alternative is to relate to the shadow, acknowledging its presence in ourselves as well as in others when appropriate. An adult accepts the fact of having a shadow side as a condition of being human. It will always be in us in some way. Likewise, in our collective history we are not trying to destroy the darkness so that only light remains but rather we are trying to accept them both. Each requires the other for existence, as thesis and antithesis are required for synthesis.

The ego usually has to deny its shadow at first in order to establish its own sense of worth. This is perfectly normal and even useful in the first half of life. A strongly developed ego helps us see why befriending the shadow is usually a task of the second half of life, when our ego is already established and is ready to be taken out and polished. Then we see how our shadow contains riches of creativity and a whole new world of possibilities for us. Only then are we likely to let go of our belief that we have no shadow. Instead we begin to look for it in every corner of our personality and *want* to know its shape so that we can make the best of it.

To continue denying the shadow is like sanding off the tail side of a coin; it loses its value. On the other hand, the shadow is valuable in the same way that coal potentially is: the pressure on it creates a diamond. Perhaps the weight of the repression fosters the hidden value of the shadow. This is the positive side of repression and denial, another example of the best being found in the worst. There is always a way to go from bad to best in our dealings with the shadow. Befriending the shadow is how it happens. The more unconscious the shadow is, the darker its effects. The more conscious we become of it, the greater the chance of finding and refining its dark gold.

Denial of the shadow is repudiation of our own reality: Denial of our positive shadow is the meaning of low self-esteem. Denial of our negative shadow makes for an inflated ego. Here are some ways we deny our shadow and some of the effects and dangers that arise from that denial:

• Not accepting criticism or admitting accountability when appropriate.

• Denying our darker side when others point it out. This is especially dangerous when the survival of an intimate relationship depends on our admitting it. Now we can understand why the conflict stage hits a romantic relationship in such frustrating ways: Here is a young man who needs to build his ego and thereby denies his shadow. Yet the resolution of a conflict with his girlfriend demands that he face it.

• Identifying too much with our self-image, our persona, so that we take ourselves too seriously. We can tell the shadow is being hidden when we see no humor in our circumstances.

• Repressing our darker side for fear of losing approval. This includes people-pleasing, which masks our shadow and thereby makes its effects more insidious.

• Professing beliefs and virtues that we lack: hypocrisy. The word *hypocrisy* is Greek for playing a part. It is the pretense that our persona is our real self. Just as a mask protects a face, hypocrisy protects our true shadow face from exposure. We pretend to be more than we are or better than we are or even something we are not. Cover-ups in politics are collective examples; shadow deeds are secreted away from public view lest the image they belie show itself as flawed. Such protected images of persons or organizations often take precedence even over human life. *A Few Good Men* portrayed this disturbingly. What is disturbed is our narrow, uninformed trust that established systems and their representatives have no shadow.

• Fearing our own shadow (like denial of the shadow in general) leads to vulnerability to predators. We are at the mercy of others' shadows when we deny our own; for example, the guilelessness of Persephone lost in a world of sweetness and light resulted in Hades' abducting her into the dark underworld. In the same way, ingenuous young people fall prey to cult leaders.

• Denying the shadow in others: "It is hard to believe that those who were protecting me were also those who were harming me." We disallow the shadow of abusers and predators, especially family members: "They were doing the best they could." "He did not mean to do that to me; he was an alcoholic." We may go to any lengths to absolve them: dissociation from or amnesia about what happened, idealization of those who hurt or violated us, fragmented identity: that happened, but to someone else. The latter might even lead to the formation of multiple personalities.

The dissociative mechanism of the self-protective psyche after trauma may be so firmly locked into place that we hardly experience *anything* with its full impact. Yet many of these strategies of denial are adaptive: they help us accommodate information and memories that might be too much for us to bear all at one time or at this time or at any time. Respect for our limits is not resistance to the truth but self-protection from further intrusion. The work in therapy is to honor the closed door and to open a little window to change when the time is right.

• Believing movies that depict the triumph of good over evil as if that were inevitable, perceiving retaliation as the most successful or only response to evil, trusting in the infallibility of the courtroom, or having any Pollyanna view of life, family, or love.

• Monster making: To the extent that we consider others inhuman in their shadow actions, we are denying that potential in ourselves. When we fail to acknowledge our negative shadow side but see ourselves as "holier than thou," we may project the "evil" onto others, for example, in witch hunts. Fundamentalists who hate and condemn others as heathens give themselves the right to harm or even kill those who are "less than human." Society projects its shadow onto minority groups in this same way. Scapegoating is a shadowy attempt to destroy an enemy. Such an enemy is a split-off part of ourselves. What we dissociate from seems alien and dangerous. Hence we strongly persecute, disdain, and seek to hurt or destroy what has been split off from ourselves.

• Idolizing: When we imagine others to be idols above human reach, we minimize our own positive shadow. Then we may follow cult gurus, fundamentalist teachers, or ego-drunk leaders. To idolize is to set apart and thereby to break apart the inner structure of our own psyche. We project our ball into the hands of a pitcher who seems more adept than we. There may be such pitchers, but the healthy choice is to learn from them, not to let them play our game.

Hitler was considered both a monster and an idol. He was a shadow figure for a whole generation whose most somber purposes he was willing to implement. Jung said about

Hitler in 1938: "He is the loudspeaker which magnifies the inaudible whispers of the German soul." Hitler did not simply lead people into evil; he received their mandate for it. This deputation came from the German people, the Nazi Party, Pope Pius XI, who signed the Vatican's 1933 concordat with Nazi Germany, Neville Chamberlain at Munich, the U.S. exclusionary laws under Roosevelt, and every silent man and woman everywhere. Silence, in this context, includes blindly believing leaders or policies without informing oneself more broadly about them or examining what their record shows.

• Denying our positive shadow, which can happen when people and their impressive lifestyles keep us so in awe that we do not acknowledge our own powers and enthusiasms. We may then lose touch with our deepest needs, values, and wishes. We may lose the incentive to rise to our true potential. We may even act in self-diminishing ways to garner the approval of those "greater than" we. Any life built around approval from people who do not help us self-activate and co-emerge puts us in danger of being controlled by them. A life that is centered around personal enthusiasms, projects, issues, service, and bliss sets us free to become all that we are. This fulfills our destiny to bring out the best of ourselves and give it to the world.

• Believing that the shadow will someday be gone and that perfect light will take its place. Shambhala is the Buddhist name for a kingdom of enlightenment that will appear on earth in only a few short centuries. It is said to last for at least eighteen centuries, since there is no permanent kingdom without a shadow. Tibetan Buddhists believe that the heinous and massive dimensions of the shadow in these times is an indication that Shambhala will not be long in coming. Yet the *cycles* of life and death, light and dark, are unalterable givens of existence and can therefore be trusted as necessary, useful, and nourishing.

There is no physical Shangri-la, no Atlantis, no Never-Never Land where every dream of a shadow-less world comes true. Wherever humans are there is the darkness that destroys. Wherever humans are there is the light that reconciles. Does this mean that appealing metaphors like "the wolf lying down with the lamb," are not true? Their truth is indeed real. It is called befriending the shadow. It awaits us in "a land of milk and honey," the one we allow to appear wherever we love one another.

• Believing that evil can be eliminated once and for all by vengeance or war: "the war to end all wars. " Vengeance and retaliation have within them an implicit belief that evil can be ended by more evil. Actually, villains in stories do not always die but rather go into hiding. New villains appear when the original ones are killed. Evil cannot be created or destroyed. It simply is. We cannot even presume the presence of a silver lining before doing the work that sews it in. There will always be a shadow as long as there are people.

When Dorothy returned from Oz, the neighbor "witch" was still alive in Kansas, but Dorothy no longer feared her. This is a way of saying that she did not kill the evil of the witch but only took back her own power from her.

• Believing that the brutality and atrocities of World War II were the worst or the last in the history of humankind.

• Believing that some specific person has no shadow. Jung stated: "People who are least aware of their unconscious side are most influenced by it." The trickster can be hidden especially in those who seem to have no shadow. Our projected beliefs about them have most seriously diminished and fooled us.

Believing that our partner is not capable of betrayal, our town is not a Peyton Place, our country is not as violent and corrupt as others, our religion not as hypocritical, our family not as inadequate, our bank not as greedy, etc. We automatically assume that if it is ours, it is somehow not shadowed!

• Equating being good and being favored, based on early messages from childhood. In a healthy upbringing, "Be a good boy" is replaced with "Be good as much as you can and make amends when you fail or harm anyone. That will make it easier for people to love both sides of you." This resolves the dilemma presented by a battle between the shadow and the persona: "I'm bad" versus "I have to look good." We can hurt someone and still love the person, but we cannot say we still love someone if we cannot make amends to that person.

• Attempting to root out a symptom denies the shadow instead of rerouting it. For example, my uncomfortable sense of obligation about calling my mother leads to my not calling her anymore. Instead I might think: "Perhaps I'm not taking responsibility for *choosing* to call. I project rather than own my desire or choice. My sense of obligation may be a projected desire that is in shadow, that is not accepted by me or known to me."

• Believing that all violence and crime is the result of early childhood abuse, which denies the fact that the shadow has a life of its own in every human heart. Early abuse certainly accounts for a great deal of adult dysfunction, but it cannot be the full and final explanation. It describes the *context* in which violence is instilled but it is not a cause of it. Human beings do dreadful things because they are human and have a shadow side. Some human beings have been so damaged by the violation of their bodies and souls that they become time bombs in later life. Some have been hurt in even worse ways and become saints. The shadow certainly thrives in an abusive atmosphere, but it is not born there. It is innate in all of us and no past can explain it away.

• Insisting that our political leaders be perfect. Ideals are in the office, not necessarily in the holder of it. Ideals of behavior are in our heads and are not meant to be in a leader's hands. We make no room for a leader's shadow and then we victimize the person for becoming vulnerable to it.

What has been called demonic possession may be another form of denial of the shadow. The medieval mind had culturally embedded in it fears of spontaneity, impulse, free thought, and ecstatic feeling. Persons who were devout externally became scurrilous, licentious, and irreverent. Polarization occurs when our positive shadow side with all its lively energy becomes verboten. What is not integrated splits off and becomes autonomous (like the cult of Dionysus in ancient times). When that which is fully human becomes taboo, the psyche rebels and sets up its own citadel of rejected feelings and heretical beliefs. These take on a life of their own and may turn against us and our serenity. Unwholesome taboos are those based on fear of the emergence of the full range of human feeling and experience. The medieval church had this fear; many fundamentalists still have it. The psyche rebels because fear-based, health-inhibiting taboos contravene bodily wisdom and alienate us from our deepest needs, values, and wishes. When there is no healthy outlet, we may become possessed and then hurt by our canceled humanity. Demonic possession is a culture-bound example of this. Multiple personality disorder (now called dissociative identity disorder) is a contemporary, culturally accepted version. No matter what the name, dissociation originates in the trauma of abuse or prohibition. The shadow lurks there and, until unmasked, continues the torture.

In the film *The Three Faces of Eve*, both Eve White and Eve Black seem incomplete and inadequate, and then a third Eve appears. She has self-assurance and sanity and is a beautiful alternative to the other two personalities. She is the healing third who transcends the opposites now that she has contained them. What a powerful and precise portrait of the results of the practice of befriending the shadow. It does not take exorcism; it takes holding, honoring, and allowing something more to emerge. That more is always and already within.

> *Suppression of the shadow is like remedying a headache by a beheading. . . . In the last resort, there is no good that cannot produce evil or evil that cannot produce good.*
>
> —C. G. JUNG

THE PRACTICE

· Find each of the forms of shadow denial in the above list that characterizes you and make a plan to reverse it. Tell the people you live with of your plan and ask them to flag you if they see you slipping back.

· Take the items on the list that you believe do not apply to you and check them against the impressions of you held by your partner or closest friend. Do you find yourself defending your position or can you hear some element of truth in your partner or friend's feedback?

• There are three main ways by which we invite the shadow into our lives: we deny the existence of a shadow by being overly trusting of others; we have poor personal boundaries and thus become easy prey to predators; we act from a fear-based motivation.

Which of these apply to you? If there is even one person in your life that you imagine to have no shadow, look again. If you constantly let people take advantage of you, look for how you are letting them inflict their shadow side on you. If you act from fear in most of your decisions, look for how you elicit the predatory shadow reactions of others.

How We Project Our Denial

Projection makes the whole world a replica of our own unknown face.

—C. G. Jung

It is not that man in Rome that is the source of my problems; it is the Pope in myself that needs to be excommunicated!

—Martin Luther,
TOWARD THE END OF HIS LIFE

We are reading and we begin to feel hunger pangs. The message is: it is time to attend to the need for food. If our life is threatened on the way to the restaurant, we will attend to that and the hunger will disappear into the background until the danger is past. An organismic urge toward homeostasis in our bodies brings into the foreground precisely what is important for survival. It makes it figural so we can address, process, and resolve it. With respect to our shadow, our psyche does this by projection: we see our hidden self dramatically before us in others who resemble or act out our shadow side. Thus we project our unconscious shadow for a positive reason: to see it and act in such a way as to integrate it. Like the bashful moon, we have a dark side, but it is only waiting its turn for the light.

Projection is our most pervasive and least acknowledged way of denying our own shadow. In projection, we delegate powers in ourselves to others. We simply see our own shadow attributes in someone else and imagine they are not also in us. It is to burn a witch when we ourselves are involved in magic. Our perceptual apparatus automatically organizes random stimuli into intelligible configurations, whether or not they match reality. Ink blots become butterflies; noises at night become the wind; a wink becomes an offer of marriage. The other person may or may not have the quality we project; usually the person does have it in some way.

Projection is looking in a mirror at ourselves and imagining we are looking at a picture of someone else. Unfortunately, we thereby put pieces of ourselves into others' keeping. We react strongly to seeing our own traits in someone else: with severe dislike to the negative characteristics in others and with exaggerated awe at the positive attributes of others. This is probably a wake-up call from our psyche because the time has come to befriend our shadow and to recover our projections of it. It is coming back home to the embrace of the authentic Self. This is the home that Dorothy said there was no place like.

Projection of our own negative shadow can cast us as persecutors or victims. Projection of our positive shadow can cast us as martyrs. Examples of negative shadow projections in society are biases toward minority groups: African Americans, gay people, drug users, and so on. This is projective identification in which we cast off what is unacceptable in ourselves, attempting to make others carry our worst self-doubts and self-recriminations.

In nature it is the wolf, falsely accused as the silent predator in the dark forest who kills for sport, who carries our projections, "the big bad wolf." Yet there is really no evil in nature. No matter how much scientific information tells us that the wolf is a necessary part of ecology, there is still a worldwide hatred and fear of this animal. We keep trying to kill off something we fear. We are attempting to eliminate evil. We are scapegoating an animal with a violent vengefulness. Are not these phrases familiar from the list of ways we deny the shadow?

When we project our positive shadow, we lose touch with our personal potential, the very stuff of our destiny. Projection is not only personal. Like the shadow in general, it has a collective side. We project our archetypal shadow onto others, inflating some people as gods and deflating others as demons. To whatever extent we are stuck in such projections, we remain unconscious of our shadow work and fail to notice the divinity or demonism in ourselves. This is how archetypal projection diminishes us spiritually. We lose sight of our own angelic and demonic potentials when we only recognize those qualities in someone else.

Projection works in our favor to grant access to secret rooms in the psyche that are ready to be opened and owned. It is an invitation from the inner Self to re-member ourselves, to recover our parts and reinstall them in our psyche. Projection helps us retrieve parts of ourselves from others. It is hard to withdraw our projections and face life as ourselves. We want to maintain the persona that has worked so well to make us liked. So we defend ourselves against insight and then against taking action.

Projection of our shadow hurts others and diminishes us. Projection in itself, however, is a normal means of knowing reality. So much of our view of the world has subjective dimensions. A subjective assessment of external reality is a psychic function and so is necessarily tied to our inner life. There is actually no reality without projection and no projection without reality. Projection in itself is therefore not a bad thing, only a human thing. The work is to remain conscious of it, to take it into account as we examine our relationships and our choices.

Our unconscious is first visible in projection. Only the unconscious part of us can be projected. What we are conscious of does not become projected onto others. A man with full and comfortable awareness of his masculinity does not project it. He may admire other men but not so strongly as to diminish himself or aggrandize others.

How can we tell healthy admiration from positive shadow projection? Appropriate admiration leads to imitation and appreciation with no loss of our sense of ourselves. We are genuinely impressed with someone's accomplishments or virtues. We are not driven slavishly to follow such a person or to give up our own freedom. We are happy there is such a person in our world and we learn from him or her. This is not an example of projection of our positive shadow but healthy responsiveness to the truth of someone's superiority.

Are anger, outrage, or indignation at an injustice all simply negative shadow projections? Is legitimate admiration a sign of projection? How can we tell shadow projection from simple responsiveness? They often occur together. Here are ways to discriminate: In projection, we become identified with something in a disproportionate way. In simple responsiveness, we relate appropriately. If something is not projection, we take it as *information*, have a feeling about it, and take responsibility for it. It is the nature of information to instruct and enlighten. It is the nature of impact to arouse:

You are aggressive toward me and I react. When that reaction is fierce, exaggerated, or intense I may be projecting my own shadow onto you. Befriending the shadow is basically a way of working with impact so that it can become information. Outrage at injustice may also be based on a sense of an affront to our entitled ego: "How dare they do this to *me!*" The shadow side of ego reacts with the wish to retaliate. This reaction does not scare the readers of this book, because we know there is a program that can be put into place that will help us find a creative alternative. None of this has to be an either-or. There can be a progression from one to the other. The work is about developing a response that is healthy and loving, one that gradually overrides the ingrained retaliatory proclivity of the shadow ego. If our outrage leads to compassion and nonviolent work for change, the positive shadow of our ego is being engaged.

Ego outrage at injustice is healthy responsiveness when it flows from a recognition of our hologrammatic humanity: "Do not ask for whom the bell tolls, it tolls for thee." If all humankind is one mystical body, each person is meant to feel for all: "I respond to your pain even though I have my own personal history or baggage. I feel compassion for both the perpetrator and the victim." Truly evolved people can feel this stirring of empathy as an alternative to the wish for retaliation. It is the initial response of love followed by congruent action. The realization that you have done something generous is better than the satisfaction of revenge.

In pure projection, something affects us strongly and is usually acted out. It *keeps* bothering us. It is not limited to one person but arises in any and every instance of our noticing it. In projection we may see truly but we unconsciously add inordinate emphasis to another's goodness or badness. Thus good becomes superb and unattainable and bad becomes evil and unforgivable. We split opposites and exaggerate their divergence, believing them to be irreconcilable. This is always a clue to the shadow.

On a scale of one to ten, with ten representing purest motivation in your concern for injustice, where do you rank yourself in your most recent response to something you considered unjust? The work you are doing in this book is meant to raise the number. Even a fractional rise is already an instance of success in befriending your shadow.

In the shadow world of projection, idealized images take the place of activating our own potential, and blame takes the place of acknowledging our own deficiency. To see truly is to observe as a fair witness who has nothing to gain or lose by how people are or by what they do. To add hyperbolic emphasis is to add layers such as control, judgment, expectation, fear, desire, blame, shame. These layers come from the scared shadow side of ego. To peel them away and thereby see what is really there (and here) is to say yes to it as pure fact, like it or not. This is mindfulness, attention to the here and now as we lighten ourselves of the layers of our ego that distract us from its truth.

> *What we conceive of as reality is a few iron posts of observation with papier-mâché construction between them that is only the elaborate work of our imagination.*
>
> —J. A. WHEELER

THE HEART OF THE PRACTICE: MINDFULNESS

Mindfulness is a Buddhist meditation technique that brings our attention to our breathing in the here and now and away from our mind's inveterate habit of entertaining us with fears, desires, expectations, evaluations, and so on. The word *mindfulness* is a poetic irony, since the practice is mind emptying, not mind filling. The practice outlined below is an adaptation of the Buddhist technique.

The shadow layers of ego are control, fear, attachment, the need to fix things, obsession with an outcome, blame of others, and shame about ourselves. (These are precisely the things that vanish from one's life after a near-death experience. Perhaps enough of the ego dies in that moment so that its limbs atrophy.)

When we peel these layers of ego away and see our present life predicament purely as it is, we are seeing it mindfully. Mindfulness entails pure attention to *what is* without the following elements: what I believe it is, want it to be, have to make it, or am sorry it is not. This is what happens in mindfulness meditation: I breathe through it all without judgment, attachment, control, fear, or any other reaction, simply paying attention to each of the ego's deceptions, labeling them, and then letting go of them. Daily practice in stripping away these ego embroideries that are sewn around us is a spiritual health habit.[9]

Practice this psycho-spiritual style of mindfulness meditation now and each day: Sit in a quiet place with your eyes closed and with attention to your breathing throughout this exercise. Keep returning to your awareness of your breath whenever you become distracted.

9. True prayer is a form of mindfulness. It is an unconditional yes to the present without the desire to change or control its direction. Ego prayer is about fulfilling ego purposes, especially the alteration of realities and their outcomes to fit its own narcissistic wishes. Spiritually evolved prayer is an assent to the unfolding of destiny in whatever way it needs to happen. Prayer does not ask for immunity; it asks for the strength to accept whatever will be, to grow because of it, and to be thankful for it. Mindfulness in prayer releases the healing power in ourselves and in the archetypal Self. Studies show that the effective prayers at Lourdes seem to be the ones that are mindfully attentive and mindfully open to whatever may result, rather than those that are insistently attached to a particular outcome.

Take a distressing event that has happened recently or the main problem you are dealing with in your life right now. Picture it as an onion with many layers. Imagine yourself holding it in your lap and peeling off one layer at a time. The layers are control, fear, attachment, the need to fix things, obsession with an outcome, blame of others, and shame about ourselves. Imagine what your problem begins to look like as you progressively eliminate each layer of neurotic, inflated ego. As each is removed, what is left? Only more and more *space*. Only the pure event or problem is real, and its reality is roomy. The heavy, smelly, tear-evincing rest of it is self-made, a product of ego.

The final step in this exercise based on mindfulness meditation makes for a powerful shift to our heart center. Imagine the face of the person in your life who brings you joy and toward whom you have always felt love. (For me this is my son, Josh.) Bask in the felt sense of this person. Now, with this heartfelt joyous love, see your problem once more and ask yourself for a solution from within that context. You will see how it does not then emanate from intellect but from caring and compassion. This is such striking evidence that letting go of ego (the layers mentioned above) leads to compassion. An actual experience of loving someone is the bridge. This is how love *is* the answer.

This exercise is powerful because it simply walks us into the spaciousness of our own reality. That proves to be the unbounded Self, the Buddha nature, utter openness, our positive shadow, our path. There is something alive and immensely sane in us that shuts down when we are caught in the drama of ego with all its neurotic layers of fear and desire. This something awakens in the gaps between the layers of struggle and disguise. Enormous lively energy happens when we stop and sit in mindfulness, when we take time to be. This is how Buddha sat. Predicaments experienced in this way look so much more manageable and they reveal how much of their so-called reality is fluff.

Since nothing less is required for wholeness than the complete undoing of ego habits, every hold-on, holdup, and holdout of ego has to go. What a paradox: *finding all through emptiness.* Meister Eckhart fearlessly and optimistically says: "Man by his emptiness has won back that which he was eternally and ever shall remain." Emptiness summarizes shadow work: Regarding the negative shadow of ego, it means nothing to hold on to. Regarding the positive shadow, it means empty of limits.

Mindfulness meditation performs mysterious and immensely valuable maneuvers in the psyche:

• In mindfulness, a conscious vision replaces an unconscious blindness. It befriends the shadow, since it is willing to see all without the distracting blinders of ego.

• Mindfulness is the fast track to building the skill of intuitive knowing. Intuition is interior access to knowledge without need for logic and without obstructions from the neurotic ego.

• Problems are always simpler than our conceptions of them. We have confounded our experience with all our mental addenda. Mindfulness defragments it so that simplicity results. Eventually this mindfulness carries over into daily life and helps us with a major and ongoing problem: confusing reality with our pictures of it.

• Mindfulness makes it possible to look at our limitations and errors matter-of-factly, without shame or self-depreciation. It allows us to ask for help without having to feel ashamed or one down. It allows others to disappoint or even hurt us without our having to recruit the ego's storm troopers of revenge. We see it all clearly as what it is without the self-serving or self-promoting ego in the way. "I am what I am" is what the mindful Popeye says, with no taking advantage and no allowing of others to take advantage either.

• In mindfulness, natural feelings of attraction or repulsion can be experienced without simultaneously feeling compulsive enticement or terrified avoidance. I simply notice and take as information and I am no longer fixated in any way. Now I am less liable to feel constrained and compelled in my way of operating and I have choice. This is how mindfulness leads to freedom. Choice is only possible because nothing has to be limited to mean anything specific. All is open potential like the positive shadow.

Mindfulness is meant not to help us feel something differently but to feel it as it is without fear or attachment. We look beyond a reality that faces us by looking at it directly and fearlessly without the screens that ordinarily negate and obscure it. The sooner we notice the self-defeating inclinations of ego and halt them, the sooner does a new mental habit develop.

• A rousing gap opens when we stop acting in accord with habit. What a wonderful way to find out who we are. Empty of attachment, we *become* perfect space, the empty circle of Zen, the unfathomed no-thing-ness. This is the pause between action and reaction, where compulsion ends and freedom begins. Fear begins to diminish because most of our fear is ill-founded and misdirected reactivity.

• Mindfulness provides a shortcut to nondual awareness. This happens because mindfulness means experiencing something without an impulsive leap into or away from it. This elicits a greater recogniton of the transient nature of experi-ence. The result is fewer automatic responses and less com-pulsion to have needs fulfilled in some specific way. This makes for less of a sense of a solid "I." Thus mindfulness leads us to see precisely and finally the illusory nature of an independent, free-standing I. "I" is really a stand I am taking: control, blame, etc. In mindfulness, that I vanishes and only utter spaciousness remains.

• Pause and poise in the center of our revolving world is the best position from which to watch the parade of our personal events and experience. Serenity in the midst of the ups and downs of life is a powerful indicator that we are living in accord with our deepest needs and wishes. Ego fixations like control, expectation, blame, etc. actually inhibit the release of our potential. Mindfulness thus contributes to the be-friending of our positive shadow. All the landscape of the path is the path.

• The effect of mindfulness that is most encouraging in our work has to do with the positive shadow. How does the limit-less potential in our positive shadow become activated? What rouses something out of its unconscious slumber within us? What activates our potential? It is this same mindful atten-tion. Mindfulness is the most precise psychic mechanics for releasing our potential powers. It is the bridge between con-scious and unconscious, the centerpiece of the work of the mature soul.

• In the moment of mindfulness, we touch the very fabric of Self, since we pass beyond the distractions of ego's embroi-deries. Mindfulness is the awareness of a fearless witness whose defenses are unnecessary because the scared ego has taken its bow, in just a breath. The sense of separateness and

separate identity vanish in the farther reaches of this awareness. We are finally not aware of objects at all but reside simply in nondual awareness itself. I am this.

In Zen such mindfulness is called the gateless gate because there is no need to find a way in. We are already in,
since we are always present in the moment by mindfulness.
Of course, it takes some breaths and some letting go to notice. "I am the space in which I sit. I am the space from which
everything in my life arises and into which everything sets."
Mindfulness is a consecration of our soul to the glittering
incorruptibility of that space. The mindful psyche is an apparatus of relentless and irrepressible transformation that can
only be impaired by ego and only limited by a lazy imagination.

• Meditation combines *shamatha,* calm abiding, and *vipas-
sana*, mindful awareness. The sense of refuge that results
makes us able to face everything with equanimity. In the mirror consciousness of mindfulness, anything is allowed and
nothing is held on to. This awareness in me is the same
awareness that is in all things. My mindful awareness is the
universe conscious of itself. Distinctions and rankings self-
destruct in the dust that ego is left behind in. This is why
compassion comes as a result of awakening. *Kensho* is the
Japanese Zen term for enlightenment—seeing one's true nature—and seeing that self-realization is the same as the realization of our abiding fellowship with all humankind.
Enlightenment means making room for that light to come
through.

• Tarthang Tulku says: "When the teachings are truly understood, there is little difference between meditation and all our
other activities. The teachings and our experience become the
same." When we relax our ego grip on events and experi-

ences, the subject-object dichotomy vanishes. We then experience the state of "one-mind samadhi" (the serene concentration that characterizes the meditative state). The alternative is samsara, captivity in the world of fear and desire with its endless cycles of loss and clinging. Whether the world is samsara or nirvana in any particular moment is actually a matter of our frame of mind. Mindfulness makes any moment nirvana. The neurotic ego makes any moment samsara.

The first line of Changling's poem speaks of "an empty autumn sky." The horseman can only ride into the "endless wastes" below an empty sky, that is, no thoughts remain. The thoughts are fear, desire, blame, shame, attachment to an outcome, and all the other layers of the self-made ego. When no such thoughts remain, there is nothing left but mindfulness, the horseman of enlightenment.

> *The All is wholly within us, . . . an object infinitely great and ravishing: as full of treasures as full of room, as full of joy as of capacity. To blind men it may seem dark, but it is all glorious within, infinite in light. Everyone is alone the center and circumference of it.*
>
> —THOMAS TRAHERNE, SEVENTEENTH-CENTURY ANGLICAN MYSTIC

6

Our Shadow Displayed

EVIL AND THE ENEMY

It is useless to deny that evil exists; we must frankly face its existence and refuse participation.

—JANE E. HARRISON

Evil is that which disrupts or destroys the flow of life, freedom, or human dignity. Evil is the shadow egocentricity that takes advantage of the rights of others. We might say it is an attack on others' right to life, liberty, and the pursuit of happiness. The happiness we pursue is the expression of our deepest needs, values, passions, and wishes. To use our now-familiar terms: evil is a deliberate violation of positive shadow potential.

The proclivity toward evil is not an inherent badness in us. It is what our shadow looks like when it is kept repressed and then explodes into conscious activity. The repression is maintained by fear. We are afraid to face or show what might be ugly or cause us to lose our friends, reputation, approval, or persona. Evil is what fear looks like after we've repressed our negative shadow for a long time. A puppy kept muzzled and blindfolded in a narrow pen for a year would not become a very friendly dog.

Human beings are essentially good. Some human motives and actions are good; some are evil; some partake of both. The luminous Self coexists with the dark shadow in the same way that good and evil coexist in humanity. The Self does not contain evil but is coincident with it, as physical things do not contain a shadow but coincide with one.

We cannot eliminate evil, only acknowledge it in ourselves and in the world and then deal with it. The bad news is that there is no idealized future day when evil will be ended. The good news is that the entire *source* of love, wisdom, and healing power is available today. The fullest opportunity for enlightenment is totally present in this very moment. Freedom from evil is not to be found on another planet or in a sweet by-and-by. Evil is a part of life, the negative shadow part of it. The wish for the end of the shadow leads to dualistic conceptions of the afterlife: heaven means no shadow, hell means no light.

There is no freedom from evil, but there is freedom to face it and not to act in accord with its rules. Evil triumphs when we join it or when we change for the worse because of it. When we go on loving, no matter what hand life or people deal us, the Self triumphs. In that moment, goodness is real and so are we. In *Faust*, Mephistopheles says: "I am a part of that power which always wills the evil and always works out the good."

Evil is one-sidedness. It results when one element of the psyche, such as greed, takes over and pushes away another possibility, such as generosity. Evil is that which makes wholeness impossible. Everything is meant to serve our wholeness in its own limited way. Greed, for instance, can serve it by adjusting itself down to healthy self-provision. Perhaps the security in that may lead to compassionate concern for the provisioning of others.

There is no concrete good or evil in nature. These are moral categories, qualities of human acts. When evil seems outside us, it gains mastery over us. Like the personal shadow, it is projected and so retains a stranglehold on our powers. In the past, evil was exclusively appropriated to demons. A nonhuman agency of evil is a "not me." Since shadow befriending begins with self-acknowledgment, this attitude cuts us off from the opportunity for personal healing.

The presence of goodness does not permanently eliminate evil but removes it in the moment. Our work is to acknowledge good in spite of evil, not instead of it. We stay on guard, since it can always reappear in our choices. We have often heard that wholeness/goodness triumphs over fragmentation/evil. The resurrection motif in so many religious traditions is a metaphor for this victory of wholeness. Jesus rises after being destroyed, so something in him cannot be destroyed: absolute goodness. This is a way of saying that the Self cannot be destroyed, especially not by the ego. Thus, when we do the work that leads to wholeness, we are not only protecting ourselves from evil but also becoming less vulnerable to it. This must be why so many martyrs welcomed death with joy. They knew that the body the buzzards were circling overhead to devour was not the one that mattered.

When I accept myself, I see that I always contain inclinations toward both good and evil. In this acceptance, I find the center. I both reconcile myself to the fact of evil and commit myself to the work of goodness. When I allow consciousness of both virtue and vice in myself, a widening occurs in my psyche. I then can play with opposites rather than be frightened by them. The healing play that emerges in the practice of befriending the shadow makes it an ally. "I'll have night's

cloak to hide me from their eyes," said Romeo about his enemies. Embracing the night as he looked with love at the light
from Juliet's window, he made darkness his ally.

Evil is the manifestation in conscious life of the unconscious shadow. As we work on our negative shadow we grow
in the freedom to choose what we may act out in daily life.
We are then never at the mercy of an evil impulse. No devil
can make us do it. (The vanity of the devil is a metaphor of
inflation of ego.) Positive shadow work leads to more autonomy, since we are no longer courting an ideal of perfection
but the reality of wholeness within our own limitation and
potential. This leads to becoming compassionate enough to
experience vicariously the pain and evil in the world and to
accept its burden with personal responsibility. This is how
we finally redeem each other. Compassion is our befriended
positive shadow aimed at the negative shadow in others.

We were programmed as xenophobes who run from
strangers and cling to those who are familiar. Yet we hear
from Saint Paul: "Do not be afraid to entertain strangers, for
thereby some have entertained angels unaware." In the heroic
journey motif, the hero is often given help by a stranger or
enemy. Prejudice makes people enemies *because* they are
strangers. We project onto them our personal shadow and
even the archetypal shadow of the world. Judging others is a
way of avoiding a confrontation with our own shadow. Prejudice in us makes us strangers to ourselves. How can we
know ourselves when we do not believe that everything
human is possible for us, good or ill? Carpocrates, an ancient
Neoplatonist philosopher, presents a curious premise: each
individual soul must experience every human possibility before it can become free of its bodily limits.

Christ's command to love our enemies seeks to override
our ego's program. He recommends that we combine the opposites. We do not make foes into friends and then love them

but love them as enemies, combining love and antagonism. This is too hard a task for the human ego with its unalterable will to divide and conquer. Confronted with this challenge, the hero consults a wise old man or finds an amulet or asks the aid of a god. These are metaphors for the grace required to complement our ego powers when they have met their ego match. The help of a guardian angel is another metaphor for this graceful part of the work.

A battle with demons symbolizes an *inner* struggle with our own shadow. Such a battle enjoins us to love the enemy within, not only the one out there. Violence results when we pit one side of ourselves against the other, the same thing that happens in war. The most effective peacemakers are those who acknowledge their own inner antagonisms.

How does one face the opponent within? The first step is to seek dialogue with the inner enemy and the second is to promote the enemy to the status of an ally by unconditional acceptance of and respect for its unique powers and by enlisting its cooperation. This work requires a consolidation of conquest and surrender and of defenselessness and resourcefulness, more examples of the union of opposites. Mere surrender is no better than mere resistance. Conscious facing of the enemy within replaces unconscious defacing of the enemy without. An unconscious action of grace that reformats and reorders us happens concurrently with our conscious work on ourselves. Even in the results of the work, the opposites attract and reconcile. To love an enemy is to love ourselves, since an enemy is a representation of our own shadow. Love integrates; fear separates. To refuse to reconcile with an enemy is to fail to integrate our own shadow. This is the challenge implicit in the consoling dictum "True love casts out fear."

THE PRACTICE

Our work is to let go of the hope that evil will end and simultaneously to work indefatigably to end it.

• Evil is anything that diminishes wholeness or takes advantage of others. Confronting our own evil and dealing with it is not only a psychological issue, it is also a spiritual one. Therefore both psychological and spiritual work are called for. The psychological work consists of making amends for evil done and making a decision to change whatever in our lives makes evil happen. It is not enough to be conscious of evil; we have to reject it continually in all its insidious forms. This is why conscious decision is required. Spiritually, the work is openness to transformative grace. On its own, even the healthy ego is at a loss in the full confrontation with evil. A power beyond ourselves has to come into play. It is the power of conversion, the spiritual equivalent of psychological change. Both paths lead to one destination: we promote the entry of light and wholeness into the world.

Evil is not meant to be integrated but to be replaced by goodness. At the same time, evil is not ever fully destructible. It remains in our psyche as both an option and an inclination. The work helps us see this and override it with alternatives that institute goodness wherever evil might have been our purpose or our choice. In the total opposition that characterizes the extremes of good and evil, there is no reconciling third. The work here is not to befriend but to overcome. The healthy response to the evil in the world is to roll up our sleeves and fight it with all our might.

Darkness is not evil. The healthy response to darkness is to bring an equal measure of light to it. Light and dark are meant to be integrated. Goodness and evil are meant to be separated so that evil goes and goodness stays. We will always see the results of the evil and injustice of others in the world around us. Our work is to fight it and not to add to it. In the face of the meaningless and unalterable suffering inflicted by evil, on others or on us, the spiritual challenge is immense; we can only abide mindfully in the utter incomprehensibility of it and take *that* as solace. Teilhard de Chardin offers a sanguine but challenging addition to this idea: "To adore is to lose oneself in the unfathomable, to plunge into the inexhaustible."

• Contemplate others' shadow but then also their divine nature, a superior object of attention. "All beings have Buddha nature. I liberate all beings who do not yet know this or act from it." This bodhisattva vow is not about inflating our powers but about acknowledging the vast potential in all beings for enlightenment. Say this: "May all beings reach enlightenment. May I be a reservoir and channel of grace in whatever way the world needs me to be."

• List the people you have considered your enemies in each era of your life. Are you still holding a grudge? How can you let go of it? Take the single worst trait of each of the enemies you have listed and then acknowledge it as somehow true of you at some time in the course of your life. Which feelings remain unexpressed about each of these enemies? Find the thread of similarity in all of them. If they have harmed you, how have you expressed your anger? Are there amends to be asked for? Are you ready to forgive?

• We are conscious of many of our negative traits and hence they are not technically part of the shadow as Jung described it, that is, they are not unconscious. However, as we befriend the dark side we know, the shadow we do not know begins to come into view more easily. In this book, we have therefore been including even our known dysfunctional traits as apt for the work of transformation. Befriending the shadow involves a total inventory of our shortcomings, a making of amends for them, and a resolve to change for the better. List your long-known negative traits in an inventory; write out the specific ways you will make amends where possible; and come up with a practical plan to change. Use affirmations that help reinforce the new behaviors. Read your list and plan to one person you trust. Notice that this practice is an alternative to shame about yourself or guilt about your faults. The inventory plan helps you contain and contextualize what you have done and who you are rather than criticize yourself for it.

• The shadow is manifested when we like and do not like people for no apparent reason, especially on a first encounter. Recall those who have struck you that way and look for your own positive and negative shadow in your reactions. We incite others' shadow when they strongly like or dislike us for no apparent reason. Consider the times this has happened to you. Have you taken something personally that may actually be a projection?

• The shadow manifested in crime and violence is too much for most people to witness. People who work with crime, abuse, and violence on a daily basis need a way of off-loading their experience. Otherwise every day is additive to post–traumatic stress. The work described in the practice sections in this book provides ways of debriefing oneself.

FAMILY STRAINS

> *The polarity to be harmonized in human development*
> *is that although our beginnings require the certainty*

that begets trust, our mature abilities to negotiate life's vicissitudes require the capacity to hold together in the face of uncertainty.

—L. W. SANDER

We were born with instinctive emotional needs: for attention, for acceptance of us as we are, for physical affection, and to be allowed to act in accord with our deepest needs, values, and wishes. These are our essential requirements for wholeness. Implicit in being born is the inalienable right to have our instinctive needs fulfilled. These needs are not subordinate to our parents' emotional needs. Parents whose emotional needs are too overwhelming to allow them to make a child's needs primary do not seem to have the calling to parenthood. Only people who can grant that priority seem to be true parents-elect. Nature has not fashioned every adult for this task. Ann Landers once asked her reading audience, if they had it all to do over, would they still have had children. She received thirty thousand letters, and 70 percent of them said no.

Childhood needs are a function of dependency, of having no alternative resources. Adults have the same needs—for attention, affection, acceptance, freedom—but in flexible, lighter forms, and they have many more resources both within and around them. Our problem is not that our needs were unmet by our parents but that they are unmourned by us now in the present. Once we do the personal work of mourning the shadow side of our past, its deficiencies or abuses, we have greater access to the enriching intimacy others may provide. We are also more in touch with our own potential and our deepest needs, values, and wishes. This is our positive shadow side that was stunted by the lack of being allowed to be ourselves and to emerge into our full psychological stature.

When our childhood needs were unfulfilled, they left a psychic wake: grief at the loss and a long, plaintive, interior cry for what we missed. This cry remains inside us all our lives. It sounds like this: "Accept me, care about me, let me be free, see me, hear me, love me." We scream it in words or in silence during all our childhood; we scream it in words or in silence in every adult relationship. It begins with hope and sometimes ends in fulfillment, sometimes in despair.

As healthy people, we do not take care of our own needs alone; we seek love in someone outside ourselves. The fern cannot provide its own environment. It requires very specific external conditions. We, like it, wait for the right conditions: mourning the losses of our past (our part) and being loved nurturantly by another person (an adult partner's contribution). Our early needs had as their purpose to engender a strong sense of self. This may not have been possible in childhood. It is possible in adulthood. Our identity is love-instigated but not time-bound.

Our early and lifelong needs for freedom, attention, acceptance, and affection have a shadow side. In the childish shadow way of construing fulfillment of the need for being allowed to be free, we may seek release from responsibility. The requirement for attention, in the shadow context, may become a need for pampering; acceptance may become the need to be conceded to as right about everything; affection may become the need for sex. The work of integrating the shadow contributes to our ability to experience intimacy in more adult ways.

The shadow of childhood is in the abuse and neglect we may have suffered at the hands of our parents and the secrecy that may have surrounded it. Every trauma of early life becomes a drama in adult relationships unless it is mourned and healed. This drama is the deepest shadow of adult intimacy. We repeat our past and do not even realize we are doing it. If we were hurt by not being listened to, we may now be looking desperately for a partner who listens and then blame the partner when he or she does not. We will be insatiable because we can never get enough of what we previously missed. The only way to deal with a loss like this is to mourn it.

Mourning is a healing of memories. It is grief work.[10] By mourning we let go of the original hurt. It consists of admitting what happened to us and what we are up to now in our adult relationship, then feeling all the sadness, anger, and fear that accompanied our past and now attends our present too. Finally a shift occurs and we let go and forgive so that we can go on in healthier ways. This going on is a combination of self-parenting and openness to healthy intimacy. We do not then seek love but we drop the walls we had erected to keep it out. Love is not pushy; it waits for a welcoming nod.

Since separation and individuation are the central tasks of development to adulthood, loss and grief are built into growth. To move on to a new stage of development is to let go of a former one that has become comfortable. It was comforting to be nursed. When we were weaned, we lost a feature of our mother's body warmth and advanced to a new way of being nurtured, one appropriate to our new age in life. But the price was loss and grief, the shadow sides of growth. Every cell in our body learned that letting go and going on has pain in it. To grow is to move from attachment to detachment and then to new attachments that more accurately reflect our new level of needs. Accompanying detachment is the

10. These are the steps of mourning the past: remembering abuses and neglect; feeling sadness, anger, and fear; reimagining the events but this time as one who speaks up for oneself; dropping the expectation that anyone can fix or restore the past; being thankful for all that was learned and gained from what happened; forgiving those who hurt us; performing a healing ritual; and self-parenting, along with making healthier choices of partners and friends who can cooperate in that.

negative shadow of anxiety about separation and the mourning of a loss. In attachment is the positive shadow challenge of a new beginning, with all its risks.

To grow up is also to engender a capacity to be alone serenely and safely. The paradox here is that the capacity to be alone develops best in the presence of someone who is consistently nurturant. In the intimate embrace, I gain the power to be alone securely. Everything is from someone, that is, a gift, grace. Mother's role was to contain us at first, then to be a safe base for us to return to as we began exploring, and finally to become a lifelong supportive adult. Our role was to be contained, to go and return, and finally to go on, as in the heroic-journey motif.

Timing is crucial in this process. Each change and separation is meant to happen in its own time. If weaning occurs suddenly or too early, it may feel like abandonment, the shadow side of comings and goings. We react to any abandonment with vehement displeasure. In a nurturant home, such cries of protest and pain will be sensitively heard. Personal power develops from precisely this parental responsiveness to the wisdom of our childhood intuitions and our inner clock. This is a feature of the positive shadow of childhood: we are free to *find* our inner resources.

When the timing is just right, early in life, we become more willing to let the old attachment go and redesign our relationship with our mother in accord with our new powers. This happens only because of grief work: we let her die to her old way of being with us and let ourselves die to our old way of being with her. This is instinctive; it wants to happen. The paradox of human growth is that we gain our identity through loss.

Grief's favorite position is piggyback on past similar events. Our tears are shed for more than this one sad thing. Our present sad or angry reaction to a painful predicament in our relationship is a signal of the need for childhood related grief work. The predicament stirs the positive shadow of ego (functional, healthy, appropriate) if we finally feel more compassion for ourselves and our partner. It is the negative shadow of ego (neurotic, dysfunctional) if we act out of vengeance.

Delilah became very upset by her boss's not standing up for her to management even though he had promised he would. Delilah is indignant about her boss's behavior because she has done so many personal favors for him and she thought that would lead to his being loyal to her. She feels entitled to that consideration and asks herself: "How *dare* he do this to *me?*" Yet Delilah herself does not stand up for her children when something happens at their school and they are wrongly accused. She takes the teacher's side against her children.

In her own childhood, Delilah's father was a weak and passive man who never stood up for her or intervened when her mother physically or verbally abused her. Her father never abused her in that way but he allowed his wife to get away with it almost every time. He was more afraid of confronting his wife than of losing his daughter's respect; his fear of his wife was stronger than his wish to protect Delilah. She felt isolated and abandoned by him in those painful moments, and that emotional reaction now automatically replays when an authority figure lets her down. Delilah's reaction to her boss is thus a clue to two elements at work: her shadow ego is affronted and her early unresolved childhood issues are aroused. If she takes the transaction between her boss and herself *literally*, experiencing displeasure at an injustice, she will lose her chance to become more conscious through her practice of befriending the shadow and grieving the past.

How can we know how much of our past to dredge up?

Under the normal surface of our daily life with all its order and functionality, there may be a hidden lake of troubled waters that holds old secrets and hurts from the distant past. For some this lake is like Lake Emerald in Connecticut: it contains only some old Coke bottles, Aunt Abigail's earring lost in 1925, and some artifacts left by the last of the Mohegans many decades ago—nothing scary. For some it is like Lake Tahoe, holding secrets of pain and crime: the gun that killed Guido is there and so is Guido—many scary things and frightening memories. And for some it is like a lake that is known to all as mysterious and sinister, holding something so terrifying that it seems better not to keep looking. Only its name is enough: Loch Ness.

If our life is basically happy and things are working out fairly well at Lake Emerald, it may be better to leave well enough alone. Not every arrowhead has to be found for us to be happy.

If our life has had its share of pain and joy but relationships have not worked as well as we would have wished, it is worth getting to the bottom of Tahoe, dredging it for its secrets and being done with them.

If our life has been full of compulsions and inner pain, if no relationship has ever worked, if our life is messed up and we feel damaged and too fragile right now to look into things too closely, we can wait until we feel ready. The monster is not to be disturbed if we cannot handle confronting him. But perhaps we at least do not have to keep feeding him. That might be the only work for now.

The family shadow appears in what our parents projected onto us: "You are the strong one" or "the weak one" or "the black sheep" or "the one expected to do what I could not." Our parents cannot come through for us; to do so would contradict their projection. A parent may project his or her own positive or negative shadow on a child. This is ultimately a rejection and is felt as one by a child.

Ruby sees her preadolescent daughter Lynn using makeup. She is experimenting in an age-appropriate and innocent way, but Ruby judges her as slatternly and as headed for an immoral life. Ruby never notices her own truly seductive and loose manner with men. As long as Lynn is the one perceived and blamed as trashy, and as long as Ruby is reprimanding her, Ruby is off the hook. She cannot accept the truth about herself and so fails to allow Lynn's normal behavior. The adult Lynn may someday blame her mother for being too strict. She may never realize the deeper failure on her mother's part: Ruby never succeeded in being strict with herself. Ruby and Lynn are missing out on the love that happens when the real I meets the real thou. Projection works against authentic love. How will either of them learn to be in a healthy relationship with another adult?

Honesty about living with all our limitations is healthier than the continual search to "do it all perfectly." It is better for children to see limitations in their parents and to see their parents' sincere attempts to deal with them than to believe that their parents are perfect. An honest self-presentation by parents is the best gift children can receive. It makes their own experience of themselves believable. Lynn did not have that chance.

When a child refuses to carry his parent's projections, that parent may be angry and reject him. To avoid this, the child may feel obliged to follow the family projections as scripts ever after, for example, "I have to succeed no matter what the cost to my health, my integrity, or my self-esteem. I am committed to acting in accord with my father's deepest needs, values, and wishes. I am living his life." When a son stops following this script, his own needs, values, and wishes become clear and are refunded to him. This is how self-esteem hangs on the withdrawal of shadow projections.

The family shadow is often hidden in the family secrets. The skeleton in the closet is really the shadow in the closet. To have to keep a long-term secret or to be at the mercy of it makes personal integration an almost impossible task. If the secret is about abuse of us by someone, we may feel isolated and split off from our own reality. This may lead to a denial of the shadow in other people, and we may then find ourselves the unwitting prey of predators in later life.

Sometimes we find out about our shadow, especially the shadow of our own childhood past, from our children. Pasquale is a divorced middle-aged man whose son, Angelo, has lived with him all his life. Presently Angelo is at home between high school and college. Pasquale knows that Angelo loves him, but he nonetheless often feels unappreciated and even used because Angelo rarely offers to help out at home except to do the few chores assigned to him. He certainly never extends himself to give back something to his dad for all that his dad does for him. Angelo's many friends are constantly at the house. But Angelo does not make time to visit with Pasquale as he does with them. He simply comes and goes at will.

When Pasquale brings all this up, Angelo tries to talk him out of his feelings by maximizing the few contributions he does make and by pointing out that fathers are supposed to take care of their sons. He even remarks that to say thank you would make him feel that he was a guest in the house rather than a bona fide member of the family.

It gradually became clear to Pasquale that his son was truly unable to see his point or to respond to his hurt. Pasquale did not want to be punitive toward his son, but he did feel tempted to cut back on favors, money, and so on. He decided simply to say ouch—out loud—when he felt the pain of Angelo's ungiving attitude or behavior toward him.

After a while, however, Pasquale began to question himself: "Why do I need Angelo's appreciation so strongly?" Pasquale did not doubt the legitimacy of his need. He recognized his desire for appreciation as appropriate. What bothered him was the compulsive flavor of it. He also did not like having his feelings be at the mercy of his son.

Pasquale particularly wondered why he felt such a strong need for acknowledgment and gratitude at this time in his life. He certainly did not feel this need in his thirties, why in his fifties? Could it be that this urgent sense of need came into play at this age because of every parent's inheritance from the distant human past? Survival of aged parents always depended on their children's caretaking of them. "Is it an old biologically ingrained programming," wondered Pasquale, "that makes me feel this need so sharply?" He guessed that probably did figure in somehow and that it gave an archetypal dimension to his experience. Parents may be calibrated to feel a need for their children to be more emphatic as they age. At the same time, Pasquale knew it was his own personal issue too.

Pasquale acknowledged that it was common for young men of Angelo's age to take parents for granted. He also knew that his son was no exception. "How much is involved in this!" thought Pasquale. "It seems complex, but my task is simple: let go *and* speak up!"

One night as Angelo and his friends were on their way out to shoot pool, Pasquale began to reminisce about his own youth. He recalled that he was exactly this same way toward his own parents, even more so. Pasquale realized what his parents must have felt and how insensitive he had been. Angelo had helped him see this part of his personal shadow by unwittingly making him the target of it. Pasquale wrote a letter of admission to his parents and expressed his appreciation of them. "He *is* an angel," mused Pasquale about his son, "he conveys a message about who I am, where my shadow lurks, how family matters go in cycles, and how to let go of expectation."

In addition to our family shadow, we may also be confronting another source of life-denying injunctions. The shadow side of our religious tradition may have contributed to the engendering of guilt and shame about our freedoms, our bodies, our spontaneity, and even our sense of inquiry. Guilt is the belief that we are cut off from wholeness. It brings up a terrifying sense of isolation, the punitive dimension of excommunication.

In Christianity, sex has often been reckoned as the foremost element of shadow guilt. (The more autonomous sex is, the less conscious we are of its archetypal and healing meanings.) The image of Pan (nature) and the devil (evil) merged in Christian tradition. Sex became the metaphor for a natural, and therefore unbridled, spontaneity and freedom that could threaten order. Freud observed that compulsive fascination with ritual may mask repressed sexuality. Actually, what our religion may have labeled as perversions might be potentialities of our sexuality, the positive shadow side of it. Homosexuality, transvestism, playful submission and dominance, fetishisms, are not the shadow side of sex. They are the side scapegoated by those who deny or fear the variety of legitimate human experience. The shadow side of sex takes two forms, inappropriate guilt in us and violence toward others. The violent shadow side of sex exists on a wide spectrum: from rape to using the body parts of endangered species to infuse sexual virility in aging men.

Reductionist religion, like reductionist physics, denies half of reality. It is founded in a Cartesian dualism of mind and body and thus condemns the full spontaneous release of the sexual drive. The religious dissociation of sex from our potential for joy in our bodies is a truly dark side of the shadow of religion. As we have been seeing in our look at the shadow, that which is repressed comes back to haunt us in a distorted way. Promiscuity may become someone's style not because the person is evil or weak but because sex has become severely dissociated from full humanity and dangerously associated with soul damnation. Seeing in integrated ways, Blake wrote: "Man has no body distinct from soul; for that which we call body is a portion of soul discerned by the five senses."

The guilt dimension of the shadow of sex comes through in Brian's story. He was the most macho guy on his high school football team. No one knew, least of all Brian, that he was gay oriented. His team spirit and his many male friendships had an erotic component to them but it never exhibited itself directly. His homosexuality was his positive shadow side, his true self, his potential to live in accord with his deepest—and most deeply buried—needs and wishes. One night when Brian was drunk he made a sexual advance toward his best friend. Brian's tenderest longings could not emerge when he was sober but only when his persona was disabled by a drug. He was rebuffed by his friend and regretted his actions the next day, the familiar "Boy, was I wasted last night!" The gentle side of Brian is wrapped up in his sexual orientation, but it is inaccessible as long as it remains in the shadows. He may live his whole life and never become who he really is or even know who he really is. What chance does Brian have to be all he can be and to make the contribution to the world he was meant to make? Look at all that is missed when one entire dimension of an identity is a missing person.

The greatest danger in the shadow of institutionalized religion is its tendency to make us doubt the abundant resources within ourselves. As long as we believe that we can find ourselves only in a source that is outside, we are caught in dualism, a form of violence and violation, and are thereby self-diminished. As long as we rely on mediators who have sole and full hegemony over the means to our wholeness, we cannot integrate our positive shadow. Guides help us but not from hierarchical or patriarchal heights. The ones who walk *with* us seem more sincerely believable as authentic assisting forces. Is this not what religion was meant to be for beings like us who are on a journey?

To be "born again" does not mean to be safely entrenched in patriarchal and divisive bigotry. To be born again is about identity, not position. It means carefully and thoroughly rearranging our lives and attitudes to meet the challenges of nonviolence. It is a total commitment to the Sermon on the Mount: letting go of ego in favor of gentle love.

The positive shadow of religion is a spirituality that respects our liberty and opens us to the love, wisdom, and healing within and around us. The heroic spiritual-psychological journey is about finding that positive source within. The source *is* transcendent but only of ego. It is immanent in the Self, available to all us human priests, inventors of our own sacraments. This is what Percival may have realized when he beheld the Holy Grail and noticed, with reverent awe and amused surprise, that he was staring into his own soul.

THE PRACTICE

• What are your personal needs in intimate relationships? Look over the history of your relationships. Which ones fulfilled your needs? What were the needs of each of your former partners? Were you able to fulfill them? Were you, or your partners, seeking too much from one another? It seems that healthy adult partners seek to fulfill only 25 percent of each other's needs; the other 75 percent we find in ourselves, our families, our friends, our careers, our hobbies, our spirituality and religion, and in entertainment and special interests. If this is true, have you been seeking too much, or too little, from your past or present partner?

• Recall the experiences of your childhood that stand out with pain or joy. What is there for you to be thankful for? What is there to mourn? Perform a ritual of thanks for what was good about your childhood.

Use this technique of grief work for that which was abusive or neglectful about your childhood: Recall the instances. Feel the sadness, anger, and fear you must have felt in the past and that you still feel now. Cradle the feelings and let them last as long as they need to, with no attempt to assuage or interrupt them. Imagine yourself going through the experiences of the past with your present strength and resources. Be thankful for how your past has helped you become a stronger person today. Let go of blame and let forgiveness flow into your heart. Resolve to parent yourself and to seek partners, friends, and teachings in life that will be assisting forces to your healthy self-emergence. This book and this work may be examples. Perform a ritual of letting go and going on.

• Here is an imaginative exercise that may help you make a connection between a shadow trait you may have become aware of and something from your past that may still be unfinished or unprocessed:

Look at what you most despise about yourself.

Trace that feeling back as far as you can to the point at which it began, perhaps as far back as childhood.

Now picture yourself at that age and recall what you were having to deal with at that time and how few resources you may have had.

Let it become clear that the thing you so condemn in yourself was originally a protective strategy to provide you with an inner resource in the face of what felt dangerous. The very thing you now dislike in yourself may have been your only way of defending yourself against real or imagined threats when you had no visible alternative.

In the present, imagine yourself sitting across from your younger self and having a talk. Listen to your past self and respond from your present adult self. Be sure to say: "You had no one to help you back then but now you have me."

Choose a symbolic object that represents that desolate early self and hold it and comfort it each day. Always add: "Now you have me."

• Rewards and punishments may characterize child rearing or schooling. They are meant to increase motivation and effort but work only in short-term ways. They are unrealistic in that they do not reflect the true conditions of our human existence. The good are not always rewarded nor are the miscreant always punished. Nor should they be. Ultimately rewards and punishments are ego generated and are disrespectful of others. They are really forms of control. Rewards control by promising; punishments control by threatening. The loving model is learning from errors and collaborating in the process of change. This is cooperation rather than constraint. Reward does not lead to intrinsic motivation toward goodness. It leads to more need for reward. As the Tao says: "It is best not to make merit a matter of reward lest people conspire and contend." Punishment certainly does not lead to internal conversion. It leads to humiliation, rebellion, and rage. Once the fear of punishment is lifted, people are more likely to want to make amends, to truly change. Piaget says: "Punishment renders autonomy of conscience impossible." The style of the Cold War was deterrence by threat of retaliation. To threaten our children or one another is to create cold war rather than peaceful love. *How did I learn at home and in school? How has that style helped or hindered me? How do I treat my own children? Have I created an atmosphere of respect or fear?*

• What are the areas of your religious past that need to be mourned as self-effacing? What are the beliefs and abuses from which you need to recover? List the ways your religion may have engendered fear and guilt in you. How was it positive and life affirming? What in it can you be thankful for? How many of your present deepest needs, values, passions, and wishes are in the hands of religion? How can you retain the archetypal riches of your religious tradition?

THE SHADOW OF RELATIONSHIP

A healthy adult relationship is a meeting of an I and a thou in fearlessly intimate contact, with an ongoing commitment to a mutual exchange of love by mirroring attention, acceptance, and affection and allowing each other to be free to live in accord with our deepest needs, values, and wishes.

We all want to be loved for our whole selves. We know we are befriending the shadow of relationship when we cease trying to get our partner to measure up to our wishes and needs exactly. We begin accepting him or her as one who, like all other human beings, will not measure up, or will for moments here and there, and that is genuinely enough. To accept someone's negative shadow side makes love more believable. To believe in someone's positive shadow makes a partner a true helpmate. *Can I be faithful to your shadow?*

Whenever we strongly react to any person with attraction or repulsion, projection is at work, the best clue to the presence of our own shadow. An invisible part of us has become highly visible in someone else. We are therefore being pushed by an image of our positive or negative shadow. Helen Luke says, "Projection is the way you see everything that is unseen in yourself." An intimate relationship is liable to contain many unconscious projections, preventing the meeting of the authentic I and the authentic thou. As we withdraw our projections, authentic relationship with another becomes more and more possible. To relate in an I-thou manner is to relate mindfully, that is, without the encrustations of ego: fear, clinging, blame, shame, and so forth. *I witness thee, not project upon thee.*

The romance phase of a relationship projects the positive shadow of lovableness. Partners acknowledge and see their full potential for love in the way they feel about one another. This is the wonderful thing about romance: the partners' most lovable attributes are being mutually mirrored, that is, loved with attention and acceptance and granted the freedom to emerge in their own way.

We may meet someone and feel an instant "chemistry" with her, an instant bond that feels self-validating. We imagine that tingling to be a guarantee of a match made in heaven. Yet such chemistry may be more accurately a sign that our own positive shadow is being constellated. Fascination is a common signal of the arising of our positive shadow. We are seeing the hidden best of ourselves mirrored in another. We may be finding out more about ourselves in that moment than about the great future we might have with the other person.

Our positive shadow is intimately bound to our sense of being mirrored and held in relationships. The positive shadow is directly related to what love is about and what our potential for it is. A clue to our untapped potential, our positive shadow may appear in any sudden reaction of joy or comfort in an interaction or ongoing relationship with someone. It may also occur as it did for Delilah, a young woman who was watching a movie and was moved to tears by a scene in which the hero risked his life to support the woman he loved. Delilah's reaction may show that she has it in herself to be that courageous for someone she loves. Her reaction may also be a clue to how Delilah herself feels most loved: having others stand up for her. The tears may also show her where she still needs to grieve her own past, in which she had no such support from her dad. Tears are one of the best indicators of where our work is.

In the conflict stage of a relationship, our partner sees our negative shadow side quite clearly as it manifests in external behavior. We see our partner's darker side too. We may not see our own projections nor take responsibility for them. Conflict with someone may actually be a battle with our own projected opposite, "shadow-boxing." Helen Luke also says: "Uniting means two unique things that meet, not two blurred things that merge."

In the world of ego projection, relationships are characterized by fascination and dependency. In the world of the Self, everyone we meet is someone we relate to without blame or expectation. This is mindful meeting and relating, without the fog of fear or clinging. Marie-Louise von Franz adds: "We meet those to whom we belong in the world of the Self."

"I hate how stubborn she is but I love how feisty she is." What we most despise in our partner is often exactly what we most admire. This is because intimacy combines our opposite reactions and elicits both our positive and our negative shadow material. Our drive toward wholeness makes us truly want the whole person. This includes his or her shadow side. We bring our own shadow to our partner for a positive reason. We hope for a mirroring acceptance of that side of ourselves: "Please befriend my shadow. I will show you the worst of myself and I ask you to continue to love me." This may be precisely what did not happen in childhood, when parents seemed not to love us when we were "bad." Mirroring—unconditional love from one person to another—helps us accept our own shadow as lovable. Befriending by others makes us more facile at self-befriending.

In a relationship, one person may hold a cherished but hidden piece of another, either positive or negative: "You attribute to me what you deny in yourself." Something intrapersonal thereby becomes interpersonal. Freud said: "All emotions are intrapsychic and intrapersonal, not interpsychic or interpersonal." In other words, they are within us, not between us. This means that problems *with* others may ultimately be problems *within* ourselves. To befriend our own shadow is to recover a lost part of ourselves and thus become present in relationship as whole persons, the only candidates for intimacy.

Fritz Perls said: "When we project our power it turns against us and we clobber ourselves with our own energy!" We do this by our resistance to our own truth, which then turns back on us and hurts us. We are hit by the boomerang we threw. An example of a projected potential is in the statement "He is superior to me." The "clobbering" is in believing the alternative: "I am inferior." As we draw in our projection, we restore equality and are empowered by the reclaimed energy.

It is sad to realize that the energy that goes into projection onto someone else is debited from our account. It is refunded when we withdraw the projection. Which account is this? It is the one that holds our own deepest needs, values, and wishes, our own creativity. Was this what we were fearing all along, the full emergence of ourselves?

Lily and Quentin fell in love while they worked on political campaigns together in college. They both thought they had found the perfect mate: equal in intelligence, like-minded in politics, mutually sexually appealing and compatible, and even with the same interest in music and cooking. They did not realize that each of them was up to something else that was likewise similar: both saw their own mother in the other. Lily's mother was controlling, demanding, and manipulative. Quentin did not manifest any of these traits in college, but they certainly came out early in married life. Quentin's mother was passive and submissive as well as completely devoted to her husband and son. Quentin unconsciously expected that same treatment from Lily, though she was a strong, assertive woman who always insisted that Quentin take care of himself. Lily and Quentin thus began their life together as mourners. Lily was grieving the replay of her mother's control and Quentin was grieving the loss of a specific brand of female nurturance that he expected of a wife.

Their work is to confront the shadow sides of their mothers, now their own shadow, in one another. Will they do this or will they blame one another and become caught in a deadlock? So much depends on their honesty about the shrouded side of their personalities.

Can Quentin and Lily trust one another enough to go into the dark together? This is the journey required in every relationship, symbolized by Orpheus's brave trek into the underworld (unconscious) to retrieve his wife Eurydice. His guide into the shadow world was Hermes, the trickster god. Shadow work is a guide to the depths of relationship, and a tricky path too. Is this a page in the relationship chapter of the treasury of wisdom that most of us neglected to read?

The shadow of romance is clinging. The shadow of conflict is the rest of the familiar repertory of the arrogant ego. Intimacy means mirroring attentive and acceptant love. The shadow of intimacy is the self-centered narcissism that refuses to grant attention to and acceptance of the other. It brings malice and the retaliatory, competitive ego reactions that kill affection. It brings control that prevents the emergence of one's true self in favor of what the controlling partner wants the other to be. Every partner has a shadow, so every relationship is in danger of its effects when it is being covered up. The shadow that enters the light cannot hurt us. Healthy partners confront their own and their partner's shadow and work together on mutual befriending.

The healthy positive shadow of relationships is the sense of personal plenitude and freedom from neediness: "I have worked on myself by knowing my needs and appreciating those who fulfilled them in childhood. I have mourned for the needs that were not fulfilled, and now take care of my own needs in collaboration with you." These are the words of someone who is not needy but need-conscious and need-fulfilled. He comes to a relationship not with neediness for fulfillment by the other but with a fullness to share. He seeks a partner in need fulfillment, one who will cooperate in it, not one who will provide it.

A craving for completeness outside ourselves prevents the maintenance of lasting relationships and at the same time makes us harder hit by the abandonment that may result. Once we no longer crave completeness, we become open to mature enrichments:

An adult relationship is free of dependency, that is, child to parent.

An adult relationship is free of caretaking, that is, parent to child.

As the negative shadow brings out the worst in us, the positive shadow brings out the best in us. One of the results of work on ourselves is an expansion of and greater access to the riches in ourselves. This is why inner plenitude and resourcefulness as well as freedom from neediness result from our letting go of the past. Our chances for happiness are diminished as long as need fulfillment from a partner is our

primary requisite for it. When relationship enlists and pro-
motes our own lively energy, happiness is much more likely.

THE PRACTICE

• Throughout this book, we are facilitating an inner work on
ourselves, hearkening to our core of personal meaning. This
legitimizes our psychic, as opposed to objective, reality. Such
interior focus sharpens our ability to tune in to others' experience. This is why growth in personal spirituality has always
meant more compassion for others. Moreover, when we situ-
ate ourselves in someone else's psychic reality, we are less
likely to be controlling. We want to experience the other and
we respect his or her inner reality. Empathy is the opposite of
projection. In empathy we respect the core of the other; in
projection we invade and displace it with our own. In em-
pathic resonance to the core of others, we make fewer infer-
ences, judgments, and interpretations. In other words, we
bring more mindfulness into our relationships. This is how
mindfulness helps us love.

How do you miss out on loving more maturely and authentically when you have someone pegged in a certain way?
Try letting go of your habitual view of someone and seeking
the person's inner core. Using examples of positive and negative reactions to people in your life, how are you projecting
your positive or negative shadow onto them? Which of your
own powers are you thereby losing?

• We may fear and hide our shadow but cannot help but desire acceptance too. This follows from the fact that our innate
longing to live out our potential tells us that creative energy
is locked in our shadow.

Are you fearing the revelation of your shadow? What

are you doing to hide it? What are you doing to show it so that it can be accepted? Can you safely show it to those you love most? Can trust mean "Will you still love me once you see my shadow?"

An unnoticed and unbefriended shadow in one partner can be abusive to the other. Mature and loving commitment means that each speaks up about the shadow of the other and each responds by working on his or her own shadow material. Does the following sound like a description of your relationship? If not, can you attempt to practice it?

In healthy relationships, the negative shadow of each partner can be integrated and held enduringly by the other. This happens even through failures at loving and refusals to see shortcomings or their impact. Yet with the holding and accepting is the gently repeated request for change so that each partner's right to happiness can be respected. "I hold your darkness and I ask you to work on it. I support you in that work by joining you in it and by understanding that it sometimes fails. I trust you more and more as I see the sincerity of your efforts."

• Examine your expectations and judgments about your present partner and former partners. How do they line up with your childhood memories of your parents' relationship to one another and to you?

• What are you secretly demanding of your partner? Of your children? Of your friends? What are you openly asking for? Can the secret demands become open requests? What are your fears about doing such a thing?

THE DARK SIDE OF ANGER

Human relationships inevitably arouse anger. Authentic anger is a legitimate, healthy feeling that is briefly expressed to communicate one's displeasure at a perceived injustice without violence toward anyone else. To exaggerate one's anger in order to hurt or change someone is not pure anger but the shadow of anger. It takes the form of drama, abuse, and theatrics. In such instances one is not attempting to communicate but to intimidate.

If someone frightens us with his anger, we have a clue that he is not expressing true anger but engaging in abuse. He is scaring us with his own fear, a clear example of projection of the shadow. The word *drama* can be used here for abuse because drama means putting on an act. The actor engages in colorful theatrics to induce in us the feelings he wants us to feel. He is in control. In true anger this does not happen. One is instead simply expressing one's authentic feeling, with no attempt to elicit a particular reaction. The actor layers feeling with manipulations, for instance, blame, put-downs, demands, aggressive actions, threats, physical or emotional violence, retaliation. These layers of drama are what scare us, not the pure feeling of anger. True feelings cannot harm us, only their shadow can. We fear violation, not feeling. (The layers of drama are the same ego layers that we let go of in mindfulness.)

True anger usually contains sadness, disappointment, and fear, the three components of grief. A responsibly angry person acknowledges these simultaneous, legitimate feelings and shares them with us but does not blame us for them. Anger comes from the healthy ego; abusive drama is from the citadel of our inflated ego. Anger says: "I am angry at you and want you to know it." Drama says: "I want to get you for daring to offend me. I want you to suffer for it and change for me."

As your partner, I simply want to share my anger and let go of it with no wish for retaliation or concession. I may ask for a change in you but I do not demand it. Only my shadow-anger drama does that. True anger is nonviolent. It rivets my attention on you and your feeling rather than frightening me away. Anger comes from attention. True feelings are forms of attention, the fulfillment of one of our basic needs. We have had this kind of attention paid to us so rarely. This is why, when it happens, *we* stop in our tracks and pay attention. True anger does not scare us away; it intrigues us and draws us in. All true feelings come from attention to attention, the direction of mirroring love. Drama-abuse comes from self-enclosed fear; its aim is intimidation. It is the scared child in me shouting at the scared child in you. True anger is respectful, though temporarily displeased, love.

True anger requires no response but asks for one. Drama-abuse demands a response. In true anger, I take full responsibility for my feeling, though I see you as implicated in it. I ask you to be accountable and to make amends but do not force that upon you. Drama-abuse is a strategy meant to punish you, make you change for me, or keep you from causing me to grieve for not getting what I want. It is often out of control (a temper tantrum, that is, a bruised-ego tantrum). True anger is always enacted within safe limits. Drama-abuse goes over the edge with hysterical theatrics. Drama represses true anger; anger expresses true assertiveness—it shows what I feel, asks for what I want, and lets go. The shadow of anger destroys safety; true anger creates safety. Drama is aggression, the shadow side of healthy assertiveness.

Drama-abuse arises from the shadow of ego, the bruised, indignant, arrogant ego that is terrified because it believes it is not getting what it is entitled to. Anger arises from an inner aliveness that is unhappy with something but also realizes it cannot always have its way. Anger is helpful in that it reveals our deepest needs, values, and wishes—by negation. Anger is expressed and let go of expeditiously and cleanly. Forgiveness is the resolution of anger.

Drama-abuse is held on to and smolders as resentment; it is meant to silence you in order to protect me. Anger is meant to inform in order to open communication. Most of us have never seen true anger, only drama-abuse.

Anything split off assumes a life of its own with purposes opposed to those of the healthy ego. It does not join in with the ego to keep it coherent but stands autonomously against it and fragments it. Abuse, the shadow of anger is the product of such fragmentation. Befriending the shadow reduces hegemony of autonomous shadow, and then there is no need to project it. The total psyche becomes assimilable.

THE PRACTICE:
DEALING WITH ANGER AND ABUSE

True Anger	*Abuse: The Shadow of Anger*
Authentic self-expression	Theatrical display: tantrum
Is meant to express a feeling	Is meant to manipulate
Arises from displeasure at injustice	Arises from an affront to ego
Informs the other and creates rapt attention	Scares the other and drives him/her away
Is meant to communicate	Is meant to silence, intimidate, or dump on the other
Desires a response from the other but does not require one	Insists the other acknowledge how right or justified one is
Allows for perspective	Is trapped in the heat of the moment
Takes responsibility for this feeling as one's own and sees the other as a catalyst	Blames the other for what one feels and sees the other as a cause
Asks for change but allows the other to change or not	Masks a *demand* that the other change

Contains sadness or fear, and these are acknowledged	Masks a dashed expectation, disappointment, or loss of control
Is assertive	Is aggressive
Is nonviolent, in control, and always remains within safe limits	Is violent, aggressive, out of control, derisive, punitive, and hostile
Coexists with other feelings	Occludes other feelings
Asks for amends or lets it go	Seeks to retaliate
Releases the aliveness in one's true self and leads to repose	Derails lively energy and creates continuing stress
Arises from a healthy sense of justice	One's bruised, scared ego impotently enraged
Is brief and then is let go of with a sense of closure	Is held on to and endures as lingering resentment or grudge
Sees the other as a confrere	Sees the other as a target
Aims at a deeper and more effective bond	Wants to get the rage out no matter who gets hurt
Coexists with and empowers my love	Cancels love in favor of fear

• Do you find yourself mostly in the right column in the list above or in the left one? Begin the *practice* of healthy anger by writing this table out longhand and placing it where you will continually see it. Every day read aloud each item in the left column, preceded by "I" or "My anger," adjusting the phrases to fit as an affirmation; for example, "My anger coexists with and empowers my love." Read each item in the right column aloud, preceded by "I let go of the habit of, " and adjust the statement accordingly; for example, "I let go of the habit of seeing anyone in my life as a target."

• Anger directed by someone toward you is best dealt with by doing what will be instinctive, paying attention. Listen to what is said, acknowledge the feeling, and ask what the angry person wants from you. If your ego gets in the way, you will be unable to hear. Instead, you will voice over the person's anger with explanations that justify you and attempt to show that the other's anger is not justified. To receive a feeling is to let go of ego and allow the other person to be right, since all feelings are legitimate. To hear with compassion is to be conscious of and responsive to the pain in anger. As you listen, remind yourself that this is the other person's issue, not yours. Feelings do not hurt; they clear the air between people.

• How can you deal with drama coming at you from someone? Drama-abuse originates from a refusal to deal with feelings or to let a person respond reasonably. The only strategy in that explosive moment is to leave the premises. It is useless to try to reason with the arrogant or hysterical ego. In fact, it may only serve to inflame drama for both of you, and violence may result. Violence does not come from anger but from indignant and frightened egos.

A loving person does not want to inflict drama on anyone. One technique that may help reduce your own drama is to cool it down until it becomes anger. How do you cool down? Scream, break dishes, pound a pillow, shout out invective, *alone*. Only when you have contained your own drama and can contact and express authentic nonviolent anger is it fair to confront someone with it.

Anger is an interior experience; pillow pounding and the like exteriorize it. This expresses the feeling, but you do not necessarily *experience* it. Discharge is not enough. The acting out may feel good for the time being, but only an *inner* contact with your anger at an interior feeling level truly addresses and releases it. Sit quietly and drop into your anger in such a way as to feel it as truly yours. Notice your felt sense of it.

Allow yourself to hear what it says to you and dialogue with it in a mindful way.

· Examine your own past. Does any of the following fit for you?

If, when you saw your parents sad, you felt you were to blame; or angry, and you felt you were in danger; or afraid, and you felt you were not allowed to feel that way too, then their distress and drama were being dumped on you. Your family may not have provided a safe context either for feeling anger or for receiving it. What chance do you have for showing and receiving it safely now except to work on yourself? This work grieves your past and befriends your own shadow, which releases your potential for authentic feeling. These are the gateways to success in intimacy, in which love and anger are meant to be expressed simultaneously. The work makes love work.

HEALTHY ANGER VERSUS RETALIATION

> *The anger, the resentment, the bitterness, the desire for recrimination against people you believe have wronged you: they harden the heart and deaden the spirit and lead to self-inflicted wounds.*
>
> —BILL CLINTON

Retaliation takes two directions at once: we feel a sense of power over the other as we gain control: "I showed her!" and we have a sense of invulnerability as we feel safe from future hurts: "He'll think twice before he does that again!"

Retaliation is sometimes acted out and sometimes repressed. To act out our retaliatory impulse directly may take the form of sadism, violence, bullying, vesuvian diatribes, tirades, tantrums, blaming. To act out indirectly may take the form of teasing, sarcasm, lateness, distancing. When we repress our urge to retaliate, it turns against us and becomes depression, bitterness, and ongoing resentment. The alternative is to state our feelings and to ask for restitution. If it is not forthcoming, we let go and move on. Can we become as careful and exact about restitution when we hurt others as we may be about revenge?

Anger is meant to be felt fully, to be safely contained, and to be kindly expressed. This conscious experience of the feeling of anger empowers us to act resolutely toward and yet respectfully of others. As anxiety decreases, so does the will to retaliate, and in its place arises the healthy, pure, and primordial aggression that is so much a part of the survival instinct in all of us.

Frustration accounts for the major thrust of retaliation. An infant bangs its crib when the bottle is not presented; an adult walks out when a partner refuses to do something in the desired way. As we grow in psychological and spiritual maturity we can intervene in that chain reaction. We can *pause* between our frustration and our will to get even. This is paradoxical work, since delay of gratification is what evinces the retaliatory response to begin with. To add a pause seems to make matters worse. Yet the conscious dimension of the *chosen* pause opens us in a sensitizing and empowering way. We stop and then find the place in our adult self where sense and sensibility reside and we act from that place with pride in ourselves.

That healthy pride makes for an exponential increase in self-respect. We are proud that we have more in us than the will to hurt. We like the fact that we can transcend the desire for revenge in favor of a loving form of anger and self-protection. What aroused us to aggression then becomes an enlivening experience, not a deadening one.

When I contain the desire to get back at someone, I discover what it takes to deal with whatever triggered it. Frustration is reframed as the excitement that can set the stage for a healthy release of nonviolent anger. A healthy adult relationship creates a safe container in which anger can be expressed, shared, and received with respect. This is mirroring, that is, lovingly accepting and validating each other's anger or any feeling. By being mirrored, feelings become legitimate and shareable, the opposite of shameful.

When we create a container for our own anger, we set it free from the embroideries of blame and demand. Then and only then do we discover the underlying feelings that may be beckoning to us from past life and relationships. We see how this present existential anger is basically simple but has gathered complicated energy from past memories or hurts. This shows us where our work is, and we no longer attempt to dump it on someone else. We cannot do this work when anger is turned into drama and we are blinded by our affronted ego. The ego is terrified of grief and letting go. Drama-abuse is its way of getting around those threatening possibilities.

And may this storm be but a mountain birth.

—COLERIDGE

7

The False Shadow of the True Self

*W*HEN OUR NEEDS are fulfilled in childhood in healthy ways, we feel safer in the world and our self-esteem increases. We are proud to be who we are. When our early needs were not fulfilled and still remain unmourned by us, we may not feel safe enough to show our authentic choices, characteristics, attributes, and feelings, since we might thereby lose approval. This creates a false self. Yet only a true self can establish and maintain an intimate relationship and a healthy self-image.

Our *true self* is who we were when we were born, the self that by mirroring and respectful love from our parents would have emerged proudly and lived on securely. This potential self remains inside us and is accessible to us all our lives. It simply waits for mirroring—attention, acceptance, affection, and allowing—to become activated. This comes from people who love us and from ourselves as we do the work it takes to love ourselves.

The true self cannot be erased, abused, replaced, or undone. This true self, psychologically, is our functional ego, the capacity in us to work toward goals, feel our feelings without being destroyed by them, deal with fear, accept the conditions of human existence, and express the joy of our lively energy. At the spiritual level, it is also the Self, our Buddha nature, having all the sovereign archetypal powers of divinity: unconditional love, perennial wisdom, and the capacity to heal. Our true self is thus both psychological and spiritual. As long as our true self is hidden, it is the equivalent of our positive shadow, a unique and untapped potential.

The *false self* is the personality we created in response to those who had power over us in childhood. *False self* refers to the neurotic ego and the persona. The false self is the negative shadow side of our true self. We learned early on that it was not always safe to show our true self—our deepest needs, values, inclinations, talents, and wishes. That self might be met with disapproval. Disapproval from those who were feeding us meant our very life might be in jeopardy, certainly our security and happiness. We found ways to hide our true feelings and reactions and instead to display faces that would win approval from the adults in authority. This is the origin of the false self with its words and deeds that emerge from strategy, reflecting not our own wishes but those of others. There is usually a connection between abandonment fear and the false self. We were abandoned every time our true self was rejected and our false self was rewarded. We abandoned ourselves every time we were so terrified of rejection that we took the reward. Terror is hard to fight, so we can have compassion for ourselves about all this.

The true self articulates by thought, word, and deed an authentic reality. It is independent, like a cat. The false self does whatever it takes to win approval. It is fawning, like a dog. The true self is a real person; the false self is a persona, an ego ideal generated by others and then maintained by us. The true self was nurtured by the adult part of our parents. The false self was molded by the scared-child part of our parents. Our mothers may have feared the emergence of our true selves, reacting therefore with anger or intimidation to behavior that represented our authentic wishes and feelings. Gradually we were conditioned to act in accord with parental wishes and expectations. Our true self went underground for safety.

William Carlos Williams wrote: "I always knew that I was I, precisely where I stood, and that nothing could make me accept anything that had no counterpart in myself by which to recognize it." The true self is a mirror that contains perennial wisdom and matches everything that is said or done against its own truth. If it does not fit, it is discarded. If it fits, it is welcomed. This is how the true self is continually enriched by the external world.

The true self is discovered; the false self is invented. The true self is unconditional; the false self is conditioned all through our lives as we encounter people and give them the authority to dictate our character to us. The true self is its own director. The false self is an actor who does what the director(s) tells it to do. We hide our true self because it is unsafe to show it, protecting it until it *is* safe. Like the explorer fig (the first fig of the season), we check out the environmental conditions, and only if they seem friendly do we give the signal to the whole tree to bloom and show its full and true harvest of fruit. Like just such a fig, we must have looked up from our crib at our parents and home and asked: "Is this the environment in which my deepest needs, values, and wishes can bloom safely and abundantly?" The answer we came up with instructed our true self to emerge proudly or to go into hiding until the season was right. This book can be your good season.

"Manners," taboos, values, and limits all help us live comfortably in society. But scare tactics, manipulations, guilt trips, shaming, insults, degradation, and belittlement are forms of control and abuse. The former can lead to a healthy true self, the latter to a false self. The former felt like reasonable advice from someone on our side. The latter felt like unsound threats from someone hostile to our full emergence as persons of unique gifts.

The false self is the outfit we learn to wear in order to make life easier. We make decisions based on what will best endorse and maintain our image in others' eyes. This may also apply to our choice of a car or a wardrobe. We say that a car is chosen for efficiency and economy and that clothes are chosen for style and weather. Actually, we may want desperately to convey a certain look that projects just the image that makes us feel safe, approved, or superior. The false self is the servant of ego. My false self is a pose; my true self is poise. "My wife brings out the worse side of me" may mean she ex-poses me. She makes it impossible to pose. To be exposed is to lose FACE. Can I thank her for that?

As we saw earlier, the persona is the face that our ego wants to show to the outside world. It represents conformity and adaptation to societal requirements. It is a mask from the collective unconscious by which we compromise ourselves with others' expectations. When we strip off our mask—or when the trickster strips it off for us—we see that under it is something collective, not personal, a compromise between us and society. If we identify too strongly with the persona, we may believe that subterfuge is all there is to us. The persona works best when it is used for adaptation and convenience. It can also placate when we are afraid: a smile to the mail carrier when we are fearing the arrival of a threatening letter.

Our persona is often rewarded by money, respect, or power. Integration of our shadow grants us the spiritual gift of becoming whole regardless of material things. It provides the sense of a coherent self and curbs the overused false persona. The persona is a necessary part of any personality; it is the legitimate clothing of ego. Shadow and persona counterbalance each other. Our persona is our ego ideal; our shadow is our reality. The shadow is welcomed as the persona dissolves. The shadow makes up for the smug complacency of the persona, and the persona makes up for the antisocial tendencies of the shadow. If we are all persona, we are phony. If we are all shadow, we are psychopathic. The more we dissolve our false persona, the more we integrate our shadow.

The false self is the persona of the shadow side of ego. It wants to make a good impression even at the cost of truthfulness. The persona of someone with a healthy ego wants to make a good impression but can handle its own imperfections. A person with this persona does not place conformity above the values of spontaneity and humble self-disclosure. The negative persona gives full priority to conformity for approval's sake. Now we can understand the ego's central wish for retaliation. It has as its purpose to protect the persona of ego, the false self.

There will always be tension between conformity and spontaneity. The healthy person survives by visits to both sides of the river:

When I am spontaneous I	*When I conform I*
Preserve my true self	Preserve my security
Trust that I can handle any consequences to my authentic self	Am concerned with my impact on others and fear the consequences to me

Why is my self so easily falsified? Fear gains ascendancy over self-respect. In my false self, I learn to want what others are willing to give me. I will be freer to want what I want if I have agreed with the condition of existence that says I will not always get it and will have to be willing to grieve my losses.

We all operate from both our true self and our false self. Our goal as adults is to live from the true self at least more than 50 percent of the time. The false self asks one question, What do others want? The true self asks, What do I want? Not to know what I want is a sign that I am not living in my true self more than half of the time.

One of our most beguiling human tasks is to discover our true self. Others cannot do this for us. Nor is our own intellect the best pathway to the true self, since it can be fooled and unduly influenced by society, parents, peers, and religion. Imagination is the pathway that seems to offer much more access. The issues that keep us captivated, the images that keep arising in dreams, the secret fantasies that occupy us, these may give us clues to discovering some truth about our true self. They are rarely to be taken literally. Usually they are signposts to an undiscovered or discredited territory of our psyche, a territory that is clamoring for statehood. Do I dare to make the choice to respect myself? Do I dare choose to be myself no matter how it hurts or how much it costs?

The true self is usually found outside the boundaries, rarely within them. Our persona may ultimately be invested in negating who we really are. We fear finding out that we are different from the way we appear. In a xenophobic world like ours, that can, after all, mean isolation, loss of rights, or shame. Adults take that chance. They look for ways to be true to themselves, compassionate toward those who do not understand, and still free to live and work unmolested as who they really are.

There is no single consistent sense of self that perdures throughout our life span. There are, rather, a variety of senses of ourselves that flow from interactions with others and from our interior world. Both of these arise simultaneously, though they may have appeared sequentially in the course of life, as we know the times tables simultaneously though we learned them sequentially. Varied senses of oneself are cross sections of appropriate self-coherence arising and receding in time. The true self is more like river rapids than like a lake.

An authentic self will require engaged focus on and commitment to who we are in this moment, an exciting existential project. All that is required for a true self is a reasonably approximate presentation of our *present* sense of self, a sense that has continually changed and evolved. Since it is an event in time and not a locality in space, *the self is no one and nowhere,* as the Zen masters have always said. Identity is not found as an object is. It is that in us which seeks no object and knows there is none to be found. Not seeking is thus the key to identity. Only when there is nothing more to seek can the vast treasure of the transcendent Self be found.

The true self is an inner wise, intuitive force, both psychological and spiritual, that is able to befriend its shadow and accomplish individuation. It clearly, accurately, fearlessly, and joyfully knows our real needs. It is all we have to give, all that can be loved about us. Our true self makes us unique specimens of our species with an inner repository of powers and creative ability. This is precisely the equipment required to fulfill our destiny of displaying in time the timeless design that wants to unfold in us.

What God whispered to the rose
to make it bloom so beautifully,
He shouted to my heart times
one hundred!

—RUMI

THE PRACTICE

• List the various eras and milestones of your life. Beside each entry list the deepest needs, values, inclinations, and wishes of that time. Who were the assisting forces in your life in each era and at each threshold? Who were the afflicting forces at those times? In which group did you stand? Did you help or hinder yourself?

In your present life, what are you doing to foster the emergence of your true self, what are you doing to live in accord with your deepest needs, values, passions, and wishes? How do you act from a false self in your home, job, and elsewhere? How does fear evoke falseness? Are you in a relationship with an assisting force, someone who encourages the full emergence of your true self? How does the work you are doing in this book help you manifest your true self more and more?

• Draw a picture of your persona. List your persona characteristics. Show these to friends and ask them to add to the list or subtract from it, based on their perception of you. Which features of your persona are helping you live a healthy, functional life, one that fulfills your goals? Which features of your persona help you maintain a false front?

• In my persona I may believe myself to be a gentle guy. Yet I know I want to hit this fellow. I do not do this, because others' perception of my nonviolent persona would thereby be tarnished. If I were to live more authentically, both gently and assertively, what changes would be required in my persona?

• Other people's reactions obviously figure heavily in the design of my false self. I grow in authenticity as I dialogue with people around me. I may disfigure my identity in the same way. Which of these possibilities fit for me:

  • I pay no attention to other people's reactions OR
  • I am aware of other people's reactions and they do not affect me OR
  • I am concerned about other people's reactions and they do affect me OR

• I am designing my life in accord with other people's reactions.

• What a tragedy for us humans that one lifetime can turn out to be not long enough to fulfill and free all of our potential. What gets in the way?

   • Old messages and rebuffs we swallowed whole that choke us now
   • Relationships now and in the past that stifle and stifled our chances at full self-emergence
   • Every attempt ever made by others to plunder our precious inner riches, to derail us from our natural inclinations, to obstruct our path toward wholeness

All these have to fade and fall flat if we are ever to become what we were meant to be. Look for them everywhere and push them aside as you head for the peak, lest you start to decline before you reach it.

In my childhood in New Haven, I was taught to be like everyone else, rather than encouraged to be myself. Normal meant safely conforming. Recently I found this quotation: "Normal is that which functions in accord with its design." It was written by Dr. Daly King in 1945 in the *Yale Journal of Biological Medicine*. So someone knew even then that being normal did not have to mean being like everybody else. Someone in the very city I lived in could have told me what would have helped me so much. Only a few streets away was the wise permission I needed. But I had stayed home that day.

A FACE TO MEET THE FACES: THE LIFE SPAN OF THE FALSE SELF

Functioning in my false self, I put on appearances that work to make me liked and keep me safe. By doing so I disown my true self in favor of the version that will win approval. The false self makes me careful about every word, gesture, and deed. This precludes the possibility of spontaneity, the very thing that reveals what a true self really contains. This is exactly how it is self-disowning and self-negating.

Why would the reactions of our parents toward us encode such a long-standing cellular program in us? Why would we have bought into their belief system, to the detriment of our own? Probably because what was at stake was loss of contact, something that we want more than self-emergence.

Fearless self-declaration is proportional to the way parents and other significant people in our early years supported our self-expressions. Did they mirror us? Did they thwart us? Did they encourage or discourage our assertion of our right to satisfy our needs, to become independent, and to express love in our own unique way? Inevitably, we were also sometimes punished for what we expressed. As children, we had to cope with or evade these constraints. When we did not succeed, we felt threatened, rejected, stifled, angry, or afraid. To deal with these feelings, we made sly, self-negating compromises. We suppressed our need for autonomy, denied our needs for nourishment and support, or held back our needs to give and receive love. To maintain these strategies for coping, we may have adopted illusions about the world and incorporated these illusions into our evolving self.

The false self might have been born when narcissistic parental needs interfered with our needs to separate and individuate. We then had to manufacture an identity that was carefully tailored to the demands of our parents out of fear that we might lose their approval, which is to say, their love. We may have been indoctrinated with two messages that could cripple us in the very areas that make for adult maturation:

Regarding separation: "Don't go" or "You can't go."

Regarding individuation: "Don't grow up" or "You can't make it alone."

We may have dealt with the threat by submerging the "culprit" (our true self). Our courtship displays for approval may then go on all our lives, but they have to end if we are ever to become real. The adult task is to locate our own freedom and declare it even without having first been allowed to have it. Our true self may never have been mirrored by another person in childhood. We may have to find it elsewhere today. Therapy, positive relationships, and twelve-step programs help us in that process. Sometimes one person accepts us totally, and that helps us know and trust the lovability of our true self. Only when it is safe to show it will it be shown. Emerson said, "We mark with light in the memory the few interviews we have had with souls that made our souls wiser, that spoke what we thought, that told us what we knew, that gave us leave to be what we inly are."

The false self blockades knowledge of the true self (not only its emergence). We may not believe there is anything inside us except the props of a lifetime: doing what others want and being what they need us to be. So how can I love myself? I can love only what I know. And how can I be loved truly if I am not truly known? Someday we realize that only the false self was really loved by those who demanded that we become what they wanted, parents included. "The love I gained with such uphill effort and self-defacement was not meant for me at all but for the me I created to please others," says Alice Miller. *I fought so hard for what they told me to want.*

In healthy development, the false self works to defend our susceptible and precious identity from those who might attempt to take advantage of it. It had a great advantage. The problem arises when we become adults who comply with the environment out of neediness and fear, begging from it like the tame wolf who begs the penurious farmer for food. We no longer relate to our world but beg to win its boon. The heroic journey becomes the beggar's opera.

The false self does not allow the emergence of the true self even when it has something safe to offer or when conditions are safe. This is because the original abuse came from those who loved us. We are now caught in the ambivalent confusion of acting lovingly for others or being ourselves.

The false self affects our freedom to express feelings: "Big boys aren't afraid" may have been an early message to me from my parents. It may have remained within me as an injunction and now I feel bad about myself if I become afraid. I may even be incapable of showing it. This is not happening because I am inadequate but because an inner, cellular taboo has been activated over which I am powerless. It is automatic and subtle. It is familiar and habitual. Is this why I can so clearly know and not follow through with doing?

Imagine at what cost to myself I formed a false self: I gave up on myself. I abandoned myself. I became unrecognizable to myself. How hard it now becomes to honor my deepest wishes, powers, and values.

The false self even creates a false body. We constrict and misshape our body in the process of getting to look like whatever model society proposes for us. The human body reveals in a truthful way just how stressed or pained a person is. Our stooped or inflated or deflated body tells the story we may be afraid to relate. *Am I trying to have someone else's body?*

Nonempathic responses to us in early life may have invalidated our sense of ourselves and our bodies as whole and good. We then do not believe that our feelings or our physical senses or even our intuitive self is an accurate observer of reality. There may have been two options for us within our family: If there was no response to us, we may have become numb about any uncomfortable feeling. If a judgmental response occurred, we may have disavowed that feeling and now, ever after, believe that our true self does not contain it.

Our heritage then became an inner program of *governing principles*. Early repeated experiences in life become dictates in our minds thereafter. The original prejudices of our parents about life and about us became the organizing beliefs of our self-image, our life choices, our hope or despair about our potential for success at work and love. Beliefs that certain feelings are taboo, that we are inadequate, doomed to fail, bad, or even worthless, keep ringing true inside us no matter how successful we have been: if, because of early conditioning, I believe that nothing I do will amount to anything, I may say "Why bother?" to a creative challenge. I have handled such challenges before and I even know, rationally, that I can handle this one. Yet some other voice chimes in and says I cannot succeed, and I give that voice more credence than what the record shows. The "voice" is that of the projected parental shadow smuggled into me and now operative as my own shadow of self-doubt.

The self-negating beliefs behind our governing principles remain well-nigh indestructible throughout life. They come to haunt us especially in times of stress or change. They can become the architects of the *automatic* persona or ego reactions we keep engaging in. This is how the worst part of our parental shadow becomes our embedded reality. The work in this book; in therapy; and in an adult, understanding love can help us reverse this.

We easily imagine these archaic introjects to be the awful truth about us. We believe they tell us what we are. Our false self tailored by others and their negative shadow projections on us seem of equal weight with our true self. For example, we may recall the shadow voice, the edge of criticism or malice or inappropriate anger in parental responses to us. We hear it over and over and we imbibe its negative verdict un-wittingly. We then hear ourselves speaking in that same shadow tone to our children or friends. The shadow side of our parents, be it voice or gesture or mannerism or some other manifestation, leaves vestiges or even exact replicas of itself in us. It is so hard to believe that this is not our real self. Yet this is someone else's self that became encoded in us when we were not looking—and certainly were not being looked into with respectful love.

The results of the negative messages of childhood are unconscious organizing principles that direct our behavior and our way of seeing the world and ourselves. This legacy is what makes early childhood traumas so relentlessly insidious. Something was programmed into us that became *personal*, something designed so craftily as to prevail again and again in our life choices. This is something structured into us to sabotage, defeat, and even abolish our chances at happiness and individuation. Since this happened to us in the context of love, we remain loyal to it throughout life, resistant to chang-ing our self-defeating programming.

We are afraid that we will *not* repeat what we have been habituated to. An archaic tie endures and remains intact. This tie is predicated on the condition that we give up our deepest and dearest personal identity, our true self. Fidelity to our own most cherished needs, values, and wishes may have been equated early on with the loss of love. The only way to retain or recover the bond was to submit to the demolition and re-construction of ourselves. This is how the very core of life and self becomes awash with fear of being who we really are. A core belief in personal worthlessness will not yield to impressive successes in the course of one's career. Only sin-cere grief and intense work on oneself, usually in therapy, can reinstate such a dolefully usurped self. Meanwhile, the great pretender sits on the throne of power.

An example of the long-term and insidious effect of a self-negating organizing principle is in the habit Ozzie has. He continually criticizes others. He feels so inferior that he puts others down to raise himself up. This is an immature solution but it comes up automatically. It shows how trapped and defeated Ozzie feels. He is highly successful in his job, but that does not reverberate down into his psyche and raise his self-esteem. Ozzie is hearkening instead to his father's voice that told him over and over he could do nothing right. That is the voice that mutters to him now at a low but constant register. It is a deeply ingrained commentary on his inadequacy that cannot easily be reached, unseated, or dispelled. Ozzie criticizes his wife continually. He blames her for anything that goes wrong. She has matured over the years and he has not. She loves him but she is ready to leave him because she despairs of his ever changing or catching up.

Ozzie needs to see the origin and the ineffectiveness of his criticizing. This will, most likely, not happen out of the blue. It will take work, a work he may be too afraid even to begin. Yet Ozzie may also surprise his wife and admit: "If I use criticism to cover my own feelings of inadequacy, I must have work to do on myself. It will be scary but I have to get on with it or lose my relationship and remain unhappy personally." He will then need to be like the boy in the algebra class who has fallen behind his classmates: he does not criticize the subject or the teacher; he simply asks for tutoring to catch up. If Ozzie can be this matter-of-fact about his needs, he has a chance of maturing. It takes a lot of maturity even to see it this way. It takes a lot of letting go of ego to admit the problem is his and the work is his too.

The false self also operates in adolescence with peers who insist on strict conformity in dress, grooming, social and sexual habits, tastes, and so on as the price of acceptance. So where can we go to find a welcome for our true self? To whom can we turn to find full permission to be ourselves as we really are? We expect that permission from our first intimate partner. We arrive in the house of love hoping to discover the porridge we could find nowhere else. We go straight up to the table and say "Feed me!" We go straight up to the bed and say "Be just right for me!" And then we might fall asleep for a long time and wake up to find a bear in the house.

We ask to be loved by our partners completely, "as we are," and then we hide who we are. It is a great gamble to show one's true self. Only those who really love one another can do it, and even for them it is a scary proposition. If, from earliest times in my life, love could be negotiated only at the highest of prices—my true self—I may still be buying it at that original inflated price.

At the same time, in intimate relationships we ask our partner for authenticity. This seems like a simple request. But do we stop to realize that to ask for authenticity from those who were trained to hide their true self is to ask them to give up their only way of being loved? Since openness may always have been associated with the loss of approval, how can we expect ease in self-disclosure? "Who has not sat tensely before the rising of his own heart's curtain?" Rilke asks.

The true self is unassailable and yet vulnerable. It cannot succumb to victimization and it dares to show softness and openness. It is courageous enough to show itself to the world, whether or not it is approved. The false self is defensive, always on the lookout for the danger of another's dislike. Love from the true self is unconditional, but love from the false self is conditioned by fear. Love in the true self is from the heart chakra (bodily center of energy); love in the false self is in the lowest chakra, that of survival. A needy person is usually operating from a false self. A person who is whole and seeks relationship only for mutual enrichment is probably living mostly in his or her true self. Such a person may say this: "I can only be loved as who I am, not as who you need me to be. Love me as I am and you will find your best needs fulfilled."

The false self is like a caged bird. It can be taught to sing by the promise of approval and rewards. You will feed it and there will be songs aplenty. Oh yes, you can make it sing to you, but you cannot make it love you.

THE PRACTICE

• Using the following outline of a possible family scenario, what fits for you? Notice the connection between this and the early critical messages discussed previously.

> • I instinctively assert my right to grow. This includes my right to feel, to love, to stand up for myself, to separate, to individuate, to be sexual, to have opinions, to be different, and to look unacceptable.
> • This may be affirmed or negated by my parents.
> • If affirmed, I proceed to self-esteem.
> • If negated, I may feel an instinctive reaction of rage, grief, or fear.
> • These feelings become signals to my parents to get out of the way.
> • If they do not, I feel anxiety (the gap between self-expression and self-negation).

While holding my anxiety, I fight it out until I feel secure, or I turn against myself and repudiate self-expression as much too dangerous, and I join "them" against me. This is self-abandonment, and the rage, grief, and fear have been likewise repressed to prevent the punishment that may have resulted.

• Ask yourself these questions: How have I compromised my self-affirmation with self-negation and invested instead in a false version of myself, that is, in the ego ideal designed by others for me? Is the energy that formerly went into self-affirmation now going into living up to a parental ideal and not into living out my own identity? Is this how I lose my birthright? Is the best I can achieve a success at compromise, that is, self-defeat? (This makes success failure. What a grievous irony!)

• What are the governing principles of your life? Who instilled them and how? Consider the lists below and mark the entries that describe you. Use a practical real-life example of how you act out each of the items that apply to you. What are some practical ways in which you can further the process of self-expansion? Ask your partner or closest friend for specific input and suggestions from both sides of the chart. Recast the right side of the chart as affirmations and recite them each day: "I believe in my own potential," and so on.

Self-Limiting Characteristics	*Self-Expanding Characteristics*
Believe that all is fated	Believe in my potential beyond limit
Inherit traits, beliefs, and lifestyle from family and never examine them	Examine my inheritance and make choices pro or con
Positive shadow unintegrated	Release my potential
Negative shadow unintegrated out of fear or despair of finding any value in it	Valuable kernel to be found in negative traits that can be transformed, e.g., control becomes leadership

Childish reactions to the conditions of existence: not accepting what cannot be changed, blaming others	Adult responsiveness to conditions of existence: accepting what cannot be changed, changing what can be
Depleted by helplessness	Animated by resourcefulness
Deficiency needs are the focus	Growth needs are the focus
Stuck and unable to mobilize myself	Move on with access to outer and inner supports
Fight or deny the givens of my personality	Accept my givens and work creatively with them to forge my destiny
Caught in drama of fear and desire	Lively energy ever renewed
Marginal lifestyle practiced shamefully or mainstream lifestyle practiced fearfully	Marginal lifestyle practiced proudly or mainstream lifestyle practiced choicefully
Main goal: advancement of ego	Main joy: freedom from ego

• Each year, on your birthday, try an annual inventory of your psyche: examine all your beliefs, habits, attitudes, relationships, behaviors, and lifestyle choices.

  • Which ones continue to reflect your deepest needs, values, and wishes?
  • Which ones assist you and which ones deter you from fulfilling your unique potential?
  • Which ones help you show unconditional love, perennial wisdom, and healing power?
  • Which ones will you keep and which will you let go of?

When there is no conflict between your deepest needs, values, and wishes and the love, wisdom, and healing powers of the Self, you are spiritually mature.

• Ethan is a single thirty-five-year old man who enjoys going on-line. He has a penchant for cross-dressing and for unconventional sex. He is a well-known tax lawyer in the small town where he lives. His sexual habits and proclivities are completely secret. He has three separate identities in cyberspace: Admitting his gender, he is Jezebel, a lady who likes to be taken out on classy dates in the nearby metropolitan city. He is Mistress Fanny, the dominatrix with ropes and boots who spanks bad boys and leads them through other arousing and playful rituals. And he is Chuck, the single male who loves uninhibited sexual fun and erotic enjoyment with a variety of women.

Ethan is a healthy, functional, intelligent, and conscientious man who contributes greatly to society and never harms anyone. He has found a way to access adults who consent to his desires. No one seems hurt or endangered by his behavior. No money changes hands. He practices and insists upon safe sex only.

Ethan says that the Web has provided space for him to explore aspects of himself that have been socially and culturally proscribed. He is psychologically literate and sees his choices as a way of exploring the positive side of his sexual shadow. He believes himself to be integrating disparate elements of his sexuality as the pathway to his own diverse identity as a human being. To Ethan, being "a man" is a construct: physical, social, cultural, religious, and political. Being human for him means deconstructing those persona demands in favor of his own deepest needs, values, and wishes. The most convenient way he has found to put this into practice is to have other identities on-line and to act them out in safe, responsible, and playful ways.

Ethan has noticed a change in himself as a result of these practices. He recalls that he felt uncomfortable in the past when his sister asked him to hold her purse in a store or walk her poodle: "not a man's dog." This ego persona is no longer inhibiting him; he is no longer threatened by what passersby may think of him. He also is wise enough to keep his sex life discreet. This is not because of shame but because he knows that society, especially in his town, is not ready for his marginal lifestyle.

Ethan occasionally experiences guilt. This seems to be a guilt by association with his necessarily surreptitious behavior. He sees this as normal given society's tyranny over the consequences of adult choices. His guilt also seems normal to Ethan in the light of his early upbringing and its cellular effects, which do not seem to yield even to a three-digit IQ. He knows his archaic beliefs do not make a case for authentic reprehensibility on his part. Ethan takes guilt for granted as part of the flora of the middle-class psyche he inherited. At the same time, Ethan refuses to believe that as a heterosexually oriented male he has to limit himself to missionary sex. He knows that his male-shaped body does not intrinsically mean that he cannot wear a dress. He knows who he is and wants to live that way, and he has found a way to do it without losing his freedom, his job, or his self-respect.

Are these aspects of Ethan false selves or only playful expeditions into the unexplored and variegated corners of his sexuality? What is your opinion of Ethan's lifestyle? Is your opinion a moral judgment of others' legitimate choices? Is it fear based? Are you in any way threatened by Ethan's behavior? If you were to generate new identities in your journal, in your imagination, in your fantasies, or in cyberspace, what would they be?

FREEDOM FROM FALSENESS

Could it be that finding yourself does not require the study of a thousand books, the destruction and reconstruction of yourself, the pleading for forgiveness for how bad you have been, the submission of your will to someone else? Could it be that all it takes is loving what you love without shame?

How do I know if I am a "nice person"? Within me is a deceit more cunning than any Judas kiss. I have become an expert at appearances. I know exactly which face will get me what I want. Only when my niceness has no such motive, when there is nothing to gain, when I am not trying to impress or manipulate, can I trust it as real. When I let go of all that, I am just myself making choices that please or displease, making mistakes that raise eyebrows or make heads bow. When I let go of it all and let myself be seen as I am without even noticing whether or how I am seen, my real identity comes to light, or rather lets the light through. Then and only then am I an honest spaciousness not filled in with attributes that aim to please. The self is true, moreover, when it includes all the opposites on the human spectrum. Accepting that I am nice sometimes and mean at other times is a greater indicator of authenticity than is a firmly embedded and reliable niceness.

Remember what your parents kept telling you to be like. Now picture how your life has been with that and would have been without it. Take back something they took from you.

It is becoming clear that most of what I think I am is a collection of others' beliefs about me that are now internalized and habitual. I am still adding layers by reacting to others. Am I a "king of shreds and patches"? Society rewards those most split and disconnected, the best at mask-making. I peel myself down to my own reality only when I stop paying attention to other people's reactions. It is difficult for any of us, no matter how healthy, to let go of the definitions that others have of us.

When those moments of utter authenticity slip into my

life, I am all one piece, a seamless self, truly alive. Only as myself is true aliveness possible. I am then an unconditional moment of the life force not filled in by beliefs or habits that are meant to win approval. I then have no image to uphold, no impressions to make or correct, no position to defend. As long as my identity is an image, a position, a list of character-istics, I am a pawn of circumstances and persons. As long as I am filled in with others' wishes come true, I am not myself, and so not really in touch with my lively energy. Enlighten-ment, nirvana, and my true self emerge when I do not want to be anyone else.

Joseph Campbell comments: "The part of us that wants to become is fearless." Fear lurks in the shadow of our ego, but fearlessness lives expectantly in our positive shadow. There is something irrepressible and exuberant in each of us: a steadfast desire to become all that we can be. Something instinctive and more powerful than the fear of not being ap-proved hangs on stubbornly inside us. It is our lively energy, the heart of our positive shadow, what Gerard Manley Hop-kins calls "the dearest freshest deep-down things." This lively energy is our personal and unique potential, and it is the very same as that of the universe. It wants to open and display how full it is of joy and love and of that rascal ego's lost face.

The meaning of *meaningful* changes as we cease living from a false-self stance and enter the true-self space. In the psychological world, something is meaningful when it has an impact on us and evokes feeling or leads to insight, creates change, helps us reach a goal, fulfills a desire, or scares us. In the spiritual realm, something is meaningful in two ways: First, it grants us contact with the inner aliveness of someone or something or ourselves. Second, we experience spiritual meaning when the transpersonal world breaks through and into our personal world and an axis is fashioned between ego and Self. Such a breakthrough means that we give up our fear-based core beliefs about control and entitlement and drop the masks that have been designed so reliably to conceal us. It means wanting every move we make, every word we utter, every unguarded moment to reveal us, ruthlessly, as we are. *Can I let myself do that?*

Only the real I has life force. The strength to face things and handle them with my unique gifts is precisely what my life force is about. Without it, I am at the mercy of circumstances and have to depend on others to bail me out. Being at the mercy of others' reactions is a two-edged sword, with both sides wounding me. I lose myself and I lose my power; I live in reaction to others and I live in dependency on others. *I take back my power to fulfill my purpose.*

I am ultimately unknown to myself. What I call my real self may be only a catalog of my needs and choices. The self I refer to as true or false is really only an ego, a convenient launching pad for my journey, beyond it and with it, to wholeness. From the Zen perspective, I actually have no solid self, true or false, but am pure space. My work is to let go of the belief in or need for a separate self. To speak of the true self as *openness* is my Western way of acknowledging the space that Oriental masters discovered. My psychological and spiritual work meet in this space. *The horseman of enlightenment meets me there.*

Letting go of my false self, the ego, is a terrifying project. It means nothing less than taking the chance that I will be no one and that no one will love me.

It will mean the disintegration of a wall around an unprotected space.

It will entail the end of all the winsome charms; the winning words; the disguised feelings; the old familiar, reliable defenses.

It will mean admitting my superficiality in favor of a life-force authenticity that makes me no promises that I will be liked or loved.

With this embrace of the simple "what is" of my identity, I enter a deep and easy poise, the poise of someone with nothing left to protect or escape. In this surrender to my true self, I am suddenly released from the fears and strategies that have been my companions for too long. I can then show the world my true self, the only self that can be intimate, the only self that can let love through, the only self that is really living.

> *Often rebuked, yet always back returning*
> *To those first feelings that were born with me . . .*
> *I'll walk where my own nature would be leading . . .*
> *Where the wild wind blows on the mountainside.*
>
> —CHARLOTTE BRONTË

THE PRACTICE

• How can you disidentify with the false self? Here are the steps: Identify with the opposite of your usual style, go out of character. Choose what you want instead of what is habitual or proper. Give up what has always worked to get what you wanted. Give up every smile and charm of the false self. Then decide what you want to keep, out of fun, not out of fear. There is usually great humor in going out of character.

• "The best I can be" may mean having to prove I am right or on top of things; that is a burden. A good motive can be used by ego for false purposes. Not perfectionism but humanity and flexibility can become the meaning of "my very best." Then my concern is not with doing it all right but with acknowledging my limits and pressing on cheerfully. I am a spectrum of abilities and disabilities, and that is to be taken into account in my definition of *best*. How does this fit for me? Am I too hard on myself? What will I lose if people know I am not perfect? What is the fear that supports and upholds my false self? I choose to show everyone my fallibility. I choose not to apologize if I miss the mark. I am authentically imperfect. "The imperfect is our paradise," says Wallace Stevens.

Am I clinging to a nirvana myth: someday the world (or this place, household, person, . . .) will be perfect? If I am, what part of the shadow am I denying? Have I reconciled myself to the conditions of existence with all their cycles of imperfection, approximation, and disappointment? Am I fearing the grief I would feel if I reconciled myself to the inadequacies I see in myself and in everyone and everything around me? Do I have a heart large enough to forgive it all and let go? As long as there is any person, place, or thing that I believe will solve everything for me, make it all come out right for me, or bring perfect closure to things for me, I am not in line for enlightenment. As long as it will be perfect there, or with her, or with this, I am running from this and now and you and me. As long as I still believe it will all be exactly as it should be someday, I am denying that the life span of the shadow is the same as that of humankind. An all-embracing yes is the only path to whatever light awaits me.

Contemplation comes from a Latin word that refers to priests performing auguries in an unroofed sacred precinct or temple. They examined the entrails of a rooster to foretell or prescribe a future course of action. In other words, they looked into the heart of nature for a divine revelation about human destiny. Notice the equation: natural, divine, human. After centuries of contemplation, mystics have realized that nature's cycle of dying and then rising *is* consciousness. Consciousness is not a separate entity facing the conditions of existence; it *is* the conditions. How do I remain wrapped in habits that are maladaptive to the conditions of a shifting and loss-laden existence? Am I ready to befriend the conditions of existence as I do my shadow? Can my yes extend into my past, through this present moment, and into the future? Try this affirmation: "I say yes to the past as it was. I say yes to the present as it is. I say yes to the future as it chooses to be."

• Consider psychotherapy as an assisting force in the work of shadow integration. Here is a way to see its value and decide whether it may be fitting for you either now or in the future:

Every shadow issue has a past: a childhood fear that drove the quality in our shadow into hiding. A shadow issue has a present: it is being projected onto someone else and denied in ourselves. The future of a shadow issue is in the opening of ourselves to the truth. By befriending the shadow, we come upon a new way of being in the world, more conscious and more in touch with our full potential.

The goal of therapy is to become an adult who is happy and effective at loving. There is a healthy ego in all of us by which we think clearly, show feelings appropriately, and relate skillfully to other people. Our ego can also be dysfunctional when it acts out of fear or goes out of control by becoming attached or addicted. It then panics, lashes out, expects too much, overdramatizes feelings, and believes itself entitled to special treatment by everyone. Psychological health means letting go of our neurotic ego and living more and more from our functional ego. This takes work, and in therapy we can learn to do it.

We can choose to live our lives day in and day out with no consciousness of our shortcomings and conflicts or of how to become more adept at loving. Or we can choose conscious work on ourselves, to see the areas in ourselves that need healing or opening and follow through with a resourceful plan. We have two choices: we can live in reaction to each life event, exercising damage control at best. Or we can learn from each event and find therein new ways to grow. Creativity is about causing. To live reactively is to be an effect.

Resourceful plans come from psychological work on ourselves. There are many forms of psychological work: problem solving, developing assertiveness, processing experiences, mourning, changing behavior, building self-esteem, facilitating catharsis of feelings, dream work, restructuring one's daily life, and so on. This work leads to insight and to change when we are ready for it. We can trust that we will see only what we are truly ready to face. A loving balance between psyche and circumstances lets us know our work only when we have the power to do it.

The method is to address, process, and resolve your conflict or problem:

Addressing means looking at the wound, admitting it is there, taking responsibility for it as yours, and assessing its seriousness and its effects on your life and on other people.

Processing means feeling the feelings that your issue evokes, seeing how they fit with your childhood experiences, looking at your needs and frustrations, and even noticing how you may be benefiting from your problem and so are reluctant to change it.

Resolving means finding a way to change something and bring closure to it so that happiness and health may result. This may mean doing things differently, accepting what cannot be changed, or letting go of something altogether. Resolution leads to restructuring your life more satisfactorily.

You know you have processed something successfully when you can state the result or realization in one simple sentence using one- or two-syllable words:

• He's growing up and I won't let go: My work is to update my way of being a parent.

• She has gone and I am trying to get back at her for it: My work is to let her go.

• This child is now in my life and I am fighting that fact: My work is to let him in.

• I'm unhappy and I can't or won't do anything about it: My work is get the help I need to deal with things and get on with life.

• Do I also have a spiritual program? This may include such practices as mindfulness, meditation, yoga, prayer. Do I see evidence within myself of letting go of ego, growing in compassion, and becoming a source of healing to others and to myself? Do I notice myself becoming a peacemaker?

Answer the above questions in your journal in an honest way. Then share what you have written with the person closest to you and ask for feedback. Finally, write a letter describing what your program is to the person you admire most in the world. It is up to you to mail it or not. Write an answer from that person to yourself.

8

Our Shadow Befriended

WHERE OPPOSITES STAND

For order and convenience, the rational ego mind separates and categorizes opposites: oil and water, food and poison, fire and ice, money and scrap paper, ballet and bowling. The healthy ego is challenged by true opposites.

Out of fear and suspicion, the irrational neurotic ego divides and antagonizes opposites: blacks and whites, rich and poor, familiar and unknown, superior and inferior. This ego is threatened by apparent opposites.

The Self, the archetype of the conjunction of opposites, out of love and wisdom, lets opposites stand as they are and reconciles them, northern blue and southern gray, Christ and "the least of my brethren," Buddha and all ordinary beings, mindful sitting in the midst of neurotic crisis, persona and shadow.

All three elements of the psyche have a built-in natural way of dealing with opposites. All three find their place in the course of a normal human life. To befriend the shadow means using the intelligent filing system of the healthy ego to find a creative use for the divisive inclinations of the dysfunctional ego. This enterprise will require the graceful transforming power of the Self for its completion.

The nature of wholeness is to contain disparate ingredients. The wholeness of our psyche consists in all its dimensions being operative. The wholeness of our work is in combining our psychological ego efforts with the spiritual practices and graces of the Self: "Where could we find two better hemispheres, without sharp north, without declining west?" asked John Donne.

The key to one part of the practice of befriending the shadow is in the phrase "let opposites stand as they are and reconcile them." When we accept opposing forces in ourselves, we find a path between them and we keep the best of each. The image of this is in the bride and groom standing apart and yet together at a wedding ceremony. This is the first way to integrate our positive and negative shadow sides.

The key to the second way to befriend the shadow is found in the sentence, "Use the intelligent filing system of the healthy ego to find a creative use for the divisive inclinations of the dysfunctional ego." This is accomplished by finding the positive *counterpart* of a negative characteristic; we find the best of the bad, the gold in the lead. The image of this is the signing of a peace treaty and the handshake of enemies.

In the section "Finding the Best of the Bad," to follow later, we look at the second way. In this section, we explore the first way, letting opposites stand.

Either-ors do not hold and embrace opposites: "In this relationship I have no freedom and so I will leave it." Compare that mutually exclusive style with this one: "I want to stay in this relationship, and at the same time, I want to pursue my interests freely, so I will negotiate for what I want." Now I stand steady *and* run with the ball. This is an example of what is meant by reconciling opposites. I hold both facts, dismissing neither, and find a third option, one that holds both and dismisses neither.

Hegel said, "The owl of Minerva flies at dusk." Wisdom

appears between day and night, light and dark. Accepting inner oppositions brings us to the *realm of the between,* where a healing third arises, the counterpart of both polarities. For instance, I accept the fact that I am sometimes rational and sometimes irrational. Between those is a healing counterpart of each of them, the nonrational. The nonrational is healing (balancing) because it enlists and opens our intuitive, poetic powers. The image of the two crucified thieves, with Jesus in the center, is another example: opposites and a healing third.

To balance opposites is to locate that ground zero where we do not take sides. It is normal for the psyche to bear opposing tensions; it is, in fact, made up of opposites. The creative and imaginative courage it takes to hold our opposites comfortably is precisely what leads to activating our potential. Our positive shadow is thus integrated automatically with this practice. The style of "both . . . and" arouses talent for inventing. If I choose to negotiate freedom in my relationship, for instance, I will more easily access the creativity to do it.

Jung suggests containing and holding our opposites through active imagination, a technique of dialoguing between tensions, even personifying them. In his view, a transcending of opposites is impossible and dangerous, since ongoing tension of opposites is a crucial ingredient of creativity. In this, he differs from the Buddhist and other liberation perspectives that propose a transcending of opposites in favor of a unity. In the work presented in this book, both views can succeed: hold the tensions long enough and they will find a point of reconciliation. Everything requires an opposite to exist as itself, but everything requires reconciliation to fulfill itself.

Our attractions and repulsions, our opposites, reveal us to ourselves. By analyzing our fascinations and antipathies we find the far-flung and exiled facets of our personality. What fascinates us usually holds our positive shadow and what repels us usually holds our negative shadow. Both these opposing directions in us lead to the same threshold of self-realization. Libido (psychic energy) is generated by playfulness with opposites. Psychically, energy flow is what counts, not whether it is negative or positive. For instance, our energy may move in the direction of fear or of desire: "I fear her coming back and I want her back." The work in such a quandary is not to choose one over the other but to hold each option for as long as it takes to see the wisdom in each. Then I may more intelligently choose the one with more wisdom and more love. The healthy choice occurs in the context of welcome rather than dismissal.

The psyche requires and subsists on a union of opposites. When one polarity gains ascendancy, the repressed one clamors for attention and can catch us off guard. Our ego prefers to maintain divisions and dualisms. Yet opposites constitute the true geography of the inner life of us humans. If I am committed to nonviolence, I can be sure that my capacity for violence remains. If I am afraid, I can be sure I have a courage that matches my fear. If I feel hopelessness, there is hope.

To integrate opposites in ourselves, it is necessary to close the gap between them. This means not projecting one of them onto others and not overidentifying with either one of them. As long as I am all good and my partner is all bad, there is no hope for integration. We have inside us what we are in opposition to outside us. To know ourselves is to accept any shape of the shadow as possible in us. We do not know ourselves until there is nothing we cannot imagine ourselves to do or be. We often identify with one opposite and project the other: I am submissive and I see my partner as controlling (and allow her to be). If my partner and I separate, my other side, the dominating side, is restored, and I may not like myself so much. I discover that I am controlling after all.

Our persona and our shadow are on a seesaw. When ego appears through its persona, the shadow disappears, and vice-versa. What is the fulcrum? Paradoxically, it is the gap, the spaciousness that is the true Self. This is why our wholeness consists in containing and reconciling opposites.

To face a decision and sit with an either-or is not to be indecisive. That is how soul making happens. The young maiden Psyche was commanded by Aphrodite to sort out an immense mound of grains. Psyche felt herself incapable of completing the task and yet could not leave it. She simply sat and stared at the menacing pile. Soon the grains were sorted by ants from under the earth, that is, from her own unconscious. When we hold the opposites of *ready to do* and *unable to do yet*, something shifts in us from a source beyond us. The spiritual solution arises precisely from the fulcrum, the Self, between the opposites we are holding in balance. To maintain our opposites is thus to return to the Source; this is why it is soul work. Staying with the tension of the warring oppositions engenders spiritual consciousness and healthy ego character.

In the Psyche story, we see the important role nature plays in the unfolding of a human destiny. Soul making is not a solely human enterprise. It includes and requires nature. In fact, this is how we assist nature in its spiritual evolution. By our attention to soul, the imaginal world, nature joins in on the individuation process. Images themselves individuate when we honor them and work with them to find our path to wholeness. Ultimately, there is no individual path, only a world path with personal trails to it.

How do we know if in such holding of our tensions we are not simply becoming stuck? Containing tensions in a healthy way inspires lively energy. We feel the *moving* reality of our predicament. Stuckness, on the other hand, will have a flat-line, motionless quality. We know we are on the right track when we have an intuitive sense that something will come of the containing, that something new is gestating within us. It is stress-free like a necessary and acceptable phase in a process. In stuckness there is no such serenity or optimism. How can we tell the difference between self-restorative abiding in the midst of turmoil and unproductive stuckness?

Calm Abiding	*Passivity*
Energy flows	Energy is stopped
Tuned in	Tuned out
Expanded	Contracted
Engaged	Detached
Accepting of what is	Denying of what is
Poised for action	On hold
Resource based	Fear based
Symbol: spiral	Symbol: loop

Trungpa Rinpoche wrote: "Hold the sadness and pain of Samsara [attachment to the passing world] in your heart and at the same time the power and vision of the great Eastern sun. Only then can the warrior make a proper cup of tea." Living between the rising and the setting sun, holding them both in view and cherishing them both equally, is mindfulness: simultaneously taking hold (rising sun) and letting go (setting sun). We do this with every breath, and mindfulness is a breath meditation.

Opposites become complementary when we look for a way to assimilate and balance them, striking an agreement between them so that they can coexist peacefully. When we do not choose sides in ourselves but enlist all sides, opposites open into coordinated counterparts. They stand, then, not in contention with one another but in cooperative relation to one another. Wholeness happens in direct proportion to this balancing of opposites. The Self makes friends of the ego's dark and light contenders in the psychic ring. Their tension does not cease but they become more creatively engaged in the central project of life, an axis of ego and Self powers. An example of this might be two boxers who go on feeling competitive after the fight but also work together teaching ghetto kids how to fight fairly.

Games in ancient times were a metaphor for the uniting of opposites: two teams are in competition, yet both remain on one field and both remain together at the end of the game. A sports event is also an alchemical vessel in the sense that it has consistent rules and a defined space in which it is played. Within it ingredients mix and something new—better skills, more mutual respect—results. For the ancients, it was not considered worthwhile to win all the time. Defeat was necessary to experience the full range of human experience. The result of the visits to both sides of the laurel is the victory of finding full consciousness.

The horseman in Changling's poem, an assisting force for us, connects sunset west and sunrise east in his ride. He does not linger on one side only. He waits for space to open in our psyche, "endless wastes where no one goes," and then he enters at his own pace and by his own choice: grace to us, not ego in us.

HONORING BOTH SIDES OF THE COIN OF OURSELVES

*Conscious and unconscious have no clear demarcations
. . . rather, the psyche is a conscious/unconscious whole.*

—C. G. JUNG

The psyche seems structured so that our lively energy originates within and between our inner opposites. Electric current is the lively energy that moves back and forth between positive and negative poles. Any attraction or repulsion in us constellates its opposite. When we allow this bond, we are truly alive. The work is simple. For every attraction I feel, I consciously acknowledge a repulsion and vice-versa. When I acknowledge that I love and hate the same person, I realize that our bond thrives on both love *and* hate. They both contribute to the liveliness of the connection as the positive and negative poles of electricity make for the juice in a wire. And they are just as matter-of-fact as that.

We see the combination of time and timelessness in high moments of spiritual, aesthetic, or erotic pleasure. We harmonize with eternal rhythms in the fleeting song of a thrush. We know of our own mortality when we stand in front of a mirror, yet we sense immortal longings when we stand in a redwood forest. We feel an abiding calm "in the solemn shadowy cedars and the ghostly pines so still," as Whitman writes. In every instance of true aliveness, the opposites meet. To contact timelessness within our mortal selves means that *we have it in us.* This is how we know we are more than we seem. Befriending the shadow is truly about discovering the meaning of being human and the meaning of being divine.

In the first forty years of life, the ego establishes and maintains itself by definite choices: "I am this and not that." The "not that" goes into the shadow. In the second half of life, the "not that" has to be acknowledged as part of "this." Such conscious reconnecting of our opposing sides is the work of befriending the shadow. Our first task was to separate opposites and set our boundaries. That was a legitimate enterprise. The mature spiritual task is to combine and compose what we had earlier divided. That is a holy enterprise.

Conscious acceptance of opposites in ourselves brings us

to the work of dealing with each of them. For instance, the ego-Self axis calls for conscious acknowledgment and a plan for the good and evil in our self-portrait. The alternative is a Dorian Gray who splits his shadow from his persona and so is destroyed by it. Dr. Jekyll was destroyed in the same way. Both chose to separate rather than face their inner opposites; neither did the serenely satisfying practice of befriending. Good is worked with by bringing it out; evil is worked with by facing it in ourselves and refusing to act it out.

Here is what health sounds like in the integrated shadow world: "I am this *and* that. Where that is, there this is too. I take back all my projections upon other humans. Everything human is what I am. I was here and they were out there; now we stand side by side." Jung says in this respect: "The one after another is a bearable prelude to the side by side. . . . The view that good and evil are spiritual forces outside us and that we are caught in the conflict between them is more bearable by far than the insight that the opposites are the ineradicable and indispensable preconditions of all psychic life."

In the course of my life I feel drawn sometimes to good and sometimes to evil. I may deny my inclination toward evil. The inflated ego wants to banish badness lest it lose approval and self-respect. It does this by projecting it outward as scapegoating, blame, and hatred. This is how retaliation became so important an arrow in the ego's quiver. (Quiver indeed, since it based ultimately on fear of acknowledging its own humble ownership of all the ordinary human foibles.)

The older we get, the less adroit we are at forgetting or denying our perversities. Our memory involuntarily brings back to us a medley of images and recollections of how bad, how selfish, how petty, how mean-spirited we were in our past life. Specific instances come up in our minds out of nowhere: things we are not proud of, memories that sting and make us squirm: "How could I have done that?" Yet part of embracing the shadow is precisely the unappealing task of not forgetting our personal history and its mistakes. Those memories are meant to ground us in humility. They remind us that we are frail humans like everyone we blame. Regrets do not help us, but empathy for ourselves and a plan to change does. We can always be cheered up by the words of Antonio Machado: "Honey bees in my heart have made honey out of my old failures."

The work is to remember our common history too. Actually, we *cannot* forget the Holocaust and Vietnam. They ground us by reminding us of the collective shadow and of our participation in it. The work is to feel our anger and sadness and then to forgive but never to forget. Refusal to forgive only embitters and injures us, a way for the violence to go on.

I am on my way to the store to buy food for the dinner I will be preparing tonight for a friend I have invited to my house. I am planning to buy some trout. On the way, out of nowhere, I remember a time a few years ago when I was stingy toward another friend, and I feel regretful and sad. I follow this three-step program: feel, voice over, and make up for: I let myself feel the sadness about my past inadequacy as fully as I can. I access my kindly avuncular voice: "Yes, you were stingy then and you regret it. Everyone is stingy sometimes. There is a fear of giving behind stinginess. You have worked on that in yourself and you are changing. Get on with life and put the past behind you. What can you do today to compensate for this old failure?" I arrive at the supermarket and buy lobster instead of trout. Like the bees, I have made honey.

All the parts that come with our nature and with our life story are useful for our unfolding destiny, just as our left hand is useful even though we will always be right-handed.

The work is to free ourselves from dualistic division, to integrate all that happens without negating any of it.

Sometimes the darkest dimensions of our behavior may have to emerge before our fragmented self can find coherence. Our task in life is not to crush anything in us but to welcome it and thereby locate its other side. Our self-centeredness, for instance, may be our only way of shoring up a flagging and tentative sense of self. We allow for this and accommodate it. At the same time, we look for its opposite, selflessness. Each of us is a tryst of opposites, so every negative quality has a corresponding positive one that waits for a chance to be blessed and to bless.

Wholeness, by definition, can never mean a cancellation of one side of us in favor of another. Nor could it be an argument with the fact that we contain all human possibilities, no matter how unappealing. Wholeness is an embrace of all that is in us and an enthusiasm for working with it all to mine and refine its buried gold. How? We give rein to each side safely, responsibly, and conscientiously. This leads to reconciling our inner oppositions and lets them take their rightful place in our psychic landscape. Yes, that pungent skunk belongs there as much as this redolent rose!

A long history of obedience may have disabled the self-trust it takes to pull this off. Authorities and institutions, such as the family and religion, may have insisted that we repudiate or overcome certain of our natural inclinations. Impolite or irreverent qualities have become highly suspect in the civilized city of ourselves. Yet we can make room for all our inner-city population of characteristics no matter how lowly or scary. Each has a right to belong, no matter how it is shaped or colored. Befriending both sides of everything in ourselves is the royal road to freedom from fearing ourselves, our impulses, our wishes, our needs, our deepest longings, the very building blocks of our identity.

We may abhor the emergence of *selfishness* in our behavior. Such abhorrence may arise from a fear of losing face or approval, not from a discerning belief that it is truly bad. Fear is a signal that we are in the court of human-made, not nature-made, judgment. The shadow of spirituality is in the ego-designed, limited view that allows only one side of the coin of ourselves to have value, for instance, selflessness. It is then unworthy of us to devote any time to self-love or sensuous pursuits, let alone sexual ones. This turns spirituality into self-sacrifice, the old familiar religious injunction we have been trying to get away from. Sacrifice in the context of shadow work consists in renouncing the pretentious claims of ego and its successes at control and entitlement. Victor White's phrase fits: "totally dispossessed of what possesses us."

Yet nothing in the healthy psyche indicates that selflessness and denial of body pleasure are the only legitimate options. A spirituality that pits us against nature or our own nature cannot be authentic. Since we probably were not trained to discern and evaluate with naturally based criteria, we may have accepted the dichotomy easily. Yet all the mystics agree that a true spirituality is never a disembodied one. Godliness has to have bodiliness, as the incarnation motif in so many religious traditions so clearly illustrates.

Can I say the self-centered part of me that always asks for something in return is as good as the selfless part of me that asks for nothing in return? Why not? Reciprocity is not an evil but the tidy completion of a human circle. Both the yin and the yang are worthy of their place in that circle. Both sides of ourselves are related as figure to ground, another name for the reconciling of opposites. Nature is replete with examples of both giving and getting in the symbiotic ecology that surrounds and upholds us. Giving selflessly and receiving selfishly make evolution possible. If one side were to be omitted, there would be no world.

Any spiritual view that denies, omits, or disparages our variegated humanness cannot be fitting for beings like us who combine matter and spirit, psyche and body, male and female, submission and dominance, and all the other sets of apparent opposites. Such an approach would only serve to deform, distort, or disable us, not to transform us. A trustworthy spirituality embraces all that is in us, takes our whole nature into account, makes room for it hospitably and enthusiastically. Why were we given a nature if we were meant to suppress or destroy it?

Saint Thomas says that grace builds on nature. A healthy spirituality contains, holds, embraces, and accepts all the forces in us with a loving gusto: selfishness and selflessness, light and shadow, unconditional love and conditional commitment, surrender and control. These are not mutually exclusive polarities. They are embedded in one another and work dialectically together en route to a synthesis. Selfishness and selflessness can coexist in us as they do in children who progress from one- and two-syllable words to three- and four-syllable words and yet still retain the original rudimentary words in their vocabulary. One does not replace the other but makes room for it.

Unconditional love occurs only in time and between humans, so it has conditions on it from the start. To insist that love be only unconditional actually places the hardest condition on it. Love is fostered in the human context of reconciling opposites. It gladly contains giving and receiving, surrender and control, openness and boundaries, closeness and distance, the essential interstices of intimacy. Such acceptance of all our life conditions gathers a living, season-respecting wardrobe of relating. Purely unconditional love is a special dress for a special occasion, not everyday clothing. It is meant to be a miraculous *moment,* not an unceasing style.

Our work is to love unconditionally and at the same time to set firm boundaries on how we show it. This means *both* unconditional love *and* conditional commitment. "I love you unconditionally in my heart but if you are an alcoholic who abuses me and our children and you refuse help, you are no longer welcome here. I set that condition not because I love you less but because I am committed more to ensuring a healthy and safe life for me and our children than to satisfying you." To choose either one *or* the other is half love.

From the holding and interplay of opposites will come a healing third, a reconciling image, a counterpart of both. This is how, for instance, an ugly *selfishness* may become a beautiful self-nurturance. When we experience (hold) unconditional love and at the same time take care of ourselves, we then see and create an image of the two sides working in unison. This is the healing third that amalgamates, assimilates, and consolidates both sides of us. We may then even dream a reconciling image: a woman working in a soup kitchen who is setting aside time to have lunch.

To mediate any conflict, it is important not to demonize one side or divinize another side. To see the value in both sides sets the stage for resolution. Two people are arguing at opposite ends of a spectrum and cannot agree. They are fighting in an aggressive or even an abusive way. I step in and help them work out a compromise: I help each of them respect the other. I do not choose sides myself but find the value in each side. I help them see a both-and instead of an either-or and thereby the antagonists find an amicable solution to their problem. In other words, I become the peacemaker. When I become a force of reconciliation, I am acting out the transcendent function of the psyche, the work of the Holy Spirit, the healing third, who broods over the chaos to create an ordered world: "In the hour of reconciliation, many marvels will occur," says the Rosarium of the alchemists.

Real intimacy between people includes both *surrender and control.* To be open is to be vulnerable, touched by what the other does, affected by the other. How can I say I love you and not be affected by what you do? To love a child is to feel the child's pain. This does not diminish the adulthood of a parent or jeopardize the parent's freedom. When we have no boundaries at all, we become vulnerable to predation. But occasional control and a push by someone we love and trust can open new worlds for us. This may be precisely what it takes for us to make new discoveries about how far we can stretch. Visits to both shores, surrender and control in daily living, do not hurt us, only lingering on one shore too long can do that.

The opposites in human development are not, for instance, dependency and independence but infantile dependency and adult interdependence. Human openness is in the constant interplay and balance between control and surrender, no and yes, tried and true and experimentation, liberality and conservatism. In this we are not totally compelled by one nor totally repelled by the other. In fact, the boundaries of a person who has dipped into the waters of surrender are more trustworthy than those of one who has kept dry and under constant self-surveillance or in safe self-control.

When we are only in the surrender mode, we may become attached to the one to whom we have surrendered. Surrender alone cannot adequately serve the human enterprise of freedom. Neither can dominance alone be adequate to the human need for respectful love. Attachment and detachment are meant to interplay continually. Detachment does not mean disengaged or unrelated. It means no longer dependently related. This style of living takes vigilant work, but our nature joins in, since we are calibrated to let all the opposites in us merge as figure and ground, each taking its turn to come into focus. Something bigger than our ego wants us to be whole. It is the urgent yearning of the psyche to fulfill itself and us. Jung says, "There is in the psyche a process that seeks its own goal [wholeness] no matter what the external factors may be." The healthy ego rides in the direction in which the horse is going. Yes, it is the horse in Changling's poem.

Regarding the *suffering* and *happiness* distinction, suffering seems necessary if there is to be any motivation to move out of our comfort zones and initiate our journey in the world. Any good story needs some scenes of suffering and of confrontation with the dragon shadow to enhance the plot and develop the hero's character. Yet happiness is equally necessary in life, otherwise there might be no desire to stay committed where we are and conserve what is good. The lifestyle of a victim or martyr does not allow for the serene enjoyment of well-being, the atmosphere so necessary for self-restoration and a recovery of powers.

READY FOR A LOOK IN THE MIRROR

Health can only manifest in a realistic context, one that is ever respectful of our nature and of nature itself. "Either . . . or" is an ego invention. In our nature and in nature, all oppositions are fired with an unflagging appetite for mutuality and convergence, standing and joining, as bride and groom do. In the higher Self, the archetype of the sacred marriage of opposites, there is only "both . . . and." Such including is also our way of marrying into nature's evolutionary style, summons, and momentum; fire burns the forest and that releases the growth of new and stronger trees.

In the story of Beauty and the Beast we see this model of human destiny. They are not discrete people but metaphorically the two faces of one person. Beauty was in the Beast and vice-versa. Their marriage is the symbol of the potential of each side of human nature to be wedded to the other. Every beastly quality waits for recognition. This is how life is in death and death is in life: paradoxical but well-matched partners waiting for the necessary, and desired, nuptials to begin.

The shadow practices that follow trace out specific and practical ways to accept both sides of everything in ourselves. Shadow work is how we make friends with, marry, the attributes that we have so strongly despised or admired in others so that they can be finally acknowledged as our personal experience. It out there has become I in here.

We repress the shadow because we fear it. We may feel that same fear as we approach the shadow and attempt to befriend it. As the powers of the shadow become more accessible to us and more useful on our journey toward wholeness, we discover more lively energy than ever because we are recovering the liveliest dimensions of our psyche.

The work first involves calling our shadow by name and giving it a face. We are then capable of assimilating its tamed qualities rather than overreacting to them with violence or denial. Wearing animal skins or masks in primitive tribes (or even now) is symbolic of shadow work. Shamans were guided by animal spirits. Unruly instincts come under the control of the healthy ego and enter its service. The shadow is ultimately meant to contribute to the best interests of the Self: to bring more love, wisdom, and healing to ourselves and others. This is how embracing the shadow helps us fulfill our destiny.

Repression binds psychic energy. We cannot relate to what we are absorbed by. The dragon who eats us cannot also be our dinner guest. The work is in making friends with what we hate in ourselves and others and acknowledging what is best in the worst. This is how we awaken our full potential and release our creativity. Without embracing my shadow, I am sleeping, that is, unconscious, on a diamond mine while complaining about the smell of coal. The work is to go down into it and find *what wants to be found.*

The disgusting can never be integrated. We have to see the beauty in our beast. We know the work is proceeding when what upset us before now informs and touches us. The ugly prime matter of our shadow is contained and cooked alchemically as we become witnesses of its mutations and allow it to expand, trusting a golden result. Sometimes all it takes is carrying it, as the ancient mariner carried the albatross. Grant hospitality to the dark guest and he will share his magic with you. The more you look, the more you find. What seems most contrary to what I am and want? That is probably where my shadow lurks.

In Egyptian mythology, Osiris is the god who represents return to the Source. The Source is the Self of love, wisdom, and healing beyond the clinging ego. The antagonist of Osiris is Set. He is the shadow because he opposes the return to the Source. Set wants to separate and divide, not unite and join. Apopis, his serpent, is killed each night but lives through the intervening days. Set and Apopis were never to be destroyed, nor were they meant to be expelled from the pantheon. They are to be reconciled to Osiris at the end of time, in the timelessness that is accessible in the here and now by those who are whole. (The traditional origin of the demonic happens when Satan envies Christ. Envy is a clue to the positive shadow, so this myth forecasts reconciliation, not eternal enmity. Some early Christian theologians believed that at the end of time, Satan—but not evil—would be reunited with Christ. True evil *is* the opposite of goodness. It cannot be reconciled to goodness, only replaced by it.)

In the tenth century BCE, Set *was* driven from the pantheon and made a devil. His statues were broken and his name erased from temple walls. As religion becomes decadent, less connected to the Source, just such black-and-white division replaces integrating unity. Set was never meant to portray the principle of evil but only the dark side of Osiris and Horus. In Edfu, Horus, the son of Osiris, is pictured harpooning Set in his metaphorical form of a hippopotamus. He does not kill him but disarms him in each of his dangerous parts and then *rides* him. Isis, his mother, steadies his hand and accompanies him to victory. This is a striking image of befriending the shadow: riding, not killing, uniting, not separating. There is full acknowledgment of the role of the feminine in the struggle. The masculine work is symbolized by active effort—the weapon-wielding of Horus—something we achieve. The feminine work is symbolized by openness to grace, the accompaniment of Isis, something we receive.

The wife of Set is Nephthys, the dark side of the feminine, a witch. In medieval times, this is the archetype that was so fearsome to patriarchal religion. Witches were excommunicated from the community by opprobrium and then execution. Male heretics were also killed in an attempt to rid the world and the psyche of the shadow. This is the equivalent of cutting off the parts of one's body that are ugly and expecting thereby to look whole. Notice the difference between this divisive approach and that of Horus in his reconciling battle with Set. Division does not have to endure and hurt. It can lead to union, as the treaty at Appomatox illustrated in our own history. Opposing forces stood in different colors, then sat mindfully together, and finally embraced as allies. It *can* happen in that way.

Hegel's dialectic states that thesis is followed by its antithesis. From the tension of these opposites, a synthesis arises. But this unity has instability built into it. Soon it disintegrates into a new thesis and the process recommences. This is not because of any frailty or faultiness in human construction. It is the evolutionary nature of living things. The uneasiness of unity is a springboard for a letting go of what has ceased to be useful. Only then can a new configuration emerge that more accurately fits new needs and changing times. A psychological example might be this: submission (thesis) becomes dominance (antithesis) and then synthesizes as cooperation. This later feels like a loss of personal autonomy, and a new thesis emerges: standing up for one's personal convictions. Likewise, a man and a woman produce a child who synthesizes their differences. Later the child individuates and becomes his or her own person, seeking a complementary partner. In our work with the shadow, we have combined opposites and created synthesis. Yet this union will eventually engender an agitation that opens a new shadow challenge. In this sense, the shadow is never totally reposed, only repositioned. Befriending the shadow has no final destination; the intention is only to take whatever the next steps may be in an ongoing and unceasing process of personal evolution.

The Dialectic at Work in the Work

Accept ourselves as we are	Change what can be changed
Mindfulness helps here	A sense of personal power helps here
Spiritual practice	Psychological work
Graceful shifts	Effortful steps

Befriending the shadow combines the apparent opposites meaningfully and is thus an example of synchronicity.

THE PRACTICE

Most of us have already been successful at combining and containing opposites in our experience and in ourselves. For instance, in sports we combine fatiguing stress and exuberance. With our children or best friends, we are able to go on loving while moving in and out of liking.

Look at this table and see where you stand:

Can I be	*While still remaining*
Committed in a relationship	Free
Angry at someone	Loving toward this person
Aware of my faults	High in self-esteem
Against an idea or plan	Respectful and cooperative
In agreement	Firm in my own conviction
Respectful and yielding	Firm in my own beliefs
A preserver of what is useful in a belief system	Free to disregard what no longer works for me
A parent or spouse	True to a career or hobby
Repelled by what someone does	Caring about the one who did it
Generous	Self-nurturant
Emotionally involved	Intellectually clear
Proud of someone	Aware of the person's shortcomings
Available for others	Able to preserve time for myself
Flexible	True to my standards
Able to see the worst possibilities	Hopeful
Able to take risks	Safety conscious
Responsibly in control of myself	Spontaneous
Limited in my commitment	Unconditionally loving
Afraid	Capable of acting
Honest in my persona	At work on my shadow

BEFRIENDING THE SHADOW: A GENTLE WORK

This thing of darkness I acknowledge mine.

—SHAKESPEARE, *The Tempest*

I will converse with this creature that he may let us borrow his powerful shoulders.

—DANTE, *The Inferno*

Here is a story that perfectly reveals what is meant by befriending the shadow: Milarepa, the great Tibetan teacher, confronted five demons in his cave who mocked his spiritual practice. He did not fight them, though he had always been a courageous warrior. Instead he looked for recognizable pieces of himself in each of them and thereby befriended them.

We have explored our shadow realms, meeting our inner demons and our inner divinities. Freud, speaking of transference in therapy, said that not working with it is like successfully summoning a spirit from the dead and not asking it a question. This applies to the positive and negative shadow sides of ourselves. The benefit is in the work that asks and answers these questions: "How do I acknowledge my shadow and turn it to its best use? How can it serve my unique and deepest needs, values, and wishes? How can it be an assisting force on my journey to my destiny?"

Shadow work is not about improving or reconstructing ourselves. The steps we take are gentle ones: accepting ourselves, befriending our worst traits. This is to mine for gold in the psyche's dark but inviting caves. Then change for the better happens automatically as a consequent shift—the refining of the gold. Improvement is the result, not the purpose, of the work. (Happiness works this same way. It too is a result, not a purpose. Like improvement, it is a graceful shift, not an effortful step.) Befriending the shadow is not a set of incidental changes; it is a thorough transformation. It is not a preoccupation with uplifting ourselves. That only reinforces and perpetuates our belief in control. Moreover, the other side of uplifting is lapse, so emphasis on one keeps us in fear of the other. We know it is true befriending of the shadow when we experience freedom from fear.

Emma Jung says: "An inner wholeness presses its still unfulfilled claims upon us." The psyche is not only yearning for wholeness but also using everything in us to fulfill that goal, as a farmer uses every part of a pig to make profit. With regard to the shadow this happens with an economy that is quite intriguing. Our personality contains two ordinary characteristics: attraction and aversion. In its vigilant and single-hearted work in the direction of wholeness, the psyche uses each of these to compensate for other qualities that are lacking in our behavior. For instance, Marcia is passive and admires the assertiveness of Melinda. Marcia's psyche "knows" she has assertiveness in her but that it has not been activated. Marcia's psyche uses her admiration of Melinda to start Marcia on the path toward opening that untapped potential in herself. Melinda's assertiveness and Marcia's admiration are also an example of synchronicity, a spiritual tool of the psyche. Just the right person comes along and just the right impact is made so that wholeness can happen. As we saw earlier, something, we know not what—call it psyche or grace—is always at work, we know not how—call it synchronicity or grace—so that the wholeness always and already in us can come out. Synchronicity is honored when chance meets choice and we act in accord with what has begun from beyond our ego. In this sense, befriending our shadow is spiritual work. It is cooperation with a power that bursts our limitations with limitlessness.

To befriend the positive collective *shadow:* The positive collective shadow is the Self: universal love, wisdom, and healing. No single individual can fully represent, compre-hend, or contain the collective positive shadow. However, saints and self-giving heroes personify it by their example and the successful contributions they make to the welfare of the world. Mother Teresa, the Dalai Lama, and most other win-ners of the Nobel Peace Prize, and people everywhere who have acted heroically for the world, are in this category. They invest their entire life in the interests of humankind. Their egoless and long-standing commitment to peace, health, free-dom, and enlightenment put them in direct contact with the Self, and they are its assisting forces in reaching all of us. We can extend their work when we join them in it or live in ser-vice to our local community. We may never have the fame and success of the great men and women we admire but we can follow their example, and this is our way of embracing the collective positive shadow in our own limited but surpass-ing way. No single person can befriend it fully. Jung says, "Only an accumulation of individual changes will produce a collective solution."

Religious figures, gods, and saints are also personifica-tions of the positive collective shadow, our disowned powers: "All these visualized deities are but symbols of what can happen on the path." This stunning and sanguine Tantric statement is expressed in a more Western way by Jung: "Equivalent images of sacred figures lie dormant in the psy-che." Roger Walsh adds: "In the utmost depths of the human psyche, when all limiting identifications have been dropped, awareness experiences no limits to its identity and directly experiences itself as that which is beyond the limits of time and space, which we have traditionally called God." Besides service, another way of embracing the cosmic positive shadow is to see the divine figures as exemplars of and meta-phors for the spiritual potential of our human nature and to act in accord with it. The shrine of the god reflects to us our own highest nature and calls us to implement its purposes. The divine has heart but no hands except ours. At the same time, to paraphrase Jung, we are not God, but our healthy ego is the only stable in which he can be born. Each of us who assimilates a piece of the cosmic shadow refines the God image in the consciousness of humankind, as Jesus and Buddha did. We present a divine gift to the world, as their mothers did. We open our gifts to the divine as the Magi did. When this happens, we have discovered the sacred.

A Vajrayana (a school of Buddhism) technique is to visualize a deity in the center of a mandala. A mandala is a spiritual cosmogram usually circular and containing four sides. It is a metaphorical design of the environment of the divine as it enters human life. In the visualization, one sees oneself as the deity: "I am a fully enlightened Buddha." In this tradition, gazing at the god is incomplete unless the devotee goes beyond the dualistic ego and enters the life spirit of the god relieved of any sense of or insistence upon separation or division.

Cosmic befriending happens also in mindfulness meditation, which takes us out of our ego concerns and faces us toward the world. When thoughts stop, the thinking mind loses its job and has nothing to do but rest in what is. This also happens in active imagination, of which prayer is a form. Befriending also entails living life compassionately as enlightened masters do and did. To befriend the cosmic positive shadow, we have to let go of ego and its limitations and thereby discover and trust the limitless capacity we have for love and service: "This very body: the Buddha." "I live now not I [ego] but Christ [Self] lives in me."

Realization of our spiritual potential, the befriending of our positive shadow, is called enlightenment. It will not be consciously accessible and reliably in place all the time. That is not humanly possible. Enlightenment is a *happening* that occurs in unique moments of time that makes time stand still. It is not a possession. There is no permanent, ineradicable enlightenment any more than there is any permanent any-thing. There are only moments when we let the light through, although it is always available. It is thus like loving, not like having.

To befriend the negative collective *shadow:* The owner of consciousness is the ego. The collective shadow is untamed archetypal energy unless it is joined by the ordering power of the healthy ego. When ego meets the unconscious with a plan for axis, a balancing direction begins. This is the healing third that arises between opposites.

Nonetheless, the collective negative shadow cannot be befriended or integrated by any one person. There are indi-viduals who appear in every generation to personify this shadow force of destruction. They are powerless to enact their dark purposes, however, without individual followers. The primary work of befriending the collective negative shadow is to refuse to follow them and to take a stand in opposition to them. This requires a personal set of standards that check the choices we make. To form a conscience and live by it is thus a way of dealing with the negative collective shadow. This means commitment to love, peaceful solutions to problems, nonviolence, and compassion. The Nuremberg trials declared to the world just how responsible each of us is to have, know, and live in accord with humanitarian stan-dards of behavior, no matter who is in charge.

We acknowledge the collective negative shadow when we listen to the news and read periodicals that tell of injus-tices in the world. Injustice has to be looked for; it may not loudly announce its presence. Then writing to a member of congress or joining an organized effort to help deal with the problem becomes the challenging task. Nonviolent protest is a powerful way to befriend a piece of the cosmic negative shadow. Sometimes it takes the form of standing in opposition to a group we are part of. We find our own personal power in our separation for integrity's sake. This power we then use in the best interests of the group. It is a feature of the hero journey to step away and then to return with news about a better way. It takes courage, but "when I dare to be powerful, to use my strength in the service of my vision, then it becomes less and less important whether I am afraid," says Audre Lorde.

Years ago I saw a grainy black-and-white film clip of Lotte Lenya singing "Mack the Knife." Her husband, Kurt Weill, was its composer. He fled Germany in 1935 when he was declared a decadent artist by the Nazis. The song describes a predatory character who has the appealing power to seduce people but is evil underneath. At the end of the song, Lotte sang "He's Mack the Knife," and suddenly a gigantic picture of Hitler dropped into view behind her. I cannot forget how intensely she pointed to the picture as she sang those last words emphatically and slowly. I could tell she wanted so much for us to know the Mack of the time, the most recent personification of the evil in the collective negative shadow. To do our part of the work, we have to learn to point that way too. It takes caring very much that others know the truth. It takes having the courage to risk danger and retaliation. Having that kind of courage is the only grace that can equip us frail humans to join in the saintly, heroic, and angelic battle with the forces of evil "who prowl through the world seeking the ruins of souls," as an old prayer says.

The shadow has a timing all its own. The Gospel account poignantly and resignedly says concerning Judas when he was leaving the Last Supper on his way to betray Jesus, "And it was night." Later Jesus said to the soldiers who came to arrest him: "This is your hour and the power of darkness." The shadow has its legitimate time in every life. This stands to reason in a psyche/world that combines and allows opposites to flourish until something greater than both can evolve. How can we tell if it is time to befriend our shadow? If the work works, it is time. Our efforts fall flat when the time is not right; results expand beyond our efforts when the time has come.

To befriend the positive personal *shadow:* Use this triple-A approach:

• *Affirm* that you have the quality you admire or envy in someone else. This can be a simple declaration or affirmation, such as: "I am more and more courageous."

• *Act* as if you have that quality by making choices that demonstrate it.

• *Announce* it: tell everybody you know that you are making these changes and ask for their support.

These are three *steps* we take. They are usually followed by *shifts* in our personality; we begin to act in wiser, more loving, and more healing ways with no further need for effort. This is the grace dimension, the spiritual assistance to our work.

To befriend the negative personal *shadow:* Practice these five A's:

• *Acknowledge* that you have all the attributes humans can have, that you contain both sides of every human coin. Acknowledge that you have the specific negative traits you see in others that evoke a strong reaction of repulsion in you. The urge to observe coexists with its opposite impulse to expose.

• *Allow* yourself to hold and cradle these as parts of yourself. Acknowledge that they may have gone underground for a legitimate purpose and are now ready to be turned inside out and become something more creative and empowering in your life.

• *Admit* to yourself and to one other person these shadow discoveries about yourself.

• Make *amends* to those who may have been hurt by your denial of your own shadow: "I saw this in you and it is in me. I have blamed you for what I am ashamed of in myself." Make amends to those who have been hurt by any under-handed ways that your shadow has had an impact on them.

• Become *aware* of the kernel of value in your negative shadow characteristic and then treat it as you did the positive shadow above: affirm it as true of yourself, act as if it were true, announce your discovery and program to others who can assist in following up on it.

As you do this work, do not scold yourself like a critical parent for all your deficits. Have a good talk with yourself as a kindly adult: "I have been controlling and that is wrong of me, but there is a kernel of positive value in that controlling. It is my capacity for getting things done, for organizing, even for leadership. I will now concentrate on and release those wonderful attributes. I will find my positive shadow in my negative shadow." To do that is to work with what is rather than attempt to eliminate what is and thereby work against psychic truth. Shadow embracing reverses self-alienation and connects us to our own rainbow reality.

Seeing your dark side, seeing what you are really up to, while not shaming yourself for it, reconnects you to your true self and reveals its spacious grandeur. Such vision is a form of mindfulness. Turning against the external tyrant is useless.

You have to see it in your own mirror: "This face is mine. I accept the fact that there is something dark in every one of my motivations. And I still see the light in me too." Jung wrote, toward the end of his life: "I am astonished, disappointed, and pleased with myself. I am depressed and rapturous. I am all this at once and cannot add up the sum."

Follow-up Steps in Befriending

• The steps above are followed by a *visualization* of ourselves acting in a way that opens us to the positive side of whatever we feared and avoided about ourselves. This is how we relativize the negative characteristic by containing it in a "greater than" ego. We hold it in the alchemical vessel of our psyche. Then we see our unacceptableness with gentleness. Nothing in us is to be thrown away; all is grist for the mill of transformation. This is how self-forgiveness works for us.

• Daily mindful *repetition* of the word describing the specific positive quality we are attempting to release from our negative shadow is also crucial to this work. Simply attend mindfully to one quality, for example, courage, and repeat it internally and aloud throughout the day. One day for each quality is sufficient, and then begin again. Mindfulness is the psycho-spiritual maneuver that bridges unconscious potential and conscious actualization.

• It may also be helpful to use *active imagination* (inner and written dialogue) with positive and negative shadow figures, both those in life and those in dreams. Shadow figures in dreams may be those who seem far inferior or dangerous to us or those who seem far superior and appealing to us. What pursues us in a dream is often our own shadow, either positive or negative. We flee that which wants to catch up with us and make friends with us. It would help to stop in our tracks in the dream, or in active imagination after it, and ask our pursuer who it is and what it wants.

• Writing a *letter* to a role model or hero and to a villain and then writing one from those persons to you helps you relate to them rather than stand in awe of them or in opposition to them. This relating helps you see that their attributes are *in* you.

• Now you have a greater sense of your own dark choices and actions in the course of your life. You can see how they have had an impact on others. You may have hurt or taken advantage of those who loved you. You can also assume that they knew about these traits of yours and remained your loyal friends. Express thanks to them in letter form or face-to-face: "I see more of my dark side now. I realize that you have seen it too over the years and even been at the mercy of it at times. In addition to making amends, I thank you for hanging in there with me. I know I was not the easiest person to love but you did anyway and I appreciate you so much for it. I am touched very deeply by your capacity to love me no matter what. That love of yours had power in it. It helped me get to this point in life where I can admit my shadow and do the work of turning it to good."

• Keep using *affirmations* that confirm and advance your work. The affirmations tell not how a quality is used but what it does; for instance, arrogance may be used to hide low self-esteem, but it acts as if you do have self-esteem: "I feel better and better about who I am."

Affirmations lead to synchronous opportunities, day by day, to live out their declarations. As we affirm that we have more compassion, for instance, we may see more homeless people and see them in a new way. When we show compassion to the homeless, we may find ourselves opening the shadow part of ourselves that is bereft and rejected by society and ourselves. This is how shadow work cycles back and reveals more to us about who we are. To respond lovingly to the homeless is to respond lovingly to our own lostness, to feel compassion for all that is bereft and unwanted in ourselves. To feel lost and to work through it in this way is a gift. Giving something to the homeless is a fitting ritual of thanks.

Director George Stevens had this to say after his stint in Germany in World War II: "When a poor, hungry, dirty man grabs me and begs, I feel the Nazi in me because I abhor him and want him to keep his hands off me. The reason I abhor him is because I see myself as capable of arrogance and brutality in keeping him away. That's a fierce thing to discover in oneself."

• Our work is always both psychological and spiritual. The psychological work consists of steps we take. The spiritual work consists of shifts that happen to us by grace:

Step: Unconditional love for yourself as you are
Shift: Feeling the same toward others, compassion
Step: Finding your lively energy and soft center
Shift: Enemies become allies
Step: Living consistently in the new, healthier behavior
Shift: Freedom from shadow unconscious behavior and taking others' behavior as information
Step: Acting as if
Shift: Becoming in reality

FINDING THE BEST OF THE BAD

Only that which is truly ourselves has the power to heal.

—C. G. JUNG

As we saw earlier, the work of embracing the shadow takes two directions: opposites combine and then counterparts appear. For every positive quality there is a corresponding opposite, and likewise for every negative trait there is a corresponding positive one. We can love the fact that all human opposites coexist in us and can be reconciled. The previous section was about how this can happen.

The second path to alliance with our shadow is to acknowledge and embrace *counterparts*. The counterpart of strong admiration is our own positive shadow potential and the counterpart of strong dislike is our negative shadow side. This was the subject of earlier chapters.

Likewise, within each unacceptable feature of our negative shadow, there is a positive kernel of goodness, as we saw in the section on befriending the negative personal shadow. Now we explore in detail how kernel counterparts can be worked with.

In every negative quality there is a positive untapped potential quality, like a pearl in an oyster. This is how "negative" is algebraic, not sinister. Buried in anything we hate in someone else is something positive about both of us that we are overlooking. This creative potency is what we lose by projection. The kernel of value will refund us our lively energy, yet we cannot get to it without breaking the shell. The title of a picture by Jung is "Shadow: Light at the Core of Darkness." *In the dark quality I have been hating in myself and you is something wonderful and bright offering all the possibilities of the enriching Self.* Shakespeare expresses it most succinctly

in *Henry V:* "There is some soul of goodness in things evil /
Would we observingly distill it out."

The ego with all its projections is the walnut shell; the
denied shadow is, ironically, the kernel of nourishing meat. It
is the legitimate feature in an otherwise unworthy or perverse
trait. The contact with and acting on the lively kernel automatically reduces, eases, and even erases the abrasive stress
of our hard shell. When I try to get rid of it, it persists. When
I hold it and let it become something more and then act in
accord with that, it desists. The original negativity abates and
its other side, its lighter side, reveals itself. The darkness lifts
with the dawn and wanderers people find nourishing manna
in the desert.

A positive counterpart is waiting to be acknowledged in
anything about us that is unlikable or despicable. Without
exception, we can locate something good in any negative
trait. For instance, power can be a tool of the ego for self-
aggrandizing domination. Within that use of power is a kernel of great value: power can be used for cooperation and for
the welfare of all. The work is to find the *heart* of the villain-
ous ego. There is an unopened rose among the uninviting
thorns.

Criminal, evil, or violent *deeds* do not have an inherent
kernel of goodness in them. The shadow refers to unconscious traits and attitudes, not conscious actions. Our dark
deeds flow from a repressed or unintegrated negative shadow.
The redemptive kernel is in the shadow itself before it does
its dirty work. For instance, we have an innate discriminatory
power in our healthy ego. If it is in our repressed negative
shadow, it may be transmogrified into prejudice and bigotry.
If it is consciously in use, it is an ability to distinguish, to
appraise, or to make constructive suggestions. When we befriend our shadow prejudice, its kernel of usefulness appears
precisely as this healthy discriminatory judgment. If we act
out our prejudice in a violent way—by anti-Semitic jokes, in

gang warfare, or by voting against measures that grant or guarantee equality—we lose our chance at shadow befriending with its resultant change for the better. Then the work can only be self-examination, compunction, making amends, and personal reformation. This is a way for good to happen after evil. The advantage of befriending the shadow is being able to deal with the dark side before it spills over into harm. Then we can do something positive with our negative traits before they go out of control and cause pain. This is why individual befriending of the shadow is such important work for society.

The lists on pages 267–270 show the traits of the inflated ego on the left and of the corresponding positive healthy ego on the right. They are not opposites but complements. We can access the useful dimension of every unacceptable thing we do or feel. The list of lively elements of the negative shadow (what we hate and fear) *is* the positive shadow (what we can become). When we deny our negative shadow, we deny our positive shadow too. When we befriend our negative shadow, we uncover and access its positive potential.

Love includes in its alchemical vessel every negative shadow quality that fear excludes. To hold an unfavorable attribute without shame, self-criticism, or denial is to free its potential for full actualization. Here is an example: I may deplore helplessness in others. As I admit my own occasional helplessness, or my disguised helplessness, and hold it without shame and with a plan to deal with it, a redeeming quality emerges in me: openness to support from others in healthy ways. This was my penicillin in the moldy bread of others' helplessness. I had been suppressing my own potential for receiving support while opposing its counterpart in others. And this same positive quality must also be in the helpless people I deplore. As I become open to my assisting forces, I will notice that the helplessness of others does not bother me as much. In fact, it arouses compassion.

The left side of the table shows what we are hiding in ourselves and projecting onto others. The right side shows its kernel of lively energy, that is, our positive shadow. Every negative human characteristic listed in the dictionary, without exception, has a corresponding positive dimension within it. When we bury an unsatisfactory trait, with it is buried its hidden value. Here is an analogy: If we were to dig deeply into the ground on which we are standing, we might locate underground springs. The springs of many positive qualities in us are in the underground, the unconscious, of ourselves, waiting to be unleashed. What we are pressing down with our weight (repression of our negative shadow) has something nourishing under it. The valuable center is like an arch that holds a structure together by receiving the pressures of both sides.

Nothing is ultimately unredeemable in the human personality. Everything human is alchemical, something common—or even ugly—that can be transformed into something precious. This is the true source of our hope as humans: no matter how bad we are or look, we have another side. The work, the program of befriending our shadow side, reveals the value in what we find worthless. Our joy is most secure, therefore, when it is in our commitment to the *work*. This is what makes equanimity possible. We can accept all the conditions of existence and personalities with evenness because we have a program in place that has optimism in it. The work makes love possible too, since, as in the example above, we grow in compassion for others as we see them fearfully sitting on the potential we know can spring up so easily.

The items in the following table are not opposites but counterparts, the obverse of one another. The items on the right do not cancel or reverse the ones on the left; they find the lively, useful, and potential heart of them. This heart is the healing third, the transcendent function of the all-containing psyche. It now becomes clear that in this transcendent function, the image or symbol presented to us is actually a precise vehicle for the activation of a potential. Both the image and the potential are unconscious, latent in our psyche. When one appears, the other is ready for activation. This is the striking way in which the psyche participates in shadow work.

The healing third dimension of the psyche arises when we reconcile two *apparent* opposites: the quality so hateful in someone out there and the humbling acknowledgment of the same quality in ourselves. The kernel of value we find in the befriended shadow is the healing third. This is a clear instance of the transcendent function of the psyche. Here are some traditional metaphorical examples of this: The Holy Spirit is the transcendent third of the Father and the Son. In Genesis, the Holy Spirit broods over the dark waters and stirs up life from the void. Saint George rides a horse as he confronts the dragon shadow. The horse represents his animal powers; that is, he fights as a whole person, uniting his earthly and spiritual dimensions. The dragon is cut up after being slain, and the villagers eat its flesh. They thereby incorporate the shadow power. This is the kernel of nourishment in the dark and scary shadow.

Ultimately, a union of opposites is possible neither through conscious ego alone, since it divides, nor through the unconscious alone, since it identifies. It requires a third force, the transcendent function of psyche, which emerges from our struggle with the darkest side of our shadow. In the ancient myth of Perseus slaying Medusa, Pegasus, the horse that rides to spiritual heights, sprang from Medusa's severed head: the healing third. The Union of today is the healing third that arose following the Civil War, from the containing room at Appomatox where blue and gray finally met and made friends, showing opposites can arrive at union.

Here is how this union might look in practical terms: I hate vindictiveness in others and cannot imagine it in myself. I work on embracing my shadow and I begin to acknowledge vindictiveness in myself. I see little ways I have of being retaliatory. What seemed to be opposites, others' behavior and mine, now are united. At the same time, if I can be vengeful, I must have a strong sense of justice, and that is the positive side of my ego's will to retaliate. I do not fully befriend my ego simply by doing the opposite, forgiving; I also have to access its creative élan, the urge toward justice. The search for an equation in the negative shadow leads to vengeance. The search for an equation in the *befriending* of the negative shadow leads to reconciliation. What furthered division now fosters unity.

The kernel indicates the *balance* between opposites. For instance, maintaining privacy is the positive core of the tendency to be sneaky. Extreme examples of secretiveness and self-disclosure are thus balanced by the sense of privacy. Befriending the shadow leads to compassion for negative traits in others, respect for the kernel of goodness that underlies them, and desire that they find it. Evolved spiritual consciousness includes just such tender caring for humanity.

The following table is also useful in finding the positive dimension of negative traits we are aware of. The negative traits are on the left; the positive kernel is on the right. For instance, I may be someone who goes on shopping sprees and overspends. It seems nourishing to me to spend on myself, but it actually depletes me. Overspending therefore has a negative impact on my life. The positive counterpart of overspending is self-nurturance. (Looked at in reverse: overspending on myself is the shadow side of self-nurturance.) The adult healthy way to be self-nurturant is to spend appropriately and to treat myself to fun but without driving myself into excessive debt or addictive behavior.

The reason the negative shadow has value is that it is full of energy. Energy of any kind can be transformed into something good. To find the kernel of a "bad" quality, it is useful to ask these questions: What energy is stirring when this characteristic comes out? What power must I have that makes it possible to be this way? What positive quality does it take to be this way? What skill is hidden in this shadow part of me? What would it have become if it had been allowed to flourish along healthy, unrepressed lines? What is the lively energy that wants to emerge in a creative and adventurous way?

Negative Shadow: What We See in Others But Do Not Notice in Ourselves	Positive Shadow: The Kernel of Lively Energy We Have in Us Potentially but Do Not See
Addictiveness	Steadfastness
Anxiety	Excitement
Approval seeking	Openness to appreciation
Arrogance	Self-confidence, self-credit
Attachment	Involvement
Bias	Discernment
Bitterness, grudge holding	Refusal to overlook injustice
Blind obedience	Loyalty
Capitulation	Compromise
Caretaking	Compassion
Clinging	Loyalty
Coercion	Persuasion
Compromise	Negotiability
Compulsion	Reliability and follow-through
Compulsive orderliness	Organization, efficiency

Conning	Persuasiveness
Connivance	Intelligent strategizing
Control, manipulativeness	Leadership, efficiency, initiative, coordinating ability
Cowardice	Caution
Coyness	Creative strategizing
Cruelty	Healthy anger
Cunning	Artful subtlety in self-provisioning
Defensiveness	Preparedness
Demanding	Asking
Dependency on others	Reasonable trust of others
Disorder	Flexibility
Feuding	Disagreement
Entitlement	Merited worthiness, deservingness
Envy	Admiration
False front	Improvisation
Fear	Caution and vulnerability
Fear of abandonment	Lining up support
Fear of engulfment	Maintaining boundaries
Flattery	Sincere complimenting
Foolhardiness	Bravery
Gluttony	Gourmet appreciation without compulsion
Greed	Self-provision
Guilt	Conscientiousness
Hate	Healthy anger
Helplessness	Openness to support

Hostility	Assertive anger
Hypocrisy	Ability to "act as if"
Impatience	Eagerness
Impulsiveness	Spontaneity
Incompetence	Willingness to experiment and to be seen as one is
Indecision	Refusal to act without sufficient facts or inner resources
Intimidation	Recognition of inadequate skills to fight back
Jealousy	Protectiveness
Jumping to conclusions	Intuitiveness
Laziness	Relaxedness
Legalism	Healthy respect for law
Loneliness	Openness to nurturance
Loquacity	Articulateness
Lying	Imaginativeness
Miserliness	Caution in the use of money
Neediness	Ability to ask for responsiveness to one's appropriate needs
Obsequiousness	Respect
Obsession	Interest, focused attention
Overcommitment	Wholeheartedness
Overspending on oneself	Self-nurturance
Perfectionism	Commitment to doing things well
Pretentiousness	Healthy narcissism
Procrastination	Honoring one's own timing
Prodigality	Generosity

Profligacy	Passion
Promiscuous lust	Uninhibited safe sex
Rebellion against a sense of obligation	Freedom and ability to choose or refuse
Recklessness	Adventurousness
Ridicule	Good-natured humor, but not at another's expense
Rigidity	Tenacity, conviction
Sarcasm	Wit
Selfishness	Self-nurturance
Self-justification	Self-protection
Self-pity	Self-forgiveness
Separatism	Clear boundaries
Slyness	Shrewdness
Stubbornness	Determination
Submissiveness	Cooperation, docility
Suspiciousness	Not hiding one's head in the sand, the courage to know the truth
Tactless bluntness	Frank candidness
Vengefulness or spite	Righting wrongs
Whining	Saying "Ouch!" and asking for what one needs

The list on the right also shows what we have disavowed in ourselves by maintaining the ego stance on the left. Every vengeful person has a strong sense of justice for all humankind. That wonderful gift is the underground spring that may never burst forth as long as the person is caught up in vengeful spite. This is how all of us lose when one of us is caught in the toils of ego.

The ego characteristics on the left are based on fear; the right side describes what healthy love looks like. Once we let go of fear, love—old faithful—gushes out. This is what is meant by true love casting out fear. Ultimately, embracing the shadow is about becoming in action the loving beings that we are at heart. Befriending the shadow is really about learning to love. We let the dark out to let love in.

Add love . . .
Then wilt thou not be loath
To leave this Paradise, but shall possess
A Paradise within thee, happier far.

—MILTON, *Paradise Lost*, BOOK XII

Using the lists above, here is an example of working with a negative shadow trait:

I am strongly upset when others are vengeful.
I acknowledge that I am vengeful, though I may not see it.
I must have a passion for justice that I have not fully expressed.
I choose to act as if I were committed to justice without being in any way vengeful.

After taking the *steps* above, an automatic *shift* may then occur with these results:

• Retaliatory behavior by others will become simply an object of observation. I will be informed but not affected by it. It will arouse my compassion, not my abhorrence or hate. I will be a fair witness, not an antagonist.

• My own subtly vengeful ways will vanish.

• My sense of justice and my commitment to enact it in the world will emerge automatically and with ease. I will want to apply my personal work to the world, working for world peace, which happens only one person at a time.

When creative courage is missing, a plan for revenge is a form of self-soothing. When courage is accessed, new healthy styles of self-soothing appear. This is another way in which befriending the shadow is creative work. Courage and all the positive qualities of love and heroism are potentials in the Self. We do not manufacture them; we locate and activate them as a result of the shift in consciousness that shadow work instigates. Every time we enter the darkness with a candle, we bring more light than our little match could make.

The true hero destroys the illusions of ego, such as the usefulness and legitimacy of revenge and killing. An authentic hero has dismantled the ego's insistence on retaliation. Real heroes are creative enough to wrestle *and* transform the foe. For a real hero, there are no enemies, only confused, pained people who need caring and a light to help them wake up. Abraham Lincoln, at the end of his first inaugural address, showed how he wanted the transformation of the Confederates, not their destruction: "We are not enemies but friends. We must not be enemies. . . . The mystic chords of memory, stretching from every battlefield and patriot grave to every living heart and hearthstone over this broad land, will yet swell the chorus of the Union, when again touched, as surely they will be, by the better angels of our nature." We can see the Civil War and the Union as metaphors for shadow work. Two sides of one nation equal two sides of one person. Union is wholeness, the internal coherence of the Self that results from a reconciliation of the opposing sides. Befriending happens at Appomatox, where the ego surrenders to union with the Self and in its bosom finds the blessings it had lost.

What you intended for evil, God intended for good.
—JOSEPH, TO HIS BROTHERS,
GENESIS 50:20

9

Shifts That Happen:
The Graces of Befriending

If the ill spirit have so fair a house,
Good things will strive to dwell with it.

—SHAKESPEARE, *The Tempest*

CHANGLING'S OPENING POEM, one you now perhaps know by heart, is about a journey from the darkness of the setting sun to the dawn of a new day. It is the journey of befriending the shadow undertaken best by those who have no ego left, no way to divide and deny. In this defenseless and resourceful moment is an ecstatic passage to human wholeness and spiritual depth. Shadow work is the initiation into the journey. The ego is dissolved and the Self emerges more emphatically. The wonderful thing about this work is that it escorts us over the threshold of spirituality: to let go of ego, act with wise love, and become free of dualistic perceptions. We experience shifts that we do not cause. Grace is at work and has complemented our efforts with powers that transcend the limits of our intellect and will.

The inflated ego may step in at this point in our work, thumping its chest and proclaiming that effort is automatically rewarded with grace. This is incorrect. Grace is free of obligation; it cannot be forced or redirected. It comes to those who do the work as well as to those who refuse to do it, as the story of Jonah and the whale portrays. It operates mysteriously and is beyond rule or predictability. Heinrich Harrer, the main character of *Seven Years in Tibet*, was the epitome of the inflated ego-driven man and seemed the least likely candidate for grace. Monks all over Tibet were meditating faithfully and had never even met the Dalai Lama. Harrar did no work on himself and yet he was granted the privilege of becoming the Dalai Lama's teacher. Grace is beyond figuring.

What follows is an exploration of what *can* result from the work we have been outlining. Yet all the work in the world may lead nowhere and no work at all may yield benefits greater than any listed in this book. The first result/shift/grace of the practice of befriending is a psychological one: letting go of our neurotic ego in favor of a healthy one, "lest the judgment come and I be found unannihilate and delivered into the hands of my own selfhood," as William Blake warns.

Another result is a spiritual re-membering, a restoration of the lost parts of ourselves. Osiris had denied his shadow, imagining himself to be nothing but light, so he was cut into pieces by Set, his dark brother. Refusal to accept the opposites in oneself leads to fragmentation. Isis re-membered Osiris, the resurrection god, by gathering the broken pieces of his body and creating the first mummy, the metaphor for the pupa that becomes a butterfly. It took forty days for the embalming to work. The embalming symbolizes the work it takes for transformation, with a dark time necessary for completion of the process.

Befriending will also result in a shift of energy previously needed to maintain the repression of our shadow side. This is an influx of lively energy into our lives that results from recalling banished allies into our psychic kingdom and thereby consolidating its strengths.

Attention leads to healing, as attention to the Virgin Mary—an Earth Mother—at Lourdes attests. As we pay attention to our shadow projections and bring them into consciousness, we become more balanced. We articulate the wholeness that was always abiding in us. "This mortal body was meant for immortality," as Saint Paul says. "This very body: the Buddha," as Hakuin says. When the shadow is integrated, we recognize the immortality of the Self. Our mortal nature articulates its immortal longings and moves toward its immortal destiny. Our identity and our destiny are one and the same.

Another result/shift is personal creativity. This happens because we are finally actualizing our potential. It takes creativity to find the light side of darkness, the best in the worst. When we befriend our hidden dimensions, we gain a whole new lease on life. We discover new sources and resources of energy within ourselves. The work is the vitamin supplement of the soul.

We also notice a new compassion for ourselves and others. "If we could read the secret history of our enemies, we would find in each man's life sorrow and suffering enough to disarm all hostility," says Longfellow. Once we befriend our own shadow, we find that we love others *because* they are different from us, not in spite of it. This results because befriending of the shadow means no longer fearing differences. We are excited by them because we have noticed how the holding of them, fearlessly and acceptingly, in ourselves leads to the emergence of the healing third, love. This love and compassion is the ultimate advantage and gift of cutting through dualisms.

The dark of dark side does not refer to color, only to unconsciousness, the origin of bias and hatred. Befriending the shadow signals the end of our fear-based prejudices. Dark-skinned Americans are no longer the shadow of white America. Gays are no longer the shadow of heterosexuality. Non-Christians are no longer the shadow of Christianity. The homeless are no longer the shadow of prosperity. Women are no longer the shadow of patriarchal society. Pluralism thrives when love finally grasps us in its emancipatory embrace. Work on our negative shadow lets that limitlessness happen. Our positive shadow potential then opens just as expansively.

THE PIVOTAL SHIFT: THE END OF DUALISMS

The major shift that results from befriending our shadow is freedom from dualisms. Dualism is the result of refusing to hold and wed our opposites. Befriending our shadow reverses that fear-based style. The human, the natural, and the divine are no longer polarized. We appreciate the interaction of all these domains of existence as our ego collaborates with the Self in its unifying purposes of love, wisdom, and healing. Grace and effort are no longer dichotomized, as we do the work in a spirit of cooperation with forces around and beyond us. Destiny is not simply a future that will one day arrive as we befriend our shadow; it is a present reality: we are in time the timelessness that once seemed so inaccessible. We are, in fact, more than we seem precisely because our full extension and dimension in the universe *is* universe; our demons are the creative rascals of our creativity; our union with the divine is our ever richer divinity.

GOD AND I

> *My being is God, not by simple participation but by true transformation. My I is God; there is no other I.*
> —SAINT CATHERINE OF GENOA

*In a breakthrough, I find that God and I are both the
same. . . . Love God as he is: a not-God, a not-spirit, a
not-person, a not-image; as sheer, pure, limpid unity,
alien from all duality.*

—MEISTER ECKHART

Befriending our shadow is soul work and it opens us to
our relationship to the divine. There is sometimes a split in
our consciousness between ourselves and what we see as God
or as any power that transcends us. Yet the transpersonal Self
includes and lovingly embraces our personal ego. We are not
the opposite of the divine but coexisting counterparts. The
deeper we go into our inner personal life the more we find of
the transpersonal that takes us beyond it. This is why Meister
Eckhart said: "The eye with which I see God is the same eye
by which God sees me." The wisdom in the Self is in acknowledging this freedom from dualism. We can divide
human from divine with sharp demarcations or we can lose
ourselves, our egos, in awe at the blurred boundary between
them. Spirituality blurs logic in order to sharpen and sustain
a wider and all-inclusive focus. *Paradox* is the literary word
for freedom from dualism.

"God" is the metaphor for the mystery of the Self. The
macrocosm (God) is reflected in the microcosm (the human
psyche): "When all things are nothing but God, there are then
no things and no God, but only *this*," writes Ken Wilber. To
transcend all and embrace all with nonpreferential love is
what happens in us when God is love.

In the *Ramayana*, Hanuman, the monkey god, is the
sidekick of Rama. Knowing Rama is in all things, he bites a
pearl to find him there and people laugh at how he takes
religious truth so literally. He then opens his heart, and behold: Rama with Sita, his goddess wife, ever radiantly living
and reigning there. The irony is that we have to look outside

to know that the mystery is inside: the God within, wholeness, the Buddha nature. "All the lotus lands and all the Buddhas are revealed in my own being," says the *Avatamsaka Sutra*. The divine is present in all things equally "on earth as it is in heaven." The divine in this fading rose is the same as the divine in the mystical Rose of Heaven.

Buddha's bliss is like a peak experience. In it, concepts—even the self (ego) concept—are revealed as transitory. The fact of transitoriness no longer leads to despair but instead provides a clue to an inner eternity, since every polarity contains its opposite. Bliss is therefore not a move from samsara (attachment to fear and desire) to nirvana (release from fear and desire) but freedom from domination by either one of them. We transcend all the opposites and feel "divine pride" that we *are* Buddha. Blake adds: "The pride of the peacock is the glory of God." When dualism fades away, so does attachment to the fading world. That attachment is replaced by enthusiasm for the transitory as most expository of the transcendent. We are led by the impermanent to the undying. Aristotle expressed how this happened to him when, at Eleusis, he grasped "the divine spectacle presented to us by the visible world." Notice the equation in his statement: divine, human, natural.

Ego and Self may say yes to the givens of existence, but neither is ultimately satisfied with the limits they represent. We are always also yearning to make the transition from time to timelessness in this moment, from secular to sacred in this world, from seasons to changelessness in our ever churning souls. Since part of the psyche, the Self, is not subject to the laws of time, space, and causation, it points to the reality of something immutable. In the religious idiom, this is part of the "authentic tidings of invisible things" that Wordsworth describes. We cannot always trust religious institutions to bring us such news. Religion can divide us from the divine or it can let those tidings ring. This is where faith walks onto the uncrowded stage of wholeness.

Faith is located in the imagination, not in the intellect, since revelation is in metaphors and symbols. Childhood religious symbols may have retained a place and power in our imagination. This means we still have faith within ourselves. The work of integrating religious dualisms is to reinterpret the images and symbols of our heritage and thus regain and reclaim them as building blocks for a new spiritual synthesis. Adult faith is thus a possible outcome of the integration of shadow and spirituality. An adult faith is one that accepts adult responsibility. Refuge in religious symbols and rituals does not mean finding in them a shelter from the world but truly becoming refugees, adults responsibly facing our world. When that happens, faith is real, as Saint Thomas Aquinas said: "Faith does not end up in notions but in the real world."

The human psyche is the heart of the universe: the heart of Jesus, the heart of Buddha. Our predicaments and encounters with the demanding conditions of our existence are the end-beams of these heart rays. They have touched our lives in sometimes strange or unwelcome ways. An adult in faith accepts and deals with the woes in his or her story line as afflicting forces that can lead to new vistas. Something in us and through and beyond us is standing firm in the midst of the changes and witnessing them all with tender compassion. Intuitive wisdom helps us not to be fooled by the dance of maya (transitory things) but to be confident through even the most frightening of its displays. This is the real victory and the real solace of spiritual work.

Thomas Merton writes: "The spark which is my true self is the flash of the Absolute recognizing itself in me. This realization at the apex is a coincidence of all opposites . . . a fusion of freedom and unfreedom, being and unbeing, life and death, self and non-self, man and God. The spark is not so much an entity which one finds but an event, an explosion which happens as all opposites clash within oneself. Then it is seen that the ego is not. It vanishes in its non-seeing when the flash of the spark alone is. . . . The purpose of all learning is to dispose man for this kind of event. The purpose of various disciplines is to provide ways or paths which lead to this capacity for ignition."

Gradually the sense of a separate self and a wholly other God gives way to a deeper mystery. We are individual vehicles of selfless divinity, the best vehicle found so far because the most conscious. We are not the only vehicle, since all of nature is included. Faith itself becomes an assisting force when it takes us beyond dualism to the inner space that embraces and is the universe. Then human, divine, and nature are one equation. This equation *is* the Tao: the governing principle of harmony and synchronicity at the origin, evolution, and completion of all things in nature and in oneself.

Jan van Ruysbroeck, the mystic and disciple of Meister Eckhart, uses the analogy of red-hot iron to show the nature of the unity of the human and the divine. The fire and iron are one but not identical. It is a oneness that honors differences: a union, not a fusion. "I am God" and "I am not God" are two halves of one statement. It is not permanently one or the other and yet they are indistinguishable *in the moment.* Separateness dissolves because it was never really there except as a perceptual convenience. Mystics use the metaphor of darkness as a way of saying that there are no distinctions, since in the dark all separate identities are lost. "The depths themselves remain uncomprehended. This is the dark silence in which all lovers lose themselves," says van Ruysbroeck. Darkness is *necessary* for union.

Idolatry occurs when dualism makes gods in the image of our ego. Mystics did not find God to be a solidity but rather an emptiness or openness that is nonetheless a vibrant presence. Joseph Campbell says that "God is a vehicle for the mystery not the mystery itself." Our religious need is, after all, our longing for wholeness, in which all dualisms end. In childhood religion, there is an insistence on dualism. The God up there seems above the disturbing conditions I face here. But the God/Self of wholeness lives within as well as beyond them. The infinite is not a supreme being above but a supreme mystery within, operating as an ever renewing source of life and love. This mystery is evolving and never expressible as a concept, except metaphorically. A supreme being estranged from our own depth is a betrayal of wholeness. Do I see God as power and domination, that is, projections of my ego, or as participation and communion, the reality of the Self?

The conventional religious attitude is extroverted. It involves going out to find the wholly other. In adult spirituality the attitude is introverted. It entails acknowledging wholeness, both within and around us, through an experiential sense of oneness. A fear-based approach may lead to a grasping for a solid and reliable dogma within one church structure. The mature religious person in today's world knows that no single religious tradition can suffice for beings as complex as we. We draw from all traditions for an adult spirituality. Charles Taylor writes: "Human life is irreducibly multi-leveled . . . there is no single construal of experience which one can cleave to exclusively without disaster or impoverishment."

Religious fundamentalism denies the value of sources of knowledge and the legitimacy of traditions beyond one's own. This is another example of religion made in the image of the arrogant ego, which supposes it needs nothing beyond its own beliefs. To disregard or disparage science and scholarship, for instance, in understanding the Bible, is to deny the value of education beyond one's own. Fundamentalism is ultimately a denial of any higher power than that which one's limited and usually frightened ego can allow. It is becoming visible more and more in our society as the freedom-afflicting force of the collective negative shadow of religion.

Numinous refers to divine presence. This word comes from the Latin *numen,* meaning "nod" or "wink," connoting a playful willingness of the divine to contact the human. This is a far cry from Rudolf Otto's distant "wholly Other." Ultimate reality is not a duality but an open unity that has room for all diversity. In the one we discern the many. In the many we are led to the one. In the transitory is the transcendent, since everything contains its opposite. The Hindu *Atman* refers to an eternal reality, or Self, that is distinct and yet abiding in all appearances. Our work is to discern and our reward is to abide. Egos end; Self abides. Unlike the ego, the Self was never born, nor can it die. This is the true permanence that ego craves.

As we befriend the archetype of the shadow, we welcome a sleeping giant, all our inner powers. Early peoples personified the powers they became aware of in the universe and in themselves as gods. Those who took things literally perceived these personifications as actual personages out there. There were always people more aware, however, who saw them as metaphors for forces in the human soul and in the universe, both immanently and transcendently. These same people eventually saw the soul and the universe as two aspects of one reality. The personifications were never meant to offer physical proof. They are psychic, not physical, facts. Adult faith takes those psychic facts and implements them in the visible world in the form of love.

Coleridge, in a translation of Schiller, says: "The intelligible forms of ancient poets, the fair humanities of old religion . . . all these have vanished. . . . But still the heart doth need a language; still doth the old instinct bring back the old names." An atheist rejects God but may still feel a yearning for an absolute. In this sense, the atheist's capacity for transcendence has become a longing for it. Is this really atheism? Or are atheists only those who deny the existence of anything beyond ego and beyond what rational traditional science can find empirical evidence of?

There are truths about us and our journey that underlie the religious conceptions we inherited. In this context, angels and devils, for instance, are metaphors of the energies that assist and afflict us beyond our control. When our accent is on proof of the factual or literal nature of these metaphors, we are caught up in a reduction of the transpersonal to the personal.

As we saw above, the Buddha who is venerated now is not the historical person Gautama but an embodiment of enlightenment patent in him and latent in us: "This very body: the Buddha." We bow to both his actualized enlightenment and our potential enlightenment, dormant in us, awakened in him. A sutra says: "Once free of ego, you will know you are the Buddha." Dogen Zenji says it too: "This birth and death [our own] is the life of Buddha." As with Buddha consciousness, Christ consciousness does not refer to the historical Jesus. In fact, Saint Paul hardly ever mentions the events of Jesus' life. In the psycho-spiritual world of the psyche, the coming of the messiah is an inner event, a realization of a salvation that means being saved from bondage to the fears and desires of the ego. It is freedom from the snares of ego inflation in favor of openness to a divine and humbling movement toward wholeness. This is "the movement but not by force" of ego referred to by Lao-tzu.

Jesus and Buddha are not gods in a transcendent, totally other, sense. They exhibit the possibility of the farther reaches of our humanity, that is, of our divinity/Self. Jesus and Buddha are not mere personifications but archetypal epiphanies of the unconditional love, eternal wisdom, and healing power realizable in all of us. This is not simple allegory but an articulation of the zeal of the Self to exhibit itself in the living images of saints and bodhisattvas. They are the timely and timeless gifts that compose our spiritual legacy. Without them, we would never have known what heights humanity could reach, which borders it could cross. We might have thought we could go only as far as Alexander the Great did or Plato said we could.

EARTH AND I

> *If personality is the universe in miniature, then each of our memories and images are as much a part of nature as the winds and the sands and the stars.*
>
> —JEAN HOUSTON

Another dualism we may be caught in is that of ourselves versus the earth. This gap creates alienation from nature. We still think the earth is flat, an object for our use. Actually the earth is a living being, since it is self-nourishing, changing, cycling through life and death, consciously pursuing unity. Its lively energy is continually moving, constantly musical, confluently loving. Once we acknowledge and honor this, our alienation is transformed into communion. The monochrome world then opens into incalculably myriad rainbows.

Human consciousness is how the universe reflects upon itself. We are not living on the earth; we are part of how it lives. We are living elements of it. We are organs by which the universe survives. Only our misunderstanding and bias make us think it is all separate or we are on it as we may be on a concrete floor. Humankind is one of the species of nature, not an opponent or ruler of it. The early humans had no sophisticated egos to separate them from the things of nature. To be more consciously one with nature, we can bravely remove what comes between us and it, the dualism of "I in here" and "it out there."

The closed ego looking out at the world as separate sees only death and the end and lives in fear. The open Self that is one with nature and sees the seasons as its own knows that death is not the end but only part of a continuing cycle. This is how nature combines opposing forces and becomes a source and cause of joy. In fact, since the universe is still evolving, it is still being created. To be "made in God's image" means that we are what nature is still imagining. We are the creation moment in which the ongoing work of creation/evolution becomes visible. Joseph Campbell said that there is a reviving of the sacred in our present reverence for the earth, a release of creative imagination, mutual love, and even mysticism.

The archetypal coalescence of human/divine/earthly was commemorated in ancient times most splendidly at Eleusis in Greece. The mysteries of Demeter and Persephone were celebrated there annually. The Greeks reenacted Persephone's return, escorted by Hermes, to her mother after being raped and kidnapped into the underworld by Hades, the shadow lord of death. Demeter, goddess of agriculture, grieved deeply for this loss, and infertility ravaged the earth while Persephone was gone. Demeter allowed the crops to grow again once her daughter was set free. Thus an accommodation was made between life and death. Demeter chose ultimately to accept the shadow (Hades) rather than to destroy him. Note the paradoxical metaphor in this combination of opposites: plant life comes into being because of a disappearance (planting the seed); Persephone disappears and then reappears, and with her comes abundant growth. The myth shows that Demeter and Persephone are not sufficient for full fecundation of the earth or of the psyche. Both dark and light seasons are required. Hades, the dark side, is a necessary ingredient in the process. Physical and spiritual fertility will require both male and female energies, both the bright sun and the cold shadow.

"The first effect of initiation into the mystical temple of the world is not knowledge but an impression, a sense of reverent awe and wonder at the sight of the divine spectacle presented by the visible world," wrote Aristotle on the rites at Eleusis. The intention of these ancient earth rites was to engender not a new knowledge but a vision of a new world *in this world*. Transitory appearances contain ineradicable realities. The initiates at Eleusis were filled with a lasting joy. They found incontrovertibly and reliably the impetus to go on with life. They knew now by experience that everything that lives dies, only to be reborn. They knew that the shadow contains and releases the light. They blazed a path between two worlds, holding and reconciling both earth to heaven and heaven to earth, life to death and death to life: all one reality. (We refer to this same reality when we say "on earth as it is in heaven.") Initiates exulted in the lyrical pageant of rebirth, the spiritual contract signed between life and death. They found a threshold to life in death's dark palace. These are spiritual nuptial rites because they join two realms: death and life as a cycle, not as a dead end.

At Eleusis eternal life was not about the preservation of individual identities but about the one divine identity that keeps appearing between the annual buds and harvests. Immortality in ancient myths was not about the preservation of any individual ego identity but about the diamond permanence of the immortal Self within and around us. Our personal identity becomes immortal when we live out in our allotted lifetime the loving purposes of the Self. Then we survive with the Self not as separate ego personalities but perhaps as identifiable electrons around a divine nucleus. Dante saw the blessed in paradise as petals around the mystical rose of light and oneness.

Nature's cycle of die-to-bloom and bloom-to-die guarantees renewal. Not static changelessness but this trustworthy cycle is what guarantees "this very place: the lotus paradise." Demeter is the goddess of life from the earth (agriculture) and Persephone is married to Death. Thus death and life are all one process. Like Persephone, we experience dissolution and then we regroup, reconstitute, and remember ourselves. We do this by our work, and it happens to us by grace. This is the style with crops too. We make the *effort* of planting and tending, and nature grants the *grace* of sun and rain. Deep in the psyche, the archetypal world mirrors and cooperates with the natural world at every turn.

The archetypal mystery of Eleusis is precisely that of Christ, Osiris, Dionysus, and others. In the Christian era, however, the shrine of Eleusis was abandoned rather than renamed and continued. But no amount of disuse or disregard could dispel its power to strike passersby with its haunting aura of spiritual aliveness: "Forsaken Eleusis celebrates herself," is a saying that comes to us from early Christian times.

The mysteries of Eleusis illustrate dramatically a parallel we keep encountering: what happens in nature—the seed is buried and then the wheat blooms—happens in spirituality. Persephone is buried and then returns alive. That happens in us. We visit the void/crisis and come back with new lively energy. In our shadow is our fuller life.

Like Persephone, I may be dragged downward by Hades, but I will also be hoisted upward by Hermes. When I know nature I know God; when I know myself I know God. This equation keeps materializing: The natural is to the divine as to the human. Jung, in his essay "Transformation Symbolism in the Mass," shows how the Catholic mass is a striking man-ifestation of this equation: "What is sacrificed under the forms of bread and wine is nature, man, and God, all com-bined in the unity of the symbolic gift."

It is all one story, one same journey, one same set of ingredients: effort and grace in the miracle of life renewing itself. In nature there are seasons with endings and begin-nings. In myths there are deaths and rebirths. In our lives there are beginnings and endings, dark shadows and lumi-nous possibilities. Walt Whitman wrote of the spiritual equa-tion in a poem about death: "Lilac and star and bird twined with the chant of my soul."

In the practical terms of our daily life, on "this little threshing floor that makes us all so ferocious," as Dante says, what is the life-renewing promise in the death-and-resurrec-tion theme? The promise is not that things will work out per-fectly or positively for us every time, no more than every spring is bright and wet enough to bring every bud to bloom or that every saint or hero overcomes every demon shadow met. The promise is only this: Overall, things will work out in such a way that we will have the chance to work through what happens to us and then look through the resultant de-bris for some benefit or boon. Can I accept that adult divi-dend as sufficient?

In my first personal journey to Eleusis, I experienced syn-chronicity and the shadow in a powerful way. I have always been especially moved by the elevation of the Host during the Catholic mass. I even dream of being at mass at that moment. When I was myself an active priest, I devotedly cherished that high point of the rite and felt a mysterious awe during it, as if it were a minibeatific vision. To me the ritual raising aloft of the white translucent Host is like a human reenactment of the sunrise, the sovereign moment of letting the light through. The climax of the Eleusinian mysteries, intriguingly, was a similar vision: an ear of wheat was held aloft for all to see, a symbol of the new life that grows from the dying of the seed. Pindar referred to this ritual moment as "the end of life as well as its divinely granted beginning."

On my visit to Eleusis, I lay down on the very spot where it is believed that the ear of wheat was held aloft. While I lay on the hard rocks and earth, l closed my eyes and felt powerful forces moving through me. It was just like the feeling of holding the Host aloft. When I opened my eyes, the first things I noticed were some snail shells. They seemed to be a gift from the Great Mother, and that fit for me, as a lifelong devotee of Mother Mary. (In fact, there is a chapel to Mary at Eleusis and a folktale that she was taken there as a child by the angels.) I gathered three of the snail shells and stored them carefully in my backpack in a tight metal container.

A month later I returned home and placed the shells on my windowsill. They were a perfect souvenir of that unforgettable day at the mysterious shrine. The next morning I saw only two shells. I looked up, and at the top of the window I saw that one of them was alive and moving. What a striking way the goddess had of bringing home to me the perpetuity of her promise: death in life and life in death. What I thought was dead was alive. How many times in my life have I made that mistake?

In Orphic ritual there is an instruction to the soul in its journey through the underworld after death: "When you reach the Black Poplar, you will be asked: 'Who are you?' Do not give your human name. Answer: 'I am a child of the earth and the starry sky.'" My identification of myself by my name or role is a product of the limited attention of my ego. I am always, only, and already all of everything. A scripture, a goddess, a saint, a poet, and a scientist join us in seeing this:

> There is nothing in the universe that is not myself.
> (Upanishads)

I will give you the life span of the sky. (Isis to Seti)
I am a changing, multiform life of immense prodigious size.
  (Saint Augustine)
Trees and stones seem more like me each day. (Rilke)
There is not one cell in my body that was not once part of a
  star. (Carl Sagan)

THE PRACTICE

There were three stages in the sacred rites at Eleusis, and they
seem to be metaphors for our spiritual journey:

• Entering the underworld (symbolized by the rites happening at night): willingness to enter our own darkness. This is
the work of acknowledging our negative shadow, a step we
take.

• Honoring and joining the god of riches (Plutus): discovery
of light within ourselves. This is the work of finding the kernel of goodness, the positive shadow that appears as a result
of befriending the negative shadow, another step that initiates
a shift.

• Being reborn: The mysteries endowed people with hope because they showed that humans *can* be reborn, in every sense.
We can go through pain and survive it, we can die and live
simultaneously, we can let go and go on. Death is not the
cessation of existence but a liquidation of our prior attachments, our limits, our ego, our fears. In fact, death has not
been reckoned as final in any rite or myth in human history.
This part of our journey is not a step but a shift, not work
but grace, the assisting force that visits us in the house of
psyche where the shadow is befriended. The belief in assisting

grace is ancient in the psyche. Aristotle observed that those who are being initiated into the Eleusinian mysteries were not obliged to do something but to let an interior experience happen. From ancient times, in the perennial philosophy, it has been known that effort is not a sufficient ingredient for transformation. For Plato our inner spark is a gift from the gods. Our attraction to light is a homesickness for the source of it. In *Phaedrus* he says that the origin and goal of wholeness is in divine hands, noting also that something wayward in us (our scared ego?) countermands our urge toward wholeness, as one refractory horse in a chariot team can throw it off course.

Contemplate the three elements above more deeply and then see how they can correspond to the features of your own personal journey toward wholeness:

• A visit to the underworld of our psyche seems necessary. It is a trip through our subconscious and subbody to find out our own secrets. Continue to keep track of your dreams and notice the shadow figures that arise in them. Establish a journaling dialogue with these archetypal features of yourself. They connect your inner life to your daily experience.

• A finding or recovery of our unique gifts means opening the potentials both in and around us, since the Self is both immanent and transcendent. Recall the characteristics of yourself that were praised in childhood: at home, at school, and elsewhere. List all the positive qualities and create a list of affirmations that reflect them. Look closely at each one and find the spiritual dimension of it, that is, how it is a challenge or call to serve the world through the sharing of your unique gifts.

• Certain things about us reveal something transcendent, not conditioned by time or life's crises. Love and creativity are examples. When love wishes for permanence, it is because it came from that realm and wants to return to it. How do love and creativity figure in your life? Are you more loving and more creative now than you were in childhood? Acknowledge in affirmation or prayer how love and creativity come from the Source of all life and help you return to it.

• A result of befriending the shadow is that dark and light are recognized as interior realities. In befriending the shadow, a form of initiation, we recognize this and no longer need to flee, control, or destroy it. Both loss and grief initiate us into the realization that all is transitory and that we are not entitled to an exemption from that stern reality. A wound is the cost of opening. How have your personal wounds opened you? How have they closed you?

• Rebirth is a crossing of the threshold from the conditions of mortal existence to the world of the Self. List the milestone events of your life, the painful crises, the failures and successes, and your strongest relationships. Each of them was meant to make you a person of more love, wisdom, and healing, was meant to conduct you to your destiny. Without "yes, buts," acknowledge that this has happened and look for ways to foster it even further. What did you lose and what did you gain in each of your milestone experiences? How have others benefited from your journey? How are you fighting the movement that wants to happen now? How are you allowing it? Who is helping or hindering you in this mysterious process? Whom do you have to thank for whatever in your journey has already been successful?

• Meditate on these passages from *The Divine Milieu* by Teilhard de Chardin: "Throughout my life, *through* my life the world has, little by little, caught fire in my sight until, aflame all around me, it has become almost completely luminous from within. . . . Such has been my experience in contact with the earth, the diaphany of the divine at the heart of the universe on fire, . . . a fire: capable of penetrating everywhere, and gradually, spreading everywhere. . . . Our spiritual being is continually nourished by the countless energies of the tangible world. . . . No power in the world can prevent us from savoring its joys because it happens at a level deeper than any power; and no power in the world, for the same reason, can compel it to appear."

BETWEEN FEAR AND DESIRE

Fear and desire are normal for and useful to our healthy and safe functioning in the world. Fear helps us avoid or fight what may harm us. Desire enlivens us and makes it possible for us to reach out for what we need. Both reveal us to ourselves. Fear and desire are not meant to be extinguished fully because then their opposite, egolessness, would be lost too. Fear and desire provide challenges to our integrative powers, but becoming caught in them or possessed by them ruins our chances for spiritual progress. To let fear and desire cycle through us, without stopping in us or stopping us, is how inner dualism yields to unity. Then dissatisfaction opens into completeness and inadequacy opens into the power to handle things. The completeness and the power are the underground springs below dissatisfaction and inadequacy.

Befriending the shadow of our ego makes it easier to hold our normal human fears and desires without becoming stuck in them, ruled by them, or attached to them. In medieval times, listing the seven deadly sins (seven articulations of ego stuckness in fear and desire) became a way of describing the obstacles to spiritual growth. And such is what they are, since they blockade the reaching and releasing of unconditional love, universal wisdom, and healing power. This is how to tell vice from virtue: one leads to ego fever and the other to the still waters of soul making. The dualism that divides good and evil can be reframed so that evil is seen as division itself and good as reconciling unity. The seven deadly vices are simply the articulations of separateness and divisiveness: pride, envy, greed, and so on. The virtues are manifestations of oneness: humility, loving-kindness, justice, and the like. Seeing God and things as separate from ourselves is the product of identifying with something. Therein lies the danger of attachment.

To Buddha the world was not "bad" or "evil" but insufficient. He proposed simply "being here now." This is mindfulness, attention to the moment without the ego's self-deceptive distractions: fear, desire, judgment, attachment to an outcome, and narcissism. It is a commitment to the authentic reality rather than to the fictional possibilities presented by fear and desire: redoing the past or planning to control the future.

Buddhist Tantra shows a path of moral virtue and centeredness: not escape *from* but stillness *in* the ongoing dramas of fear and desire. This stillness/mindfulness is our sitting squarely in our reality without being crushed or pushed by it. It is only when we get up from that position, stand against our own experience, that we are at the mercy of fear. Freedom from fear is, paradoxically, staying in it as *ours*. Govinda says: "The certainty that nothing can happen to us that does not in our innermost being belong to us is the foundation of fearlessness." As we remain faithful to our own reality, we are one with our universe and trust that precisely our own tailor-made destiny is unfolding within it.

As long as we see ourselves as separate, we will be at the mercy of desire. Things will stand out as real and graspable rather than as products of our dualistic habits of thought. The Buddhist Tantric solution is simple: we sit in desire without denying it. From that position we give up the sense of separate selfhood by letting go of ego and entering the emptiness of unconditional reality, that is, life unconditioned by attachment and desire, "under an empty autumn sky." The compassion of the horseman of enlightenment is stirred by such emptiness. He is not stopped by it; he loves to ride into it. "So nigh is grandeur unto our dust," as Emerson says. There is something about lowliness, freedom from the arrogance of ego, and spaciousness, freedom from ego solidity, that invites the grace of enlightenment. As we lighten ourselves, we let the light through. (In fact, once we see how much of what we think is illusion and how few distinctions are relevant, we can only burst out laughing.)

Notice the striking similarity between the opening poem by Changling and this passage from the Book of Job, where the same compassionate responsiveness is revealed: "Rain may fall on land where no one lives, and the deserts void of humankind, giving drink to the lonely wastes and making grass spring where everything was dry." (Job 38:26–27)

Nirvana is a way of describing the bliss of liberation from the self-deceptions of the ego. It is the reality of who we are once we let go of the comforting limits in our attachment to a wholly other rescuer god. One does not go to nirvana as we traditionally say one goes to heaven. One simply awakens, in the here and now, to what has always and already been the case: "This very place: the lotus paradise." There is a change in perspective though no objective change has occurred: like finding out one is (always and already) a twin.

The joy of realizing our true nature creates an exuberance in us to engage in the world with love. The awakened Buddha never tries to become compassionate. He is that automatically by awakening. What is awakening? It is freedom from the dualism of ourselves and our fears, ourselves and our desires, ourselves and all that is. Then compassion is the only option.

The goal of our evolution is not to be free from fear or desire but free from attachment to either one of them. Our work is to hold the tensions between them with a *relaxed grasp*. This is the path that opens between polarities when both are held in our embrace like twin babes at a mother's bountiful breasts. These are the little ones who grow up to be Braveheart and Cornucopia, with sleeves rolled up to garden the blossoming world and gather in its enriching harvests.

None of the above can cancel the one final and ironic possibility that the Zen scholar Hubert Benoit expresses so movingly: "It is precisely the fruitless attempt to seize the unseizable that results in awakening!" Sometimes vehement desire is just what it takes to show us the emptiness of desirable things. The Tibetans say disappointment is the swiftest chariot to enlightenment. Grave disappointment hurls us into the spaciousness where the epiphany of the Self appears: "the endless wastes where no one goes"—or can be stopped. "An empty autumn sky" betokens harvest time, but here instead we see only "endless wastes," and so there is a pervading mood of disappointment.

Only when every expectation disappears does the horseman of enlightenment appear. When no one has come through for us, he gets through to us. In our defeated ego's understanding of the mystery of our life we finally gain a glimpse of a transcendent plan that has always been at work; the horseman had been riding in our direction all along. We have only to stand mindfully when the horseman of enlightenment, silhouetted in the sunrise, waves us on.

THE PRACTICE

Read the following aloud. Write it out in your own words and repeat it each day until you finish reading this book:

I have it in me to enjoy desire and be free of its grip over me. I can become free of the habit of grasping the transitory and believing it has permanent gifts to give me. When I am caught in desire, I exaggerate and inflate the value and appeal of what I want. I act as if it were all there could be for me. Under the spell of desire, I go to sleep and become obsessed at the same time. As long as I act as if such delusions are all that compose me, I cannot contact the profound depths of my own potential. Potential means power, and my power is in the hands of the tyrant of ego as long as I remain imprisoned in my illusions.

The most inveterate and insidious habit of my ego is to believe that what I need is outside myself. To be fooled by such an empty promise is the most intrusive obstacle to enlightenment. When I renounce my preoccupation with the necessary outside, I liberate my boundless inner untapped potential. Renunciation does not consist in giving up my human pleasures but in giving up my unproportional expectations from these pleasures. Once I stop searching the streets, I can go down to the wine cellar of my own house, where so many vintages are gathering dust as they await uncorking. What is missing has always been and only is I, the best wine saved till last and waiting, wanting to be poured. "Be not afraid, *it* is I."

REALITY AND I: THE FARTHER REACHES OF MINDFULNESS

> *When the mind rests serene in the oneness of things, dualism vanishes by itself.*
>
> —SENG TSAN

We are on a spiritual path when we accommodate and then transcend the warring opposites that tug at us from ego. We become sane and awake when we stop struggling with them but simply hold them until a healing reconciliation occurs. We do this by giving to ourselves what we always wanted from others: we pay active attention to the reality that faces us without judgment, fear, control, expectation, or clinging. *Attention* means *pausing*. We tarry between stimulus and response, between thought and action, as we do between every breath we take. This is mindfulness, our breath-conscious meditative response to the here and now. It is a form of self-mirroring. In this attending to what is, I mirror and pledge my allegiance to the reality behind my present predicament rather than to my ego beliefs and images about it. This is the power of mindfulness to wake us up, "Like to the lark at break of day arising / From sullen earth, sings hymns at heaven's gate," as Shakespeare says.

Behind appearance (conventional reality) is formlessness (invisible reality). This invisible reality has no separate, inherent (freestanding, noncontingent) existence but is only space. The soul mediates this connection. Appearances are yang, a masculine energy of standing out. Yin is feminine energy, the void, a spaciousness within, not limited by form. The whole reality is figure and ground combined. So wholeness must be what we miss when we see in the ordinary way. I do not see the whole picture when I focus on one thing or when I am caught up in the dramatic embroideries around things or events. I see even less when I am obsessed or addicted. This is the ultimate danger in attachment to fear and desire. (At least we can be consoled by the fact that fear and desire are not absolutes. They are always relative, moving along a scale of one to ten.)

How can I contact the ground of my reality or the figure that has become ground if I am mired in ego layerings? There is no way to catch the difference, as to the eye ice and steam seem like totally different things. I need more than my eye, more than focused attention, to see fully. When I pay close attention, I see only figure. Diffuse attention is necessary, that is, attentiveness without attachment to any one thing, mindfulness. Then the ground of it all appears.

The Sanskrit word for *mindfulness* means "attend and stay." We simply stay with and attend to our reality long enough to access both figure and ground and so find the balance of wholeness. Here is a simple example: You and I are walking on the beach and I am listening to you speak. Meanwhile, I am also hearing the sound of the waves, which is the (back)ground to the story you are telling me. Your story is enriched by my attention to it *together with* the waves' sounds. It is all one rhythm. To my ears your story is the figure (what I attend to by my listening); the sound of the waves is the ground (what I hear without zeroing in on it). *Listen* is to figure as *hear* is to ground. Together they form one engaging image. Remember what Lorenzo said to Jessica in *The Merchant of Venice*: "Here will we sit, and let the sounds of music creep into our ears . . . such harmony is in immortal souls."

Figure and ground operate continually in the psychospiritual synthesis. Appearances are the visible figure, and behind appearances is the invisible ground of being, no-thing-ness. A form of mindfulness is to attend to the ground of being directly, letting go of attachment to the figure and allowing a shift of attention to the ground from which it has emerged. Here is an example: I drop my devastation with being left by my partner long enough to enter the archetypal ground below it, the orphan dimension of the child I am and always was. I thereby contact two underground springs in my present crisis: I have personal grief work to do about this loss and all the losses of my past that it revives, and I have a spiritual challenge to face and integrate the shadow side of the archetypal orphan child-hero's predicament. Much is afoot in my psyche, triggered by the abandonment, and it is out for higher stakes. This calamity is not only about my being left; it is about my being found. By mindfulness I left the figure and found the ground. A crisis may wash over me, after all, like the flooding Nile that fecundates the arid lands.

The ground of the visible is the invisible. It is Wordsworth's "a flash that has revealed the invisible world." Resting in this is pure mindfulness, the flash that finds the pause. The pause is to time what the emptiness of intrinsic separate existence is to being. Mindfulness brings us to the place where time and being, mutability and unconditionality, are one.

To believe that appearances are all there is means attachment to appearance. Wisdom is discovered when attention to an appearance reveals it to be a figure that has behind it the ground of another reality. This deeper reality is a pure spaciousness, an open potential that, unlike the limited appearance, is limitless. It is precisely the distinction between ego and Self.

In the Eastern view, around every figure is space and between one figure and another is space. This space is *shunyata,* the void that proves to be fertile because it offers us the fuller context, the ground of our reality, void of limits. Shunyata means that nothing exists independently of anything else; all is interdependent. It is not nihilism but an affirmation of the nature of everything as spacious. Wisdom is insight into this emptiness that is precisely the openness described in Revelation 19: "I saw Heaven open."

Existential guilt results from ego alienation from the Self. The anxiety of the existentialists about the void may not truly have been about an "ultimate condition." It may have come from their insistence that ego is the only reality. Ego loves linearity and hates cycles. If the existentialists had closed the gap between themselves and everything else, their angst might have become a sense of belonging to the earth, with all its legitimate transitoriness and seasons of change. Without the transitory, we might never have looked for the infinite. As the story of Demeter illustrates: to say yes unconditionally to shaky impermanence is, simultaneously, to be blessed with its stable promise of renewal. The paradox is that embracing the cycles *is* transcending them. It is individuation that creates the dialogue between ego and Self, instituting a transition from alienation to reconciliation. Opposites no longer contend, since the Self *is* conjunction.

THE PRACTICE

Mindfulness meditation is the daily practice that cuts through all our dualisms in one fell swoop: "Swiftly, with nothing spared, I am being completely dismantled," as Saint John of the Cross says of his ego once he is in meditation.

Another practice is *attunement* to the deeper, hidden implications of a concern. I tune in to the felt sense of the issue I am facing. (I thereby find the immense range of tunefulness in me.) This felt sense is the ground behind the figure of my issue. It is the soulful space around and behind the external drama. I locate the true essence and impact of the problem facing me by finding this fuller feeling sense of it. Using the example given earlier: When I have been abandoned in a relationship, I may feel totally isolated and unwanted. The archetypal orphan is visiting me. The hurt, indignant I has become the obsessive figure in my consciousness. I am now so caught up in this forlornness that I am actually joining in on the abandonment of me. I thereby feel trapped.

In the attuning way of focusing, I can experience the felt

sense of forlornness and trappedness and eventually contact the larger spiritual challenge of embracing the Adam and Eve condition of exile that all heroes have faced. (A hero is anyone who has lived through pain and become transformed by it. Pain is precisely about transformation and the deepening of character.) I am then locating an expansive spiritual ground in my ego-absorbing crisis. My exiled orphaned state is a heritage I have carried, and all humankind has carried, throughout the centuries; it must have meaning and usefulness in my soul's journey. This realization does not come through when I am concentrating on how bereft I am or on how bad someone was for leaving me. Then I am imprisoned in judgment and blame. Ego layers have become figure: "How dare she do this to me!" In attuning and focusing or mindfulness, I hit the pay dirt of my own newfound land, the ground of egolessness.

Thus an active visit to ground is freedom from the figure in the sense that I no longer have to identify with it, that is, remain attached to it. There is no it. I can watch the movie in my head and in my life without binding myself to any one character or plotline. When I drop attachment to outcome, a gap opens in my ego's vicious cycle of fear and desire, and surrender is the shift that results. Surrender of ego means letting go of the multiplicity of our fears and desires in favor of the unity of unconditional love, perennial wisdom, and healing power. This is also true devotion.

The Western psychological equivalent to all this is simply to take something as information and not have to act on it. Ken Wilber says: "Mysticism is not regression in the service of the ego but evolution in the transcending of the ego. . . . Ego strength is in our capacity for disinterested witnessing." This is how attunement and meditation, staying with what is, increases ego strength. Ego strength makes us confident enough to look beyond ourselves, and thereafter we see all humanity. Compassion opens from confident strength.

"One sees one's heart in all beings and all beings in one's heart. The love is the same for enemies or friends. One is the same in honor or in disgrace, in heat or cold, pleasure or pain, free from the chains of attachment," says the Bhagavad Gita.

It is a short step from "stay with what is" to "be what is." "This is my body," that is, this here-and-now reality, is my universe/Self. This is how *what is* becomes what everything is, the human, the divine, the natural. I am more than meets the eye, and so is everything. I and everything are the same. The space around me and everything is the same. Transcendence and immanence unite.

We fear this space and yet it grants us room to move. Are we ultimately fearing the opportunity to go on? This is the challenge that faces us when heaven opens.

This space is another entry into the unity of all beings, all equally arising from a deathless pure open ground of existence. This is the ground we go back to at death, a living ground, as Persephone goes back to the ground from which she will come to life again. This is the ground on which Jacob lay and there discovered the stairway to heaven. From it grows the tree under which Buddha sat and the cross on which Jesus hung.

Where is my ground and where is my tree? What in my life creates space for an unobstructed view of my real nature? What makes room for everything? What in my life and relationships is conducive to the emergence of my inner wisdom? What will I have to let go of to be free of the maintenance of separateness from which so many distractions are derived?

BEHIND APPEARANCES

The oneness is gently and graciously present to anyone who wishes it.

—PLOTINUS

Once wholeness is acknowledged as figure and ground:
Behind the negative shadow is the positive shadow.
Behind the appearance of dualism is the ground of oneness.
Behind the friend-enemy division is the love that chooses reconciliation over retaliation.
Behind the life-death polarities is not an ending but a cycle of transformation.
Behind restless desire is plenitude and serenity.
Behind fear is an alternative: the freedom from having to be ruled by it.
Behind alienation from nature is communion within it.
Behind our mortality is the immortal diamond.
Behind the ephemeral is the everlasting.

All of *it* is I. How well this fits with Freud's view of the happy result of therapy: "Where it was, there I shall be." By this he meant that there is no longer any dualistic split between ourselves and our experience of the world. Before working on ourselves, we imagined that everything in our life was an it, over and against us. Afterward, we saw that the so-called it is actually ourselves projecting and introjecting. When "it" is restored to "I," we take responsibility for all that seems to be coming at us as an integral part of who we are. Then there is no it, only I. Wallace Stevens stated it this way: "I am what is around me." Giordano Bruno does not go far enough when he says: "Through the light that shines in natural things, one mounts to the life that presides over them." Rather, it is that through the light that shines through natural things, one *is* the life that *resides within* them. Only one life, not one below yearning for one above. We are already on earth as in heaven.

THE PRACTICE

• Why am I on earth now? Two facts help me know the answer: (1) Since I am here only at the instigation and by the ongoing cooperation of others, my presence seems to have something to do with them, and (2) the whole universe is evolving, so I, as part of it, seem to be here to cooperate in that continuing evolution. This must be why I was given this lifetime and why I am equipped with exactly the potential gifts to make my unique contribution in it.

How do I know what these gifts are? They are found in two places: where my bliss meets my talent and where my unique needs, values, and wishes abide.

When I follow my bliss, when I live in accord with my deepest needs, values, and wishes, I am self-loyal. When I find ways to do this with and for others, I can trust I am making my appropriate contribution, since the two facts of human life are now fulfilled in me. The sense of something missing in my life or the sense of emptiness in myself may be about a lack of this very ful*fill*ment. Something in me is calibrated to live out this gift-giving mission and I am restless until it happens. This may be why fearless freedom of choice is so important. It is important because only through that freedom in my choices can the world move on through me.

I am not alone. I have models, assisting forces. There are also afflicting forces. The work is to ally myself with the forces that lead to love, wisdom, and healing power and to oppose compassionately those who would lead me to hate, fear, and division, and then to bring them along. It takes hope and pluck. The afflicting forces in my life so far were necessary for my full evolution as a person of depth and compassion. These qualities do not emerge when "all is calm, all is bright." They come through only when the witches have their chance to mix up my brew.

All that has happened and all that others have done to or for me has been what it took. This is why an unconditional yes is the only legitimate response to it all. I say yes now to all that has been, is, and will be. I am on love's path.

• Am I living out my destiny? Am I loving with all the force and to the fullest extent of which I am capable? I know that it is happening when these conditions prevail:

> I am living the life of my true self rather than any false self based on others' expectations or demands. This means that I am living in accord with my own unique needs, values, passions, and wishes.
>
> I have found ways to activate my potentials, to be all I can be, to open and use my gifts.
>
> I am following my bliss and have, or am gaining, the talents to meet it and make it a career or lifestyle.
>
> I am activating the spiritual powers that are portrayed in the saints and sages whom I admire or venerate: unconditional love, perennial wisdom, and healing power.
>
> I am giving the fruits of all the above to others near and dear and, wherever possible, far and wide. Full humanity is my destiny and my best and only contribution to the universe. I am richly and enduringly supported in this venture of finding my wholeness and sharing it. My whole being is calibrated for this wonderful project. An inner urgency for wholeness and the giving of it is, and always has been, working in me. My work is only to cooperate in what is already at work within and around me.

• On what threshold do I find myself standing now?

> What is behind me?
> What is before me?
> What are my griefs about what I am leaving?
> What are my fears about what I am entering?
> Who or what assists me in going on?
> Who or what attempts to hold me back?

• Answer the above questions in your journal and share them with one other person.

An Alchemical Adventure

We are approaching now the alchemical courses, which transmute while they raise the vibration. For what is maturity but the turning of basic substances into rare and precious ones with the skillful addition of just the right thing at just the right moment?

—Jean Houston, *A Mythic Life*

Alchemical work is a long-standing metaphor for befriending the shadow and finding the Self. Alchemy is the ancient spiritual science of transforming prime matter into the philosopher's stone. Prime matter is the apparently useless material the alchemist begins with: lead, earth, offal, anything contemptible. The philosopher's stone is symbolic of the spiritual Self of wholeness. The stone was thought to be the emerald that fell from the crown of Lucifer in the battle in heaven between the forces of light and darkness. The stone is thus directly representative of the shadow and the power-conferring results of our work with it.

Standard alchemy was an antecedent to chemistry in that it had to do with substances and elements—transforming lead into gold. Gold is an element that resulted from the expanding and contracting, heating and cooling of hydrogen sixteen billion years ago. Gold, like all of creation, is the result of the combination of opposites. It is star stuff, like us. It is precious, universal, and eternal like the Self. The gold that adorns our finger today was once, perhaps, the gift of Caesar to Cleopatra. Thus gold is about transformation and about time, the enduring elements of befriending the shadow, the dark gold of the psyche.

Spiritual alchemy was an anticipation of depth psychology more than chemistry. Its concern was not about physical gold but about the gold of the true Self that is born from the ashes of the shadow ego. The aware alchemist saw the unconscious in the darkness of prime matter and thus came to understand its correspondence with the psyche. The work of alchemy is the befriending of the shadow to release its emerald-gold of wholeness, the Self, Buddha nature, Christ consciousness.

Our bodies and limitations are, paradoxically, the very and only stuff of wholeness. Marie-Louise von Franz says: "It usually takes prolonged suffering to burn away all the superfluous psychic elements concealing the stone. . . . But some profound inner experience of the Self does occur . . . at least once in a lifetime. From a psychological standpoint, a genuine religious attitude consists of an effort to discover this unique experience and to keep in tune with it so that the Self becomes an inner partner toward whom one's attention is continually turned." The "tune" is the harmony of the spheres that "is in immortal souls," as Shakespeare notes in *The Merchant of Venice.*

Alchemy and, later, depth psychology were the first attempts of humankind to find a path to wholeness outside the parameters of religious dogma. As von Franz says above, the truly religious person is the one who makes a personal unique journey, entering the forest "where there is no path," as the knights of the Grail did. Why seek the Grail of the Eucharist far and wide when it can be found in any parish church? The ritualized path is not enough for beings like us who have to find out for ourselves. We require the advice of conventional sources, but we are also calibrated to find the Source itself in our own way. It will be discovered inside, in the only room in us that convention never reached, our pilgrim soul. That soul is always and already at the holy shrine of wholeness.

The alchemical opus does not end with individual work and achievement; it is also a consecration for service to the world. We become whole for one another. Alchemy, our shadow work, replicates the spiritual journey from personal work to world work in three stages:

1. Separation of body and soul creates a union of soul and spirit.
2. Soul-spirit unity rejoins the body.
3. Soul-spirit-body unity joins the world soul.

Alchemy, like Buddhist Tantra, is thus a form of continuity, since the work does not consist in evading chaos and confusion but in staying with it and working with it till it yields renewal. As lead has the makings of gold, so the shadow has the makings of wholeness. Grace broods over the chaotic deep as the Holy Spirit did at the dawn of creation. We turn the base metal of our limitations (negative shadow) into the gold of liberation (positive shadow). How? It happens in every little letting go of fear and attachment. This exponentially unleashes the untapped potential of our true Self. Attempts to eliminate anything imperfect vitiate the work of alchemy. This is why the spiritual gold is wholeness, not perfection.

The goal of the work of alchemy was the philosopher's stone, the Buddhist *vajra,* the diamond essence of the human heart, radiant and indestructible. Our enlightened consciousness is like that diamond, containing and refracting every nuance of light. It is also like emptiness because it is without color and yet receives all colors. Emptiness in the psyche is a metaphor for spiritual liberation, freedom from conceptual habit and from captivity in fear and desire. We then ride to enlightenment freely and proudly like the horseman in Changling's poem.

Lumps of coal, with time and under pressure, can become diamonds. This is a metaphor for us and the universe as well as for our crises and their possibilities. Both coal and diamonds are ultimately carbon, the same substance, visible differently at the two ends of the same spectrum, like our bodies and our world. This shows the potential of our lowly ego for transformation and the psychic forces that animate it once we free it from the clutches of the neurotic ego. Jesus was born in a stable, a way of confirming that in the most despicable place in us light can appear. "He who has found the philosopher's stone, the jewel of an enlightened heart, transforms mortality to immortality, and finitude into infinity," a Hindu sutra says. The perennial philosophy appears in the similarity of worldwide metaphors.

There are examples in the Western psychological tradition of the alchemical shadow work. Jung declared the remedy always to be in the symptom. In fact, whenever we work on a problem that disturbs us and find within it a source of healing and transformation, we are befriending our shadow in the context of spiritual alchemy. Opposites attract and help one another. "There is a budding morrow in midnight," writes Keats.

Finally, in alchemy, elements relinquish their individual characteristics for the sake of a universal goal. Once the particularities of each element are burned away, the essential oneness of the world soul appears in all its glorious simplicity. This is another metaphor for how our individual ego traits can be thrown blithely into the bonfire of universal purposes and nothing is lost. The renewed phoenix-ego in the desert only finds more effective ways to live out its radiant destiny among the dunes. The contours of the dunes may change with the burning rays of the sun and the torrential winds, but the mysterious and ever shimmering desert abides in all its dramatic glory.

In alchemy all is useful in the ongoing release of wholeness. Buddhist Tantra is an Eastern equivalent of this. *Tantra* means "thread." It is the fundamental and elemental continuity of human, god, and nature. Tibetan Buddhists call Tantra "the express train to enlightenment." It is a meditation style that does not propose eliminating attachment and fear but using their energy to move us on. This is like our practice: *befriending* the shadow. Attempting to root out fear or desire causes a logjam in the psyche. We befriend and capitalize on attachment by allowing anything to arise, attending to it, calling it by name, experiencing it fully, and letting it go. This lets its creative energy through. We befriend our fear by admitting we feel it, letting ourselves feel it fully, and then acting as if fear were not stopping us. Why would we kill the shadow of our ego to live fully? We would thereby throw away our best chance at creativity. We would be like alchemists who were burning down their laboratories.

Tantra honors the Buddha nature, continuously enlivening and renewing everything by the full experience of it. In alchemy the unacceptable is used for the achievement of the more than acceptable. In Tantra the same thing occurs: our worst becomes the best vehicle for the very best. The negative shadow befriended becomes the positive shadow released. We transform the useless rather than discard it and then its usefulness recompenses us abundantly. Liberation becomes possible without our first having to clear up all our neuroses. We can rewrite rather than eradicate.

We may identify with the worst in us. This is a distortion of fact that blocks access to wholeness. It is possible to acknowledge what we dislike about ourselves without construing ourselves to be only that. Tantra is based on trust in the essential wholeness always and already in us, our Buddha nature. When we say "I am Buddha," we begin to expand our vision of ourselves. We see the whole picture: "I am the limited person who makes so many mistakes and fails so often at loving, and I am also the limitless love that wants to give itself to everyone." (That sentence is a very powerful affirmation.) The work is not to identify only with the good, nor always to run from what is bad. It is to focus on our Buddha nature, which contains all our opposites and reconciles them to us. As Dante says: "The infinite goodness has such wide arms that it takes whatever turns to it."

Whatever forces designed us built nothing into us that could not become and lead to good. Our psyches were furnished in such a way that everything about us is good or redeemable, not good or bad. Evil is a choice, not a characteristic. We flawed humans with all our symptoms and fears remain, nonetheless, the rightful heirs of glory. No matter how badly we may behave, we can still find the spiritual path. Now, on these pages, we have been learning how to do the work that can make that happen. We are also finding out that there were always people on this planet who knew it too. We join the alchemists, cabalists, mystics, Tantrists, and clowns who saw that everything about us has good humor. As with pigs, everything about us is of value, no matter how ugly and apparently useless. Only the oink of complaint cannot be turned into gold.

Alchemists *did* succeed in finding gold; they brought the opportunity for wholeness out of the grim prison of dogmatism and religious parochialism and into the concrete grasp of individual experience. The practice of befriending the shadow is meant to contribute in that same alchemical way, to find practical and personal ways to transform ego limitation into wholeness.

An oracle represents sources of knowledge that are beyond ordinary ego consciousness. To be open to that voice within ourselves and everywhere around us is the equivalent of a pilgrimage to Delphi. The Delphic priestess sat on a stool deep in the earth. Buddha touched the earth as the witness to his truth. Wisdom thus arises *from deep in nature* and speaks *through* us. In ancient Rome women checked out a new plan or intuition by pulling up a clod of earth. If it yielded easily, the answer was yes, if not it was no. Earth was respected as an arbiter and collaborator in human decision and destiny. This respect for the camaraderie of nature and ourselves is soulfulness. It is not transcendence of nature but embodiment in it.

Deep in earth is molten fire, so oracular wisdom is an alchemical reality: a promise of the spiritual from the material. Perhaps anything we imagine as ordinary or useless has great possibility. A stunning fact then emerges into consciousness: the vast potential we see in our own positive shadow is also in nature, in the moment, in images, in our problems. Everything has a positive shadow. Every wasteland is a garden in waiting.

> *For I am every dead thing*
> *In whom love wrought new alchemy.*
> *For his art did express*
> *A quintessence even from nothingness,*
> *From dull privations and lean emptiness:*
> *He ruined me and I am rebegot*
> *Of absence, darkness, death, things which are not.*
>
> —JOHN DONNE

THE PRACTICE

Befriending the shadow requires the determination to do the work *at any cost*. The dark side of ego is in its willingness *to get its way at any cost to others.* Arrogance is autonomous self-assertion at the expense of others. The bright side of the Self is its enthusiasm *to elicit wholeness at any cost.* Here are some sentences from the preceding pages that trace this ironic theme. Consider them and notice which ones fit for you *before and after* your work in this book:

- What an image of the self-defeat awaiting the ego in its compulsion to win at any cost!
- I have to be loved, be respected, and given preference by everyone, all the time, no matter what!
- Bruce never grieves; he only looks for ways to make up for what he has lost, no matter who else may lose in the process.
- "I have to succeed no matter what the cost to my health, my integrity, or my self-esteem. I am committed to acting in accord with my father's deepest needs, values, and wishes. I am living his life."
- The path of egoless love is not about safety. It is about love at any cost.
- Do I dare choose to be myself no matter how it hurts or how much it costs?
- This is the true source of our hope as humans: no matter how bad we are or look, we have another side.
- To be creative requires that we be able and willing to visit all the dark regions of our psyche, no matter how primitive or disturbing.
- This is acting in accord with a standard of friendliness no matter what someone has done to you.
- When we go on loving, no matter what hand life or people deal us, the Self triumphs.
- The Nuremberg trials declared to the world just how responsible each of us is to have, know, and live in

accord with humanitarian standards of behavior, no matter who is in charge.

- I am touched very deeply by your capacity to love me no matter what.
- "There is in the psyche a process that seeks its own goal no matter what the external factors may be." (C. G. Jung)

Throughout this book you have encountered "The Practice." At the same time, the theme of grace has balanced that of effortful work and practice. Toward the end of his poem on the dark night of the soul, Saint John, after describing the steep and toilsome ascent to the divine, says: "From all endeavor ceasing." The mystical union and fulfillment begin only when the work yields to surrender. This crucial and humorous irony is the only fitting close to these chapters. All the work has been but a prologue to an alchemical opus by something, we know not what, always at work doing, we not how, just what it takes for our enlightenment. Changling's poem said it all: the horseman of awakening arrives only in the land of no-thing when there is no one left working. Jacob, in the Bible, stops when the sun sets—when there is no further chance to keep going—and only then is he greeted with the conjunction of the finite and the infinite, a ladder in a dream connecting heaven and earth. Only in a dream could it happen, that is, unconjured by conscious exertion.

As a final exercise, congratulate your healthy ego for all the work you have done. Thank your higher Self for leading you to this work and assisting you in doing it. Now lie back, close your eyes, let your hands drop, and breathe out a heartfelt sigh. As you breathe in deeply, feel yourself totally opening to whatever may now come to you, through you. There is nothing left to say or do. All has been done. All is immemorially known. In this moment, you are utterly receptive to what is next in your life, utterly trusting of its appropriateness, utterly excited by what surprises it holds in store.

> *Things are losing their hardness. Now even my body lets the light through.*
>
> —VIRGINIA WOOLF

Epilogue: Jacob's Ladder

$\mathcal{J}$ACOB'S STORY IN Genesis is full of shadow references. Jacob was a fellow who always found a way out of things, one who could always charm his way to what he wanted. When his charms failed, Jacob had to run from his homeland. This was out of character for someone as shrewd and resourceful as Jacob. He was bereft of his ego resources, and his familiar landscape was left behind. This is how we know something spiritual is afoot. The puny ego is ready to be nurtured to greatness by the Self.

"Jacob stopped for the night because the sun had set." This is the stop moment, the necessary pause, when we can achieve no more by the light of consciousness. We have to visit the underworld, the shadow unconscious where effort ends and ancestral wisdom begins. It is the dark night of the soul that grants access to the deepest reaches of the positive cosmic shadow, the God who will be encountered in the darkness of our personal shadow.

With a stone for a pillow, Jacob dreamed of a ladder connecting earth and heaven, with angels ascending and descending, a metaphor for the end of dualism, affirming that all the possibilities of spiritual access are now activated. Angels are the healing third that arises between earth and heaven. God appeared at the top of the ladder, promising: "I will give you the land on which you are lying; I will increase your descendants and be with you always."

When he awoke, Jacob exclaimed: "Surely the Lord is here and I was *unaware* of it! How awesome is this place! This is none other than the House of God and Gate of Heaven!" He then stood the stone upright, poured oil on it, and named the place Bethel, house of God. "Unaware" refers to his unconscious state. The shadow is a suitable locus for his vision of the transcendent because it is beyond the reach of his conscious ego's intellect and will, the familiar inner shelter he has finally relinquished. Jacob then shows ritual reverence, that is, conscious attention, to the place in nature where the vision occurred. This is mindfulness as well as an active-imagination response to his dream.

Jacob received his spiritual mandate in and through nature. He was granted a sense of trust that safety would attend him in life and he would be supported on his journey. Jacob was headed for Haran, but now he realized that this very place was his destination. He had found the passport to paradise in the shadow of his own tradition. The place he stopped at was once an ancient pagan shrine to a stone god, hence the stone that becomes a shrine. A shrine is a holy place, a place where wholeness can be revealed and granted.

Jacob was grieving the loss of his family. Grief is often the prelude to spiritual riches and awakening in heroic stories. Remember that Demeter was grieving the loss of Persephone when she gave the gift of agriculture to humankind and the promise of an endless cycle of fecundity from barrenness, life from death, light from darkness. Here is also the connection between the psychological and the spiritual: we grieve psychologically and grow spiritually. Ego opens by its yes to the work and is then confirmed by the transforming power of the Self. In Christian myth, Mary mournfully holds the broken body of Jesus as depicted in the Pietà and is thereby the midwife to his resurrection. The broken and disintegrated is reconstituted and integrated; this is the sanguine mystery of destruction and regeneration.

Jacob is not at an oasis but in the midst of the wasteland. Jacob is a wasteland *within* too, full of remorse, grief, and fear. In the midst of the darkest despair is the opening to revelation: "because the sun had set." In the most desolate and darkest place we find the stairway to heaven. In other words, what looks to the ego like unpromising barrenness is readiness for abundance. Opposites combine and paradoxes abound.

Changling's poem becomes even clearer: The horseman of enlightenment comes from the west, where "the sun had set." The wasteland is the only suitable ground into which the figure of enlightenment can enter. This is the same land referred to by Emily Dickinson: "Hope is the thing with feathers. . . . I've heard it in the chillest land." Even a Christmas carol of our childhood said it: "In thy dark streets shineth the everlasting light." We have known all this for years.

We may wonder why Jacob chose a stone as a pillow. Yet every reader of this book has many relatives who sleep against a stone: tombstones represent the immortal durability of the soul. There is an archetypal—and alchemical—theme in human history connecting stone, the unconscious, the divine, and destiny. In ancient times, a practice in a temple was the incubation of dreams. One contacted an oracle by sleeping with his or her head against a sacred stone, the abode of the god. A dream was sent from the god in response to a question or as a healing of a malady. There is also the story of Pharaoh Thutmose IV, who was sleeping under the stone head of the Sphinx when he dreamed that his destiny was securely promised by the gods.

Jacob's dream is a healing and empowering theophany. He finds the numinous residing in nature. The stone becomes the launching pad to the nondual dimension. "This [earth, my soul] is the House of God and Gate of Heaven." Is this the same philosopher's stone of alchemy that fell from the crown of Lucifer in the battle between the opposing forces of good and evil?

After his vision, Jacob is no longer arrogant and wily. Now his humbled ego faces an immensity that loves him unconditionally. Since this happens to him while he is guilty and a fugitive, he receives what he does not deserve. This shows he has left the ego world of retaliation behind and entered the kingdom of reconciling grace. The divine has befriended the human shadow. Jacob has been given the grace to see the spiritual figure and ground, the Self's design behind the ego's display. "God was here and I did not know it." We saw this before in Hakuin's poem: "This very place: the lotus paradise." Perennial wisdom is one unanimous chorus about the dismantling of the fortress of inflated ego and the befriending of its shadow so that it can become part of what protects us.

The story of Jacob gathers so many of the themes of this book and of our lives. It contains grief, as does every human story. It also presents the theme of a journey. In it nature is the locus of the spiritual. Jacob's story is about an encounter between the divine and the human and the connection between the persona and the shadow, both negative and positive. In this story psychological issues mesh with spiritual issues. It promises that we can work on ourselves by saying yes to a moment that wants to happen and be worked on by the graceful momentum that follows: Jacob's steps to Bethel are followed by shifts in Jacob's heart. These are the steps and shifts that connect effort and grace and that constitute the integration of the psychological and spiritual dimensions of our humanity.

Jacob's ladder seems to symbolize the spiritual shape of our human journey. It is an ellipse. We begin on the ground, in our daily-life grind with all its upheavals and challenges. Then we rise, like kneaded dough, to the light of the transpersonal dimension of our life and identity. "Rejoice that your names are written in heaven!" We then return by way of descent, as Moses did from Sinai and Jesus did from Tabor, with gifts of wisdom and compassion to share.

Jacob's vision *is* the combination and composition of opposites: ascent and descent. The ascent is about our yearning for the spiritual. The descent is about the zeal of the transcendent for involvement with us. The whole ladder and its traffic is about the integration of our psychological and spiritual work.

We might also say we descend, by force or choice, into the lonely void, to face our own darkness. The void is the shadow side of fear. Yet void is also unbounded potential, since it is spacious and presents no obstacle to exploring our depths. This is the descent that rescues and releases the pieces of our souls that were awaiting reunion with the wholeness of the Self. In both the ascent-descent and the descent-ascent, we return with riches and fluent in love. By descending into the negative shadow work we ascend into our positive shadow possibilities. Our best is in our worst when these opposites unite. Then effort yields to grace and darkness to light. Our very nature is, and always was, the light that is transmitted to us and through us. It took this long to know it—and we knew it all along.

The world is a smiling place.
—Saint Augustine

David Richo, Ph.D., M.F.T., is a psychotherapist, teacher, and writer in Santa Barbara and San Francisco, California, who emphasizes Jungian, transpersonal, and spiritual perspectives in his work.

Richo gives workshops around the country, some of which are available on CD. Visit davericho.com for a complete listing of workshops, books, and CDs.